The Art of
SpeedReading People

Other Books by the Authors

Do What You Are

Nurture by Nature

The Art of SpeedReading People

▼

HOW TO SIZE PEOPLE UP AND SPEAK THEIR LANGUAGE

PAUL D. TIEGER
BARBARA BARRON-TIEGER

Little, Brown and Company
Boston   New York   London

Originally published in hardcover by Little, Brown and Company, 1998
First Little, Brown paperback edition, 1999

SpeedReading People is a trademark of Communication Consultants, LLC

Library of Congress Cataloging-in-Publication Data

Tieger, Paul D.
    The art of speedreading people: how to size people up and speak their language/
by Paul D. Tieger and Barbara Barron-Tieger.
        p.   cm.
    ISBN 0-316-84525-6 (hc)   0-316-84518-3 (pb)
    1. Interpersonal communication.   2. Behavioral assessment.   3. Myers-Briggs Type Indicator.
I. Barron-Tieger, Barbara.   II. Title.
BF637.C45T54   1998
158.2—dc21   98-2364

10   9   8   7   6   5   4   3   2

Q-FF

PRINTED IN THE UNITED STATES OF AMERICA

To Danny and Kelly—two of the best SpeedReaders we know

CONTENTS

Acknowledgments

This book is the culmination of fifteen years of studying and applying Personality Type in a variety of exciting and challenging ways. During that time we have been very fortunate to study with and learn from some of the world's foremost authorities on Type, including Mary McCaulley, Gordon Lawrence, and Naomi Quenk. We are especially indebted to Terry Duniho, whose generosity in sharing his knowledge with us has been particularly instrumental in helping us develop the SpeedReading system.

We also wish to thank the many attorneys and their clients whom we served in our capacity as trial consultants, for their faith and trust and for the opportunity to apply our SpeedReading skills to assist them in their search for justice. We also appreciate the competence and professionalism of our associates Carolyn Koch and Brigid Donohue in applying their considerable talents on our behalf.

We thank our editor, Geoffrey Kloske, for his responsiveness, many good suggestions, and especially for his patience in dealing with such "involved" authors. And, once again, we are grateful to our literary agent and good friend, Kit Ward, for her continuous faith, support, encouragement, and, of course, sound advice.

In researching this book we called upon many of our friends in the Type community, including Gerry Macdaid and Jamie DeLong of CAPT, and Beatrice Kallungal of Type Resources. For their responsiveness, expertise, and generosity, we are most grateful.

We wish to thank our family and friends who, for lo these many years, have endured (with extraordinary patience and good humor) our grand obsession with Personality Type. This especially applies to Bob and Susan Stern, Bert Miller, Bob and Martha Baumwoll and the entire Baumwoll clan, Keats Jarmon, Jesse Treff, Helen Barron, Debbie Barron, and Marc and Judy Tieger. Your encouragement and support, although not acknowledged nearly often enough, are everlastingly appreciated. A special thanks to Glenn Orkin for his thoughtful review of the manuscript and talented collaboration on the SpeedReading video.

And, finally, thank you to Evelyn, whose reminder "When you're right, you're right!" gives us confidence to follow our inspirations. And to Herbie, who gave us the best advice about understanding and communicating with others. You're right, Dad, people *are* funnier than anyone!

The Art of
SpeedReading People

PART ONE

What *Really* Makes People Tick!

Please Read This First

THE NEXT BEST THING TO "X-RAY VISION"

Rob and Stephanie are both marketing representatives for competing health maintenance organizations (HMOs). At a local Chamber of Commerce luncheon, they both met George, the vice president of employee benefits for a large manufacturing company. Eager to sign him up as a client, each made a point to talk with George and give him his or her business card.

Rob and Stephanie have something else in common besides their jobs. Both are outgoing, friendly, resourceful, and spontaneous people who pride themselves on their natural warmth and ability to establish personal relationships with their clients.

Rob followed up with George the way he pursues all of his leads — by immediate personal contact. The day after the Chamber luncheon, he stopped by George's office, hoping George would have time to talk with him. With a full schedule of appointments, George was mildly annoyed by the intrusion, but managed to spare a few minutes for Rob, who tried his best to quickly sell George on switching to his company.

But unlike Rob, Stephanie had quickly pegged George for the thoughtful, methodical, organized, practical, and logical person he is — someone who is most impressed by data, facts, and demonstrated past experience. And most important, she realized that his natural personality style was very different from hers. Understanding George's personality type and his preferred way of communicating, Stephanie realized that he would *naturally* want to think about something before discussing it, would want to know all the relevant facts and details, the specific advantages, and, if convinced, would be most heavily influenced by the bottom line. She also "knew" that he was a person who scheduled his time judiciously and wouldn't appreciate her dropping in unannounced. So Stephanie took a different approach. She drafted a short letter to George highlighting the practical benefits of her company's products, including information about its long-term track record. She followed up by scheduling a meeting to answer any of his questions or address any possible concerns.

Stephanie's approach paid off and won her the account—a major coup for her and her company. Although both Stephanie and Rob's products and companies were similar, Stephanie was the more effective salesperson because she had learned what George was all about, how *he* made decisions, preferred to communicate, and how to speak *his* language. But how did Stephanie know all this about George? After all, they'd only just met briefly, days before. What really gave Stephanie the advantage over Rob? It was as if Stephanie had x-ray vision into George's mind.

Wouldn't it be great to have x-ray vision into people's personalities? To be able to look at people and instantly know what they are thinking, what they care deeply about, their likes and dislikes? If we did have x-ray vision, then we'd know how best to approach them, how to pique their interest in our ideas, resolve a conflict, strike a bargain, or simply help them feel more at ease relating to us. While no one can *really* give you x-ray vision, we

can provide you with the next best thing—the art of SpeedReading People™—a scientifically validated system that allows you to gain invaluable insights into others by observing a variety of clues relating to their appearance, vocabulary, body language, occupation, education, and interests. This unique system of decoding personalities will give you a powerful advantage in communicating more successfully with all types of people.

One of the most important skills that any of us can possess is the ability to understand what motivates people and influences their behavior. This is just as true for you and me when trying to convince our bosses we're entitled to a raise as it is for a secretary of state negotiating a complex and delicate peace treaty.

As we all know, people are different. What motivates one person often has no effect on another. The key to reaching others, whether to make ourselves understood or to influence their decisions, lies in understanding their motivations and being able to respond to their needs. All of us can enhance our natural ability to pick up these sometimes very subtle signals.

While each person is certainly unique, personality differences are not random. Human characteristics are identifiable, and often predictable. This book is based upon a powerful and well-respected model of psychology called Personality Typing, which has been used in business, education, and counseling for over twenty years. The art of SpeedReading People represents a genuine breakthrough in interpersonal communications, for it harnesses the power of Personality Type, enabling people to quickly and accurately identify key personality traits in others and communicate with them in the most effective manner.

DO I NEED THIS BOOK? . . . WHAT WILL I GET OUT OF IT?

This book will be of enormous benefit to anyone who enjoys dealing with others or who needs to. For some readers, the primary motivation for learning the art of SpeedReading People is to become more effective in their work. If you are in sales or service, you already know that different customers and clients need to be handled in different ways. This book will help you instantly identify the preferred communication style of each customer, and show you how to talk to them in the way that is more likely to get them to say yes to your pitch or request, or know just what to say to make them feel confident about your company.

If you are a manager or executive seeking better ways to motivate your employees or promote more productive work teams, you will learn how to identify the natural strengths of your employees and learn how to encourage them to make the best use of their gifts. If you are a teacher or trainer, you will discover which teaching styles work best with different types of learners and how to deliver information in the way they can best process and respond successfully to. If you are an attorney, SpeedReading will help you in all your interpersonal interactions — including dealing with difficult colleagues, keeping clients happy, assessing

adversaries' strengths and weaknesses, and communicating better with judges and jurors. And if you are a doctor, nurse, therapist, or other health care provider, you will learn how to make your patients feel more comfortable, and enable them to share vital information more freely, so you can better help them.

Perhaps you seek to understand and communicate better with the important people in your life. If so, *SpeedReading People* will provide a wellspring of insights that might otherwise never have come to you, or may have taken years to acquire. We know from years and years of experience that, as a result of this new understanding, many men and women will feel they finally understand their spouse, sometimes, *for the first time!* Others will learn how their natural differences cause predictable conflict, but that they can also be a source of great joy and help both partners to grow and develop in ways they never could if they were more similar. And parents and children will find Speed-Reading a remarkable tool for understanding each other in new and exciting ways by resolving conflicts and communicating more effectively. Finally, this book will give thoughtful adults searching for life partners a better sense of themselves and their needs, so they might find a truly compatible mate.

HOW TO GET THE MOST FROM THIS BOOK

Reading *The Art of SpeedReading People* will be unlike reading most other books for several reasons.

In fact, we encourage you to think of *The Art of SpeedReading People* as more of a life course, instead of merely a book of information. And like any life course, this book will likely have a profound effect on you, and, quite possibly, will change the way you look at and relate to people . . . forever! Admittedly, these are heady claims, but our prediction is based on having taught Type to thousands of people from all walks of life over a period of fifteen years. Be prepared to experience more "Aha's" than you have in a long time. Insights will come fast and furiously!

THE ETHICS OF SPEEDREADING PEOPLE

One question we are sometimes asked is: "Doesn't this book give people who have mastered the SpeedReading techniques an unfair advantage over people who haven't? Doesn't it really just teach someone how to manipulate others?

We've wrestled with this question and its many implications, and feel this way about this issue: SpeedReading is a tool. And *any* tool holds the potential for misuse. A hammer in the hands of a Michelangelo can be used to sculpt a breathtaking masterpiece such as the Pietà. In the hands of a madman, the same hammer can be used to smash someone's skull. The difference lies in the skill and the intention of the person holding the hammer.

We are well aware that the art of SpeedReading People constitutes a powerful tool. And we recognize that some people may abuse the skills they acquire, just as there are those who use their physical strength, superior intellect, or natural charisma to manipulate others. **We wish to be very clear about our intention in writing this book: it is not designed to help people hurt or take advantage of others. It is designed to help people better understand themselves and others, so they can communicate more successfully. Ultimately, in deciding to share what we've learned, we believe the benefits to be gained by the many far outweigh the possible harm that may be inflicted by the few. With better communication come increased understanding, tolerance, and even peace. We strive for those goals.**

HOW THIS BOOK WORKS

SpeedReading People is divided into three parts. Part 1, "What *Really* Makes People Tick!" provides a thorough introduction to Personality Type and helps you identify your own type. In Part 2, "The System: Learning How to SpeedRead People," you will discover how to identify key personality characteristics in others based upon numerous clues relating to their appearance, language, body language, occupation, and interests. You will also learn the profound ways that Type affects the way people communicate with each other, and how to SpeedReach people — using proven techniques to increase your ability to communicate with all people more successfully. And in Part 3, "Getting to Know the Sixteen Types," you will gain insights into the subtleties of each of the sixteen types. The book concludes with a list of resources that will help you increase your ability to SpeedRead people.

Throughout the book we have tried to anticipate any questions you may have, and address them as they arise in the text. You will also find lots of real-life examples, bulleted lists, helpful charts, and graphic illustrations—all designed to make *The Art of SpeedReading People* an enjoyable, as well as valuable, learning experience.

ABOUT THE AUTHORS

The authors, Paul D. Tieger and Barbara Barron-Tieger, are partners in Communication Consultants, LLC. Over the past fifteen years we have become recognized nationally as experts in the application of Personality Type with the publication of two previous groundbreaking bestsellers. Our first book, *Do What You Are: Discover the Perfect Career for You Through the Secrets of Personality Type,* pioneered the use of Personality Type to help people find truly satisfying work and conduct the most successful job searches possible. Our second book, *Nurture by Nature: Understand Your Child's Personality Type—And Become a Better Parent,* helps parents more fully understand their children and provides effective strategies for parenting children who are very different from each other and from their parents.

As an organizational consultant, Barbara has consulted with dozens of businesses, hospitals, and school systems, and has trained thousands of managers, counselors, teachers, and others in a variety of uses of Type. In his work as a jury consultant, Paul pioneered the use of Personality Type as a tool to help lawyers uncover biases in potential jurors, and develop communication strategies that would effectively persuade seated jurors.

CHAPTER ONE

The Principles of Personality Type: Why We Do the Things We Do

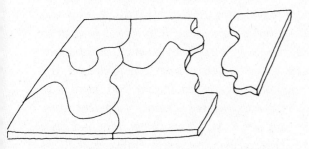

People come in all shapes and sizes, and, certainly, every person is unique. But you'll probably agree that some people are much more alike than others. And behavior that may seem random is, in fact, quite understandable and often even predictable, once you understand that person's inborn, natural personality, or genetic blueprint, if you will, which describes basic psychological characteristics. And one's personality is by far the best and most reliable predictor of behavior.

There are a whole host of factors that influence behavior: genes, upbringing, innate talents and abilities, cultural background, time period, and location, as well as the specifics of a particular situation. Human beings have a huge repertoire of behaviors. We all act differently during a job interview than we do at a rock concert. We behave differently when socializing with our families than we do with our closest friends. That's because the situation calls for different behavior. But that doesn't mean our *personality* changes with each new situation we encounter. To the contrary, as human beings we approach most situations with a set of automatic responses, acting in ways in which we are most comfortable. Evidence of this abounds and is easily seen when we consider that most people's personalities are quite consistent. For example, let's say you have a friend, Ed, whom everyone describes as responsible and hardworking and whose demeanor is almost always pretty serious. He may occasionally lighten up and deviate from that style — for example, at his brother's wedding reception, when he was dancing in a conga line.

But for the most part, he acts true to his conservative character because that's who he is. In fact, if he were serious and careful one day, and the next he was turning back flips in the office, you'd probably have good reason to worry something might be wrong with him! Perhaps you have another friend, relative, or coworker who is very different from the fellow just described. She is, instead, perpetually lighthearted, loves to laugh and enjoy herself, and almost seems immune to the everyday pressures and worries that plague most of us. It is unlikely that she is merely acting that way. She probably is more naturally carefree and easygoing than serious, steady Ed. And while, undoubtedly, some of every person's behavior is learned — from parents, siblings, and teachers — a greater portion of it is the natural manifestation of his or her inborn personality.

While there are many different models of behavior — a fancy phrase for saying ways of understanding people — we have found Personality Type to be the most insightful and useful. One reason is that it so accurately identifies key characteristics of personality that are present in all people. Personality Type is also useful because it describes behavior in positive, nonjudgmental terms. This is not an approach that says it is better to be one way or another, nor that it is better to be one type than another. But it helps us to recognize, and very clearly identify, our natural strengths and potential weaknesses. And by allowing us to understand the ways we are alike and different, it helps us not only to value our differences, but to celebrate them as well.

Before you begin an introduction to Personality Type, it might be helpful for you to know a bit about its history. The basic ideas behind Type are not new. In fact, they were first written about by Swiss psychologist Carl Jung more than seventy years ago. But it was two American women, Katharine Briggs and her daughter, Isabel Myers, who were really responsible for building on, including developing the fourth type dimension, and making these ideas useful in practical ways to so many people.* One of Isabel's major contributions to our understanding of human behavior was the development of a psychological instrument that reliably identifies sixteen distinctly different types. She named this the Myers-Briggs Type Indicator (MBTI)®, and over the past several years, millions of people around the world have been introduced to the benefits of knowing about Personality Type through the MBTI[†]. It is routinely used in business to help managers motivate employees, develop more-productive work teams, and enhance communication. It is also heavily used by counselors and therapists to help individuals, couples, and families understand and communicate better with each other. Hundreds of thousands of people have found Personality Type invaluable in helping them make satisfying career choices. And these are only some of its many applications!

*If you would like to learn more about these remarkable women, we suggest you read *Katharine and Isabel*, by Frances Saunders.

[†]The Myers-Briggs Type Indicator and MBTI are registered trademarks of Consulting Psychologists Press. People interested in taking the MBTI should contact CPP. Their address and phone number are listed on page 194.

THE BIG PICTURE: AN OVERVIEW OF PERSONALITY TYPE

There are four components, or "dimensions," that make up a personality type. They are: how people are energized, what kind of information they naturally notice and remember, how they make decisions, and how they like to organize the world around them. As you can see, each of these dimensions deals with an important aspect of life, which is why Type provides such accurate insights into our own, and others', behavior. It helps to picture each of these four dimensions as a scale — a continuum between two opposite extremes — like this:

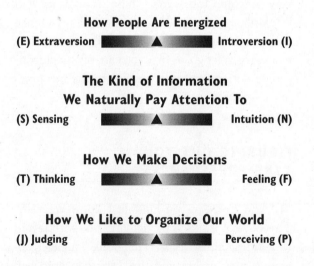

How People Are Energized

(E) Extraversion   Introversion (I)

The Kind of Information We Naturally Pay Attention To

(S) Sensing   Intuition (N)

How We Make Decisions

(T) Thinking   Feeling (F)

How We Like to Organize Our World

(J) Judging   Perceiving (P)

You will notice there is a midpoint in the center of each scale. This is important because everyone has an inborn, natural preference for one side or the other on each of these dimensions.

Some people resist the notion that they have to fall on one side or the other, insisting that they are able to use either side, depending on the situation. And while it is true that all of us use both sides of each dimension hundreds of times a day, we do not use them with equal frequency, energy, or success. A simple exercise will help you understand this concept. First, find a pen or pencil and a piece of paper — any scrap will do — you can even use the margin of this book. Now simply write your signature. How did that feel? . . . Pretty easy, we would guess. Okay, now write your signature again, only this time with your pen or pencil in your *opposite* hand! How did that feel? If you're like most people, you would use words like "awkward," "difficult," "uncomfortable," and "unnatural" to describe the second experience. Also, it probably took more time and energy, and the product wasn't nearly as good.

When you are using your preferred side on any of the four type dimensions — like using your preferred hand — you are doing what comes naturally. And when you are required to use the opposite side, it takes a lot of extra work and you're not as good at it; hence, the experience is usually not as satisfying.

You might ask: "Isn't it possible to be both, say, an Introvert and an Extravert?" The answer is no. But just as we can and do use our less preferred hand, we also use our other side on each type dimension, at times. Another way to think of it is that everyone is *primarily* one way or the other, but not *exclusively* that way. Those of us who have been studying and using Type for dozens of years have little doubt that every person really does have a natural, inborn preference for one side over the other, although in some people it is quite strong and apparent, while in others it is less strong and may be harder to identify.

Because there are four type dimensions, and each person has one preference per dimension, there are sixteen different possible type combinations. A personality type is really a four-letter code that reflects a person's preferences on each of the four dimensions. For example, a person can be an ISTP (Introverted, Sensing, Thinking, Perceiving) type, or an ENFJ (Extraverted, Intuitive, Feeling, Judging) type, or one of fourteen other type combinations.

It is helpful to spend a few moments talking about some of the language used to describe Type. For example, when we refer to a preference, we're not talking about a conscious choice, but rather an inborn tendency. We can't choose to be an Extravert, for example, any more than we can choose to be born right-handed or have blue eyes. Nor can we change any of our type preferences. We are born with a type and we remain that type our whole lives. While some people don't particularly like this idea, it is not bad news. For as we said before, it is not better or worse to have one preference over another. Nor is any one type better or worse, smarter or duller than another. Rather, each type has natural strengths and potential weaknesses, due to its tendencies and inclinations. And although every individual is unique, because

they have their own genes, parents, and life experiences, people of the same type share a remarkable amount in common.

Over the years, it has been pointed out that the language used to describe type preferences can sometimes create an unwanted distraction, because most of us have heard words like "Extravert" and "Introvert" and associate them with a meaning that is not the same when they are used to refer to Personality Type. For example, many people think of Introverts as being shy and withdrawn, and Extraverts as gregarious and talkative. This description is neither adequate, since there is so much more to this dimension than just the amount of social interaction people desire, nor accurate, since there are some very shy Extraverts and some very outgoing Introverts. These distinctions will be clarified when we discuss each type preference in depth, in the following section. But for the time being, try to let go, as best you can, of any preconceived notions you may have as to the meanings of these words.

FIGURING OUT YOUR TYPE PREFERENCES

"To know others, you must first know yourself." This old expression is particularly true with regard to learning about Type. Therefore, your first objective is to understand the Type concepts well enough to be able to accurately identify your own type. Look at reading this book as a series of learning adventures. And while it is important for you to get the fundamentals down, like millions of others you'll find reading, thinking about, and discussing Type with others to be interesting and fun.

In a moment you will begin to read about the four type dimensions, in an effort to determine which preferences fit you best. To help you decide, we've posed several questions that reflect the differences between opposite sides. Most of what you read about your preference will ring true for you, but in order to clearly make the distinctions, the preferences are presented as generalities, which really represent extremes. Try not to focus on any one specific example of each preference, but rather on a pattern of behavior that is more consistently like you than its opposite. Even if one example sounds just like you, see how all the others fit before making up your mind.

THE FOUR TYPE DIMENSIONS

Extravert or Introvert:
The "Inner World" or
the "Outer World"?

The first type dimension is concerned with the two different ways people orient themselves to life, either as *Extraverts* or *Introverts*. Contrary to what most people may think when they hear the words "Extravert" and "Introvert," this first type dimension is really most concerned about people's energy—where they get it and where they direct it.

Many behaviors are influenced by a person's preference for one or the other; two of the most

helpful questions to determine whether you are an Introvert or an Extravert are:

**What energizes me most—Interacting with other people
or
being by myself?**

**Where do I like to focus my energy—in the outer world of people and things
or
in the inner world of ideas and thoughts?**

Extraverts are "other centered." By this we mean they both get energy from and focus their energy toward people and things outside of themselves. Think of Extraverts as possessing a sort of radar that they turn outward to constantly scan their environment. The more blips on the screen (the more interactions), the more energized they become. But Introverts are really more "self-centered." This does not mean they are selfish; rather they are more self-contained and self-reliant. Introverts tune their radar to an internal frequency because they are more interested in applying their own perceptions and experience to a situation rather than looking outside themselves for the answer. Extraverts naturally (and unconsciously) ask themselves: "How do I relate to other people and things?" While Introverts (again, unconsciously) ask themselves: "How do people or things relate to me?"

Because Extraverts are energized by being around people, they naturally seek out others more often than Introverts do, which accounts for why Extraverts typically have huge collections of friends and associates.

Two very clear Extraverts, Chas and Elaine, offer a good example of this phenomenon. Friends who often socialize together, Chas and Elaine have a running competition: who knows more people? Whenever they're out together, the game kicks into high gear when one of them recognizes someone that the other doesn't know. Instantly, the other starts scanning until he or she "gets one," that is, locates someone not known to the other. While they obviously enjoy this game, their friends are constantly amazed at just how many people, individually and collectively, these two actually do know.

While Extraverts like to focus their attention on what is happening in the world around them, most Introverts prefer to immerse themselves totally in a project that interests them. Naturally independent, they find the solitude of working alone and thinking things through carefully both stimulating and refreshing. This concentrated single-mindedness can even make them oblivious to what is happening around them.

Shawn is a case in point. A very clear Introvert, Shawn loves nothing better than fooling around with computers. As he often does, one night he sat down to his computer to figure out a particular program. The next time he got out of his chair, he was surprised to learn it was 7:00 A.M. He had been so engrossed in his work that he had been sitting at the computer for eight hours straight.

By contrast, Extraverts are notorious for finding excuses not to focus on one thing because they are much more interested in and energized by a variety of external stimulation.

Throughout college, Tammy preferred to study at the library. While initially impressed to learn their daughter was spending so much time there, her parents were not really surprised when she revealed her true motivation. Sure, she got her work done, but she chose the library so she would be around other people and not have to work alone. In the library, she often ran into lots of her friends, and she took frequent bathroom and social coffee breaks. Like most Extraverts, especially younger ones, Tammy found just being in the same room with other people was more comfortable than being by herself.

Another example of the different needs Extraverts and Introverts have for interaction and concentration can often be seen in their work styles. For example, Extraverts are much more likely to keep their office door open so they can see what's going on and not miss any of the action. And most Extraverts embrace the concept of managing by walking around. On the other hand, Introverts are more likely to keep their door closed so they won't be distracted or encourage unwanted interruptions. They prefer fewer, more substantive interactions. And their management style, like everything else about them, is more thoughtful, contemplative, and deliberate.

Which do I prefer <u>more</u> — to be around others or to spend time by myself?

A popular advertising campaign encouraged telephone customers to "reach out and touch someone." While Extraverts don't really need prodding, a common complaint among Extraverts is that their Introverted friends seldom initiate contact.

> Anna and Susan have been close friends for over twenty-five years — since they met at college. But nine times out of ten, it will be Extraverted Anna who calls Introverted Susan to catch up on news, or to try and get together. It has taken Anna many years to finally understand that Susan's lack of initiating contact doesn't mean she doesn't care about her friend. In fact, when the two women are together, Susan is a very attentive and concerned friend. But since her own life is so self-contained, it seldom occurs to her to seek the company of others, even those she cares deeply about.

A car battery serves as a good metaphor when describing the different amount of interaction preferred by Extraverts and Introverts. With Extraverts, it's as if their batteries get charged up by being around people, while with Introverts, their batteries are often drained by too much or sustained interaction, and they need time alone to recharge. The fact is, an activity that will energize an Extravert will probably have just the opposite effect on an Introvert. A very common scenario: a couple, one Introvert and one Extravert, are invited to a party. Quite "naturally," the Extravert is eager to attend, anticipating all the people he will be interacting with. The Introvert, on the other hand, would prefer to stay at home, or spend the evening together or perhaps with just with a few close friends.

And lest you think this is gender based — you know, a male/female thing — there is no difference in the percentages of men and women who are either Extraverts or Introverts. In other words, it is the preference for one or the other that influences behavior, rather than the gender of the individual.

As with all of the type preferences, people with one preference often find it hard to understand and appreciate people of another. Most Extraverts have such a strong need to be around others, they have a hard time believing Introverts really do like spending that much time alone. Consequently, Extraverts are notorious for trying to get their Introverted friends, coworkers, spouses, or children involved in activities they would rather avoid. Which makes us think Introverts must often feel like the old woman whom the well-intentioned Boy Scout kept trying to help across the street. The only problem was, she just didn't want to go!

It's not always possible to look to your work to determine your type, because many people's work is not well suited to their preferences. Frequently, Extraverts end up doing jobs better suited to Introverts and vice versa. If you are an Introvert, imagine what it would feel like to work as a tour guide or receptionist, where all day, each day, your job required you to meet and greet dozens of strangers, engage them in small talk, and make them feel comfortable. Now for you Extraverts, imagine a job as a researcher, working on one project for weeks at a time, completely alone, without the infusion of energy you get from interacting with other people, or talking about different projects. Neither is a bad job, but both are potential prescriptions for frustration and burnout if held by people not naturally suited to them.*

Looking back at your childhood can sometimes help you determine your true type preference. Even as very young children, one's preference for either Extraversion or Introversion is often quite obvious. Typically, Extraverted children jump into new social situations with wild abandon, while Introverted children tend to study the activity from the sidelines before (and if) they decide to get involved. Predictably, Extraverts surround themselves with lots of friends, join many activities and clubs, and enjoy being at the center of the action. Introverts tend to have one or two best friends whom they keep for a long time, and are happiest working behind the scenes, rather than in the spotlight.

"Never talk to strangers" is an admonition Introverted children are much more likely to follow than Extraverted ones. And more than one Introverted child has been embarrassed by an Extraverted parent who is quick to strike up a conversation with anyone, anytime, and under almost

*For more information on Type and careers, see *Do What You Are*.

any circumstances. Although men usually get a bad rap for being too sure of themselves to stop and ask for directions when they are lost, it is an Extravert/Introvert issue more than it is a male/female one. In other words, Extraverts are more likely to stop and ask a stranger for directions than are Introverts, regardless of their gender.

Would I rather work on several projects at the same time
or
focus my attention on one task at a time?

We are often reminded of the many contributions that are made to the world by people of different type preferences. The gift of Extraversion is breadth, for by their nature Extraverts prefer to know a little about a lot of things. This makes them well equipped to fill the role of life's generalists. For clearly, we need people who are so tuned into what is happening around them that they can see things coming, and respond quickly to them. In contrast, the gift of Introversion is depth, for by their nature Introverts are interested in fewer subjects, but study them in much greater depth. They are life's specialists. And likewise, we need people who are willing and able to consider issues thoroughly, deferring action until it is appropriate. But this difference in outlook and emphasis is profound, and would be quite obvious were you to eavesdrop on the conversations of two Extraverts talking to each other and two Introverts doing the same. The Extraverts are likely to hit on several topics, bouncing from issue to issue, like the steel ball in a pinball machine. Each person freely offers many observations but doesn't explore any one issue in great depth. Two Introverts talking are more likely to spend time discussing fewer issues but considering the other's points thoughtfully and in much greater depth. (And depending on whether *you* are an Extravert or an Introvert, you would find one conversation infinitely more interesting than the other.)

Am I more comfortable acting first, then thinking about it
or
thinking things through before I act on them?

Extraverts and Introverts often have very different work styles. Typically Extraverts prefer to work at a rapid pace, moving quickly from one task to another. They are driven by action. Given their druthers, Introverts would rather work at a slower, steadier pace, carefully thinking through how they will do the job before they begin, and then taking time to assess their progress as the project unfolds. The popular expression "Measure twice, cut once" might well be the Introverted carpenter's mantra.

Many years ago, our friend Mary McCaulley explained a classic distinction between Extraverts and Introverts. She said: "If you don't know what an Extravert is thinking, you haven't been listening, because he'll tell you. On the other hand, if you don't know what an Introvert is thinking, you haven't asked." And we would add: ". . . or waited long enough for the answer." If someone were so inclined, he could actually measure the difference in the number of words spoken by Extraverts and Introverts. And the reason for the great disparity

is simple. Extraverts think out loud; in fact, Extraverts often need to *talk* in order to think. Introverts, on the other hand, think inside their heads. Much like a cake that is baked, then presented to the world after it is finished, Introverts "bake" their ideas inside their heads. Then, when they are well thought out and ready, they share them with others. In contrast, Extraverts only partially "bake" their ideas inside, preferring to finish them out in the world. (This, of course, occasionally results in the presentation of some pretty half-baked ideas!)

Although Introverts don't usually speak nearly as much as their Extraverted counterparts, what they may lack in quantity is more than made up in quality. Perhaps you've been to meetings where a few people (normally the very Extraverted ones) dominate the conversation. Then someone will ask for the opinion of someone who's said very little up until then. Often, the reaction is like the old television commercial in which a room buzzing with conversation suddenly becomes stone quiet as people crane their necks to hear the wise stockbroker's recommendation. This demonstrates quite well the fact that because Introverts do their editing inside their heads, what emerges is often a very good finished product. With Extraverts, you actually witness and hear the editing process as it occurs.

Am I more of a "public person"
or
more of a "private person"?

If you haven't yet determined whether you are an Extravert or an Introvert, this last question may help you decide. While history is full of Introverts who have played very public roles — including many world leaders — Extraverts are normally much more comfortable occupying the spotlight and sharing their lives with the public. This is certainly not to imply that all Extraverts enjoy public speaking. The real question is how comfortable are you with letting people really get to know you? A common complaint among Extraverts of Introverts is that they are secretive, withholding, and difficult to get to know. In fact, Introverts value their privacy so much that they usually only allow those closest to them to really get to know them. While this may be hard for Extraverts to understand, it is because Introverts are naturally more selective than Extraverts. By this we mean that Extraverts welcome all kinds of external stimulation and often feel the more the better. What doesn't interest them, they simply disregard. But because Introverts are so much more selective, they tend to be comfortable allowing only a certain amount of external stimulation in. They simply screen out the information or stimulation that doesn't apply to something that interests them. Whereas Extraverts tend to share more of themselves with the outside world, Introverts keep more to themselves. Introverts therefore have a lower tolerance for the invasion of external stimulation — whether it's from information, sensations, or people.

Although there is some controversy as to how many Extraverts and Introverts there are in the world, the latest research suggests that the American population is about equally divided between Extraverts and Introverts.* However, because Extraverts tend to talk more and louder than Introverts, there seems to be a strong bias toward Extraverts in our culture.

At this point you should have a fairly good idea of whether you are an Extravert or an Introvert. You may be very confident about it, or you may still have some doubts. This is perfectly normal. And if you aren't yet able to determine your preference on this dimension with certainty, you will have many other opportunities later in the book.

Below you will find a scale showing the Extravert/Introvert continuum. Please place a check mark at the point that most accurately reflects where you fall. The closer your mark is to the center of the continuum, the less clear your preference; the farther away from the center, the stronger you think it is. Even if you're not sure which side you belong on, try to indicate which side you *probably* fall on, even if it is just over the line. This requires an honest evaluation, for you are trying to determine which is the way you are, not the way you might want to be or think you should be. And remember, what is most helpful in determining your type is which side of each scale you prefer, not the strength of your preference.

(E) Extravert ◀▬▬▬▬▲▬▬▬▶ **Introvert (I)**

*The percentages of all four type preferences were calculated by averaging results of several studies. For the most recent and comprehensive research results, see Allen Hammer, CPP, and Wayne D. Mitchell, University of Alaska, "The Distribution of MBTI Types in the U.S. by Gender and Ethnic Group," *Journal of Psychological Type,* vol. 37, 1996.

One down, and three to go! Next we'll explore the second type dimension: Sensing and Intuition.

Sensor or Intuitive:
The Forest or the Trees?

The second type dimension describes the two different ways people perceive, or take in, information. The words we use to describe people who have these two opposite preferences are *Sensors* and *Intuitives*. Each of us continuously takes in millions (perhaps billions) of pieces of information every day, the great majority of which are processed unconsciously. Some people take in this information primarily through their five senses—what they see, hear, touch, taste, or smell—hence the name Sensors. Others take in information through their sixth sense, focusing not on what is, but rather on what could be. We use the word Intuitives to describe these people. Remember that no one is a pure Sensor or Intuitive any more than a person is a pure Extravert or Introvert. Each of us has the ability to use both Sensing and Intuition, and all of us do use both every day. But we have a natural, inborn preference for one over the other.

Below are several questions to ask yourself to determine whether you are a Sensor or an Intuitive.

Do I usually pay more attention to the facts and details
or
do I try to understand the connections, underlying meaning, and implications?

Sensors see the trees, while Intuitives see the forest. By this we mean that Sensors naturally pay attention to what they are experiencing at the moment. Handed a flower and asked to tell you about it, the Sensor will note how vivid the colors are, the smooth texture of the leaves, the delicate fragrance, and how light and fragile it is—in other words, what her three senses tell her about the flower. Hand the same flower to an Intuitive and ask her to tell you about it, and you are likely to hear something more like: "This reminds me of my grandmother. She used to have these growing in her yard, and when we'd visit each summer, we'd pick them to put on the table for family meals." You'll notice that the Intuitive perceived the flower in a very different way than the Sensor. Instead on focusing on what is, she immediately focused on her connection to the flower, and her associations with it.

Here's another metaphor that can help demonstrate how different the focus is for Sensors and Intuitives. Imagine a photographer taking a picture with a single-lens reflex camera (the kind of camera that you focus by turning the ring on the lens). The photographer is shooting a person who is standing in front of a huge panoramic view of a mountain range. With Sensors, it's as if they turn the lens until the person in the foreground (the detail) is in sharp focus, while the view behind (the big picture) is blurry. With Intuitives, it's just the opposite: they turn the lens so that the view (the big picture) behind the person is in focus, but the person in the foreground (the detail) is blurry and out of focus.

Arnie, a very clear Intuitive, learned just how attentive to details Sensors are when his apartment got robbed. Fortunately, he was away at the time and discovered the intrusion upon returning home. When the police arrived, they gave a cursory look around the kitchen first and asked him: "Was that drawer open when you left the house?" So inattentive to details was Arnie that he was embarrassed to admit he had never even noticed there *was* a drawer where the officer was pointing!

While Sensors tend to think in a linear fashion, one thought following the next, Intuitives frequently engage in intuitive leaps in thinking.

Jessica and Ian were driving in their car one afternoon, when she happened to notice and point out an exceptionally beautiful tree they were passing. After only a few seconds of looking at the tree, Ian turned to Jessica and said: "You know, I'm really ticked off at Jimmy." Now Jessica and Ian had been together long enough for her to understand the way his mind worked, and to often be able to track the origin of his many intuitive connections. But she was at a total loss this time. "Okay, explain how you got from seeing that tree to being mad at Jimmy [one of Ian's oldest childhood friends]." Ian explained: "When we were growing up, Jimmy had a tree house in a tree that looked a lot like that one. As soon as I saw it, it reminded me of him and the fact that he hasn't called me in two months. So that's why I'm mad at Jimmy."

These fundamental differences also may be seen early on in children. While one child has memorized every one of his favorite baseball player's stats,

and can reel them off with impressive accuracy, his brother can't remember where he left his sneakers five minutes after he took them off.

Am I a more down-to-earth and sensible person or an imaginative and creative one?

It bears repeating that it is not better to have one preference over another. However, there are definitely gifts that are unique to each. Intuitives are often (but not always) creative; able to see possibilities and alternatives that aren't immediately apparent. Typically, they have rich imaginations, which they use to engage in fantasies of all kinds.

By this, we do not mean to imply that only Intuitives possess creativity, for this is certainly not the case. Creativity, like intelligence, takes many forms. But the ways that Intuitives express their creativity seem to be in seeing or doing things differently from the way they've been seen or done before. Sensors more often demonstrate their creativity by finding a new application for something that has already been invented or established. This tendency stems from their natural inclination to trust what they know from experience, their own or others'. One of the reasons Sensors like data so much is that data are just facts that have been collected in a purposeful way. Intuitives are generally satisfied with less empirical proof in order to believe something is possible, or doable, since they have greater faith that although an answer may not be apparent, it just means it hasn't been found . . . yet!

Which do I trust more: my direct experience
or
my gut instinct?

Am I more tuned in to the here-and-now
or
do I often imagine how things will affect
future events?

Many Type experts believe that of the four type dimensions, the Sensing and Intuition scale represents the greatest differences between people, since it really influences one's worldview. A research project we conducted demonstrated this vividly. People were presented the facts of a murder case that involved a young woman accused of stabbing her live-in boyfriend. The boyfriend had abused the defendant in the past while intoxicated. Her attorney argued that she suffered from "battered woman syndrome." And so, at the time of the incident, she had reason to believe that her life was in jeopardy, and acted in self-defense. On the other side, the prosecution claimed she offered no proof that she had reason to fear for her life, could have left the scene, and therefore had no justification for killing her boyfriend.

While the majority (75%) of both Sensors and Intuitives voted "not guilty," Sensors were *more than twice as likely* to vote for murder as were Intuitives. These results were consistent both with Personality Type theory and with our experience as trial consultants. "Battered woman syndrome" is a theory; an idea, a concept that requires jurors to imagine how an abusive relationship can cause a particular psychological response. It is not a

condition that can be documented or verified scientifically. Since Intuitives are naturally interested in the psychological workings of human relationships, they are much more likely to accept this theory as valid than their Sensing counterparts.

Sensors, on the other hand, prefer clear, tangible proof, and are naturally drawn to practical, rather than theoretical, explanations. In this case, the Sensors focused on the murder itself, and the fact that the defendant was physically able to leave her boyfriend that evening, while the Intuitives focused on the defendant's motivations and psychological justification for her behavior.

Sensors and Intuitives tend to have different attitudes about important issues such as crime and punishment, as their answers to this question demonstrate:

To fight crime, tax dollars would be better spent on (1) more police, tougher sentencing, and more prisons or (2) more social programs for disadvantaged youth.

Twice as many Intuitives as Sensors answered "social programs," and Sensors were more than three times as likely to answer "more police and prisons" as Intuitives. Predictably, Sensors favored established actions designed to have an immediate effect (such as adding more police or building additional prisons), and whose effect could be somehow measured. Intuitives sought solutions that took into account the underlying causes of societal problems (such as how the lack of social programs is related to increased crime), and were more eager to seek new, untried, and innovative solutions. And their focus was on how actions taken today would affect future generations. The results reinforced the belief that, politically, Sensors tend to be more conservative and Intuitives more liberal.

Do I like new ideas just for their own sake
or
only if they have practical utility?

Many Sensors are most comfortable with what is familiar, while Intuitives are usually drawn to what is new and different. Theories, concepts, and hypotheses appeal to most Intuitives because they represent possibilities. The fact that something is untried and unproven is not a turnoff to Intuitives. Rather, it is the potential offered by the new idea or situation that excites them the most. Sensors, of course, are also interested in new ideas, but only once they are convinced that something real and useful will come of them.

Sal was always inventing something. If it wasn't a brand-new idea, he could find ways of improving just about anything. His latest idea was a new kind of bracket to hang pictures on the wall that would keep them straight — eliminating the need for constant straightening. As he had with countless other ideas, Sal discussed this with his brother-in-law, Jack, with hopes of persuading him to invest the necessary seed money to make a prototype. Jack, a clear Sensor, had his doubts. First, he questioned whether the world really needed a better way of hanging pictures. After all, the old way must be good enough, since it had been around forever. He was skeptical that this new mechanism would really work as Sal promised, and, even if it did, wondered whether Sal had the patience and single-mindedness required to make his idea a reality. Fortunately, Sal met another amateur inventor, who had a contact at a fastener company. Sal met with a representative there, who expressed genuine interest in his project. When Sal reported this to his brother-in-law, Jack's attitude changed completely. Having received validation from a credible source that Sal's gizmo might really be marketable, Jack became more enthusiastic and eventually provided Sal's seed money.

If Intuitives are the "thinker-uppers" — people who love to invent the better mousetrap — then, certainly, Sensors are the "getter-doners" — the people who actually make the idea work. As we've said before, people of both preferences have different gifts, and it is easy to see the important role each plays in so many areas of life. Take business, for example. Each year, thousands of new businesses are started up in this country. Many are franchise operations, which duplicate already successfully tested ideas. But others are truly entrepreneurial, the result of someone's vision (or intuition) about a product or service which doesn't yet exist, but that the entrepreneur believes people will want.

Would I rather use an established skill
or
do I become bored easily after I've
mastered it?

For many Intuitives, it is the creative part of the process that is most energizing. Once their inspiration has been given life, and the bugs have been worked out, they would rather go on to something else, leaving the details to others. Fortunately, those people are usually Sensors, who often enjoy and excel at setting up systems and following procedures so that things run smoothly. This is called being efficient. While the exact statistics of all the many hundreds of new businesses started each year are often disputed, it is common knowledge that a high percentage of them fail. Although many reasons are cited for this, including undercapitalization, lack of experience, and unanticipated market forces, there is another possible explanation that has a lot to do with Type preferences. Quite simply, the people who are talented at thinking things up are seldom as talented at making them work. This rests primarily on the fact that they dislike, and therefore avoid, any routine or repetitive activity for any period of time. Their interest tends to wane as soon as the creative challenges have been met.

Conversely, Sensors enjoy learning a skill, then using it repeatedly in an effective way. Whether as a surgeon performing an operation, an artist painting a portrait, a bookkeeper tallying figures, or a plumber installing a toilet, Sensors' combination of being very aware of their bodies and living totally in the present moment enables them to derive pleasure from performing the act itself. Intuitives often have a very different experience. For them, what the act means or represents is often more important than the act itself. And coupled with their future time orientation, they are often less than fully engaged in whatever task they are performing at the time. Therefore they don't usually experience the same pleasure Sensors take in re-

peating a task or using the same skill once they've mastered it.

From the time he was a young boy, Thomas, an Intuitive, thought he wanted to be a dentist. Of course the fact that both his father and grandfather were dentists may have influenced his decision a little bit. By his second semester of dental school, Thomas realized he had made a big mistake. For while the other students enjoyed learning standard tooth repair techniques, such as filling a cavity, Thomas thought he would go crazy if he had to do the procedure the same (excruciatingly boring) way, even one more time. When he found himself fantasizing about all the other ways a tooth could be filled, even outrageous ones like going in through the ear, or removing the top of the head, he realized he would never be happy as a dentist and fortunately (for him, and future patients!) changed professions.

That Sensors and Intuitives are often drawn to different subjects in school should come as no surprise. Intuitives are often more interested in theoretical studies like philosophy, psychology, sociology, and literature, while Sensors are often interested in more tangible subjects with practical applications, such as engineering, science, and business. This is not meant to imply that there are no Intuitive engineers, or that Sensors can't be successful psychologists, only that they don't tend to gravitate to these types of occupations in nearly the same percentages.

Sensors represent about 65 percent and Intuitives about 35 percent of the American population, giving Sensors somewhat of a numerical advantage. By now you should have a fairly good idea of whether your preference is for Sensing or Intuition. Again, if you are unsure, don't worry about it — you will have several other opportunities to clarify which one it is. As you did with Extraversion and Introversion, please place a mark on the continuum below to indicate where you think you fit. And again, even if you're not 100 percent certain which side you belong on, try to indicate which side you *probably* fall on, even if it's just slightly over the center line.

(S) Sensor ▲ **Intuitive (N)**

You're doing great! Now we'll move on and describe the third type dimension: Thinking and Feeling.

Thinker or Feeler:
A Matter of Principles or Values

While Sensing and Intuition describe the different ways people take in information, Thinking and Feeling describe the very different ways people make decisions, or come to conclusions. Clearly, each of us has the ability to make a decision based on logic or on our personal feelings and values. And, while no one is a pure Thinker or Feeler, each of us has a natural inborn preference for one side over the other. Here again, the everyday usage of these words may initially give you an inaccurate impression of their true meaning. It's important to understand that Thinking and Feeling both describe rational decision-making processes. It's not that Thinkers have no feelings, or that Feelers are incapable of logic. But Thinkers and Feelers use very different criteria to make their decisions.

The questions below should help you figure out which decision-making process is your natural preference.

Do I make decisions more objectively, weighing the pros and cons, or based on how I feel about the issue, and how I and others will be affected by it?

For Thinkers, logic rules. When making a decision, it's as if they take a step back and analyze the issue logically and impersonally, asking themselves: "Does this make sense? What are the pros and cons? What are the ramifications of the decision?" In other words, they *objectify* the decision. For Feelers, the process is just the opposite. They take a step forward, injecting themselves into the equation, and ask: "How do I feel about this? How will it affect me and others? Is this the right thing to do? What are my personal values telling me to do?" In other words, they *personalize* the situation.

Jean faced the kind of dilemma not uncommon for Feeling types. She needed to travel from Boston to New York for a conference, and a colleague invited her to ride with him in his car. Under normal circumstances, this would have been an ideal arrangement, but there was a hitch: Jean didn't respect her colleague, and, more important, she didn't like him. The only other feasible option was to take the train, which would be a major inconvenience. Not only would it cost a lot more, but it would take almost twice as long, since she would have to take taxis to and from the stations. Her Thinking friend Sandra's reaction was typical: "Are you nuts? You're going to waste two days and who knows how much money just because you don't like this guy? Nobody's asking you to marry him—just to spend four hours in the car with him!"

Still, Jean decided to take the train. Although she agreed with her Thinking friend that it might not be the smart thing to do, she believed it was the *right* thing to do. For not only would she feel like a hypocrite taking the ride with a person she clearly disliked, but she would have to pretend she liked him for several hours, and that felt phony and went too much against her values.

Might another Feeling type have handled the situation differently? Of course. But this demonstrates how important personal feelings and values are to Feeling types, and the length to which many will go to remain true to their beliefs.

Laura and Ted both sat through the same conflict-riddled staff meeting, in which they found themselves on opposite sides of a heated debate about whether to go ahead with a public relations campaign that Ted found offensive. After the meeting adjourned, Laura, a Thinker, calmly suggested she and Ted have lunch together. For Ted, a Feeler, the idea was crazy. How could Laura be so calm and unaffected after that painful and contentious meeting? And how could she be so unaware of how rattled Ted still felt? He certainly didn't feel like spending any time with her now. And, in fact, he

was still too upset to even think about eating. Ted remained focused on the disharmony, and felt a personal reaction to it, whereas Laura had never taken the argument or campaign to heart, and remained objective and detached.

Which words describe me better: logical and analytical, or sensitive and empathetic?

Naturally, Thinkers tend to be better at some things than Feelers, and Feelers better at some things than Thinkers. Since people enjoy using their natural strengths, it comes as no surprise that preferences for Thinking or Feeling will often influence career choices. The helping professions, for example, attract larger numbers of Feelers, because these jobs give them the opportunity to satisfy one of their greatest needs, to help people. This is certainly not meant to imply that Thinkers, by definition, are insensitive and self-centered. But Feelers tend to have an innate drive to understand others, and derive great satisfaction from helping them in whatever ways they can. For this reason, medicine (nursing, in particular), teaching, counseling, and sales are just a few of the areas that attract large numbers of Feelers.

Thinkers also derive their greatest satisfaction from using their natural gifts, one of which is the ability to analyze situations logically and objectively. Business, and especially management, for example, attracts a lot of Thinkers, in part because when it comes to making the hard decision—decisions frequently based primarily on the bottom line, and what's best for the company (even when that may have negative effects on its employees), it's Thinkers who are more easily able to do this with clarity and conviction.

The discussion was getting pretty heated between Jason and Richard. The decision to relocate the clothing manufacturing company they both worked for to Mexico had already been made. At issue was how far the company should go to salvage the jobs of the seven hundred workers — many of whose parents and grandparents had worked for the company. In a last-ditch effort to save their jobs, and their town, the employees proposed they buy the facility and operate the plant themselves. That model had been successful in similar situations, but they needed the company to finance the buyout.

Jason, the vice president for finance, argued against the deal. "First, let me say, I am very sympathetic to the plight of the workers. I've known several of them for years and, on a personal level, feel terrible about what they are going through. But my first concern has to be the economic well-being of the company. And, frankly, what they are proposing is a highly speculative venture. If we weren't able to make enough of a profit for it to make sense to stay here, how can people without professional management expertise be expected to? Besides, the rate of return we will receive on our investment *if* they should happen to succeed is simply not as high as we can get from a dozen other proven investment vehicles. Regardless of how unpleasant the situation, our primary obligation is to our stockholders, and I just can't, in good conscience, recommend a deal about which I have such serious reservations."

Richard, vice president for human resources, was turning redder by the minute. "First of all, I don't agree that investing in the employees is any riskier than any other venture we might get involved in for one big reason: they are highly motivated to make it work. For Pete's sake, their lives — the life of their *town* — depends on their succeeding! How can you have any doubts they will work their hearts out to make it work? Second, yes, we are in business to make money — and we make lots of it. But we owe something to the people who have helped us make all that money for close to a hundred years. We're not talking about a few jobs here. We're talking about closing down the biggest employer in the county and moving away to Mexico, not because we're going out of business, not even because we weren't making a profit, but because we want to make *more* of a profit. All I'm saying is many things go into the bottom line, and profitability is surely a big one. But in order to be a responsible corporate citizen, you have to take into account how this decision will affect real people — and not just our stockholders — for years and years to come, and don't do just what is financially conservative, but do what is right!"

While one decision-making process is not better than the other, Jason the Thinker and Richard the Feeler offer a good example of how different types use different criteria to make decisions. It's not that Jason is heartless, but like a classic Thinker, he simply stepped back from the decision, analyzed it logically, and came to his conclusion, based on what he believed was best for the company. Richard, like a classic Feeler, stepped forward and put himself in the employees' shoes. Strongly influenced by his personal beliefs and values, he fought for what he felt would be best for the employees.

Thinkers are often attracted to careers that deal primarily with goods, rather than services: for example, manufacturing, engineering, and research and development. It's not that Thinkers don't like to or can't work with people, but jobs that require them to constantly pay attention to, anticipate, and respond to people's feelings are just so much less clear cut than dealing with products, or commodities, that are constant and predictable. Many Thinkers are most satisfied in jobs where there is a minimum of employee hand-holding or caretaking. They like working with other people just as competent as they are.

Is it more important to be truthful, even if it hurts someone's feelings or to be tactful, even if it means telling a little white lie?

Feelers are naturally more attentive and concerned with other people because they have such a strong need to be liked. Consequently, they will often go to great lengths to please others. This can take such simple forms as just being helpful and friendly, which most Feelers genuinely are, to the sometimes unhealthy but common tendency to take on other people's problems and burdens as their own. In practically every organization across the country, you can find the nurturer, the person to whom coworkers go for emotional support and comfort. And while not a formal job title, it might

just as well be, for it is what he or she does really well — listen to people's problems and sometimes give them good advice. Whether appreciated by the company or not, these people provide a valuable service.

However, in their desire to help and please others, some Feelers are also notorious white liars. Anxious not to deliberately cause someone discomfort, embarrassment, or hurt feelings, they will often engage in half truths, or avoid unpleasant subjects altogether, if they can get away with it.

One morning, after being away for a week on vacation, Tim walked into the office with a new look. Possessed by who knows what, he had shorn just about all of his normally long, yet stylish, hair. In its place was what could best be described as the kind of ubiquitous crew cut ten-year-old boys were commonly given by their mothers in their kitchens in the 1950s. Jill, his colleague, and a strong Feeler, was the first person he encountered.

"So, what do you think?" asked Tim excitedly. Jill was taken aback. What she honestly thought was that this former hunk looked like a refugee from a third-world country. But she wouldn't actually admit that in a million years. What she managed to say was, "Well, that certainly is a look! You know, that cut really accentuates your eyes," and she fled down the hall to avoid offending him or further embarrassing herself.

True to their style, Tim's Thinking colleagues were more honest, and more blunt. Alex's response pretty much summed it all up: "Two questions: one, what did you do to your head?, and two, what could you *possibly* have been thinking at the time?"

Thinkers don't mean to be cruel, any more than Feelers mean to be dishonest. It's just that, above all else, Thinkers value truth and honesty, and if that occasionally hurts someone's feelings, so be it. Feelers highly value tact and diplomacy, and believe it should be used whenever possible to avoid causing anyone unnecessary pain or discomfort.

While Feelers are often criticized for being too soft and emotional, and Thinkers are often criticized as being cold and insensitive, neither of these is an accurate characterization. But to each other, they often do appear this way.

Which usually persuades me more?
A good logical argument,
or
a strong emotional appeal?

Just as Thinkers and Feelers make decisions based upon different criteria, so, too, are they persuaded by different arguments. Feelers are naturally empathetic and value the feelings of others, even if they do not make sense or are not logical. Thinkers, on the other hand, are usually not convinced of anything unless it is logical. Feelings are valid, if they are a logical reaction to the circumstances. Because of this difference, it's not surprising that Thinkers and Feelers misunderstand each other so often. Feelers tend to be hurt more easily and more frequently, and Thinkers are often surprised and confused to learn they were responsible for making it happen.

Thinkers also pride themselves on their ability to rule fairly in disputes. They are keen on the principle of one standard or rule, applied fairly and justly to everyone. Even if they do not personally like the consequence of the ruling, they respect the idea of fairness above all. Feelers are much more concerned with mercy and harmony than they are with justice. So they look for and usually find the extenuating circumstances that necessitate the exception to the rule.

Which is the greater compliment:
to be tough
or
to be tender?

While all of us need to be tough sometimes and tender at others, it is typically the Thinkers who pride themselves on their ability to remain dispassionate and firm in their actions. But it's important to make the distinction that if the issue is a personal one, or the people involved are loved ones, Thinkers will often claim they are just as tenderhearted as the next person. And Feelers, usually quick to claim tenderhearted as the more apt description, can be surprisingly tough and unyielding when it comes to their personal convictions.

Rachel and Suzanne, two Feelers, held opposite views on the controversial issue of abortion. On the morning of an anticipated court ruling, both stood out in front of the courthouse with signs and voices raised. They were equally passionate, equally unwilling to compromise their beliefs. A friend commented that no one would ever believe it, but the two women had been best friends in college. But the abortion debate had caused a rending of their friendship that would probably never be mended.

Had the two women been Thinkers, they might have been able to put the issue aside and maintain their friendship in spite of their differences. As Feelers, it was impossible for either of them to separate their values from the rest of their lives.

Thinking and Feeling is the only dimension of Personality Type in which there appears to be a gender difference. That is, in the American population, roughly 50 percent are Thinkers and 50 percent are Feelers, but of the Thinkers, about 65 percent are men, and of the Feelers, 65 percent are women. In addition to these biological influences on Type, the American culture overtly and subtly encourages males to act more Thinking and females to act more Feeling, which often imposes an unfair and unwelcome burden on Thinking women and Feeling men.

Okay, you know the drill. Try to figure out which you are — a Thinker or a Feeler. Then we will move on to describe the fourth and final type dimension.

Thinker   Feeler

Judger or Perceiver: Planning It or Winging It?

The final type dimension describes the very different ways people like to organize their world, and how they like to live their lives. And, once again, we need to clarify the terms. Being a Judger doesn't mean a person is necessarily judgmental, any more than being a Perceiver means a person is particularly perceptive. Perceiving refers to one's innate drive to keep things open, to keep taking in information, to keep perceiving. Judging refers to an opposite innate drive, to close things down, make a decision, or to judge.

Do I tend to make most decisions quickly and easily
or
does making decisions often make me anxious and unsure?

Would I rather have things settled and decided
or
be able to leave my options open, just in case something unexpected comes up?

The reason Judgers like to decide and Perceivers like to keep things open has to do with tension. This tension is often experienced on an unconscious level, without the person even being aware of it. Since experiencing tension is uncomfortable, human beings naturally try to reduce their discomfort. Judgers feel tension until an issue is decided, so they move to closure as soon as possible. This can take many forms, but usually involves making a judgment or decision about something. And usually the more important the decision, the stronger the need to resolve the issue quickly. For example, when a Judger is invited to a concert, he experiences an urge to decide. Whether or not he wants to go, he feels a need to make a decision. And unless he has a lot of ambivalence about accepting, he usually feels relieved once things are settled.

But Perceivers experience an opposite tension, for it is being forced to decide that causes them pressure and discomfort. Therefore, they alleviate the tension by not deciding, by keeping their options open as long as possible. If a Perceiver were invited to the concert, unless she really wanted to go, she would likely feel uncomfortable deciding or making a commitment too far in advance. After all, she would reason, something better might come along!

These are such opposite styles that Judgers and Perceivers often miscommunicate. Because Judgers are more definitive about everything, they tend to speak with authority. During a discussion, a Judger tends to hear decisions being made, even if they have not been. Conversely, since Perceivers are more equivocal about everything, they may even hear firm plans as undecided, as if they were only options being considered.

Since their desire is for closure, Judgers generally require less information to make decisions than do Perceivers. A scene played out every day at lunch counters across the country illustrates this point.

It's lunch time and Robert and Alex are deciding what to order. Robert, a Judger, looks over the menu quickly, decides on a tuna salad on wheat toast with iced tea — the same lunch he has on most trips to this diner. After several minutes, the waiter appears to take their order, but Alex is still looking. He asks the waiter a series of questions regarding how lean the roast beef is today, whether the soup has a chicken or beef stock base, and if the chicken salad is made with white meat or dark. Still not sure, he asks for a few more minutes while

Robert scowls and his stomach growls. Even after Alex finally chooses the turkey club, and the waiter walks away, he looks wistfully at the menu again, and says, "Maybe I should have ordered a burger."

Because Judgers like things decided, they are most comfortable when they can make a plan and stick to it. Conversely, they can find it disconcerting when plans are changed unexpectedly.

Planning a vacation together became a torturous exercise for new friends, Lucy and Jean. Since Lucy had won a trip for two to the Caribbean, the destination was never at issue. But Lucy's clear preference for Judging and Jean's equally clear preference for Perceiving became obvious early on when Lucy surprised Jean with a detailed itinerary for the entire week. Not only was there a plan for each of the seven days, but she had even included times when they would eat, swim, and shop.

Jean was shocked. Although Lucy didn't present her plan as a take-it-or-leave-it proposition, Jean had imagined a very different scenario. Since she would be visiting a place she'd never been, she was eager to explore. She had pictured herself wandering the winding streets leisurely, shopping and sightseeing, and just letting herself be swept along by the natural rhythm of the island. She craved the freedom to respond spontaneously to whatever new adventure she might encounter. The more she thought about having her time so planned out and controlled, the more uncomfortable she got.

Happily, Lucy and Jean were able to discuss their personality differences and very different expectations and arrive at some creative compromises, involving more independence for each. This arrangement allowed each to have the kind of experience they desired.

Lucy and Jean's story also illustrates how different Judgers and Perceivers are with regard to order and structure. Judgers are usually more comfortable with the notion of rules and place high importance on following them, while Perceivers view rules as unwanted restrictions on their freedom and their ability to be spontaneous. Likewise, Judgers are generally more comfortable with authority and have a natural respect for hierarchy. Perceivers are more naturally inclined to rebel against, or at least question, authority and often feel it's better to ask someone to pardon their behavior—*after* the fact—than to risk asking for, and being denied, permission *beforehand*.

Is it very important for me to be in control of most situations
or
am I often comfortable letting others call the shots?

Everyone likes to be in charge of himself or herself. But the strength of the need for control over others and situations is often significantly different for Judgers and Perceivers. Because they like things settled, Judgers are less patient waiting for things to happen by themselves, and more apt to step in and take charge. Whether in small things, such as rearranging the chairs in a room to make a meeting more functional, or in large things, such as encouraging a friend to accept or reject a certain job offer, Judgers often have strong opinions and are generally not shy about sharing them.

While Perceivers can also have strong opinions, they are more likely to see things in shades of gray rather than as black and white. It is important to reiterate that neither style is better than the other. Rather, each has strengths the other doesn't, and often envies. For example, many Judgers admire Perceivers' ability to stay open, see both sides of an issue, be spontaneous, shift gears quickly, and not take themselves too seriously. Many Perceivers admire Judgers' ability to make quick decisions, be organized and productive, fulfill their responsibilities, and set and reach their goals. But no matter which is our natural preference, the great majority of us have good access to our other side. This helps us become competent individuals. But occasionally, we encounter people who do not have this balance. If they are Judgers, they may be rigid, inflexible, and incapable of compromise. And Perceivers without the balancing attributes of Judging may be so indecisive that they procrastinate their lives away and never accomplish anything meaningful.

Am I very conscious of time, and almost always punctual
or
do I frequently run late and find time has somehow slipped away?

It is widely assumed that President Bill Clinton is a Perceiver. In fact, he has such a reputation among the Washington press corps for being late, he inspired a new expression: "Clinton Standard

Time"—which means "about an hour after he was supposed to be somewhere."

It's not that Perceivers have to be late, but they view the concept of time differently than Judgers. Judgers often plan their lives in fifteen-, thirty-, and sixty-minute increments. Since they have such a strong inclination toward productivity, they view time as an essential tool to accomplish their goals: time is a precious, finite commodity that should be used thoughtfully and respectfully. And above all, they don't waste time!

Perceivers view time as somewhat of a renewable resource, something of which there is almost always more. In fact, they are fond of saying: "Oh, I'll make time for that."

A friend reported that in the army, he encountered two types of time: "general time" and "private time." The difference, he explained, is this: "Eight o'clock private time is eight o'clock on the nose, because when ordered to be there, that's when a private has to show up. But eight o'clock general time could be eight o'clock, nine o'clock, or basically whenever the general feels like showing up!"

While Judgers are more likely to be punctual than Perceivers, this is not because Perceivers are any less conscientious about their obligations. It's simply that they lose track of time so easily because they are busy experiencing and perceiving the moment as part of a process. This is in contrast to Judgers, who are more focused on the product and often view the time it takes to do something almost as a necessary evil—an obstacle to getting to the rewards of finishing a task. In fact, many Judgers

feel an infusion of energy when they finish a task, while Perceivers feel that energy boost when starting a new project.

Clearly, courses offered to help people manage their time better were designed for Perceivers by Judgers. And although many Perceivers sign up for such sessions with the best intentions, they often find the methods and techniques are too uncomfortable, limiting, and boring to create a permanent change in their behavior. For Judgers, deadlines are for the most part, helpful, honored, and strictly observed. But for Perceivers, deadlines are sort of like an alarm clock going off, a signal that now it's time to get started.

Which is more true of me: I'm generally very organized
or
I often have trouble finding things and keeping organized?

Most Judgers are usually well organized, especially compared to Perceivers. "A place for everything and everything in its place" might be the motto for Judgers, while Perceivers are more likely to be overheard saying: "I don't understand, it was here a minute ago!" (When considering your answer to this question, remember that we all have to be organized to a certain extent or we could not function in the world. And no one is accusing you of being a bad person if you admit to having trouble being organized!) But it is an important difference between Judgers and Perceivers, and therefore helpful to explore.

The reason Judgers and Perceivers differ in these

ways is connected to the central issues of closure and decision making, as demonstrated by the experience of Doreen and Ruth.

Although job sharing worked out well financially, and fit their schedules well, there was one constant strain in their relationship: "the desk problem." Working the same job but at different hours meant Doreen and Ruth shared a desk. Ruth, a Judger, kept the desk in a predictably neat and orderly way. She liked to work on one project at a time until it was completed, and at the end of her shift, she typically tidied up, and made sure to file all necessary papers in their proper places. She would then place her "to do" list — all items duly checked off upon their completion — in her designated drawer. And she didn't seem to have a problem storing all her files in the filing cabinet assigned to her. At the end of her shift, she left the top of the desk clean and bare for Doreen.

Doreen's style was quite different, for she preferred to work on many projects almost simultaneously, and never seemed to have enough room to store her files. In fact, she had long ago outgrown her one filing cabinet, and her files had spilled over onto the small credenza and even the guest chair in the office. While Ruth resented this intrusion on her space, it was the desk problem that irked her the most. For not only had Doreen appropriated the only two other pieces of furniture in their office for her additional filing space, but she would also often leave piles of file folders on the desk at the end of her shift. So annoying had this practice become that Ruth threatened to end the job-sharing arrangement.

In considering this dilemma, it would be reasonable to ask the question: "How can two people with the identical job generate such different amounts of paperwork?" The answer lies in their different type preferences. Ruth, the Judger, makes more and quicker decisions. When a memo announcing a professional conference three months hence arrives on her desk, her normal response is to look it over and decide a course of action. If she wants to attend, she will send it to her boss with a request for funding. If she doesn't want to, but thinks it might benefit a coworker, she will pass it along. And if she considers it worthless, she'll simply discard it. In any event, like most Judgers, she has made a decision, and the paper is *gone!*

Doreen, being the strong Perceiver she is, handles the same situation very differently. Her reasoning goes something like this: "This looks great, but this conference isn't for three months. Who knows what I'll be doing then, whether I'll want to go, be able to make the time, or have the budget for it. Now, if I put this away in some file, I'm sure I'll forget it. So . . . until I can make a decision about it, I'll put it over here, in my to do file . . . *just for now.*

It must be clear that in her drive to keep her options open, Doreen simply has not made a decision, hence the need to hold on to yet another piece of paper. But, in reality, many of the files that have overtaken their office are full of paperwork which falls into this category. An interesting addendum: Perceivers often make decisions by default — that is, after a deadline has come and gone. At that point, they are often (but not always!) willing to discard the offending paperwork.

A compounding reason that Perceivers often have more paper than Judgers is that Perceivers like to collect as much information as possible, figuring: "Maybe I don't need this right now, but I might sometime in the future." This is true whether it is paper, old clothes, books, household gadgets, or just about any other object. Perceivers tend to be pack rats. Conversely, Judgers often take the position: "If in doubt, throw it out!" They reason that if they own something but haven't used it for a long time, they probably won't need it anytime soon.

Which is truer for me: I prefer to get my work or chores done before I relax
or
I can often find compelling reasons to put a task off until a later time?

Sometimes we describe Judgers as having more of a work ethic and Perceivers as having more of a play ethic. By this we mean that Judgers often feel compelled to finish their work before they play or relax, while Perceivers are often comfortable deferring work until after they enjoy some compelling experience. Whereas Judgers often derive their greatest satisfaction from completing a task, for Perceivers, enjoying what they are doing is often equally important.

This is not meant to suggest that Judgers are conscientious and Perceivers are lazy. It is Perceivers' attitude about time, coupled with being more interested in and energized by the process, and placing a higher value on having fun, which contributes to their feeling that "there will always be time later on" to finish the job.

The difference between Judgers' work ethic and Perceivers' play ethic is often reflected in their attitudes about taking time off from work, and how they spend the time when they do. Taking a "mental health day" is definitely a Perceiver concept, sort of the grown-up version of playing hooky. In general, Judgers are loath to take time off from work to begin with, frequently accumulating more vacation time than they will actually use. And on those rare occasions when Judgers do take a day off (not a scheduled vacation or a bona fide sick day), you'll seldom find them lying on the couch watching television. More likely, they will use the time to do all those chores they've been meaning to, like cleaning out the attic, washing the windows, or painting the porch. The idea of just hanging around makes them uncomfortable because they aren't being productive. Perceivers, on the other hand, are more naturally inclined to follow the admonition of the character played by Robin Williams in the movie *Dead Poet's Society* and "seize the day!"

The latest studies indicate that Judging types represent about 60 percent and Perceiving types about 40 percent of the American population. You now have a good idea of whether you are a Judger or a Perceiver. And once again, we ask you indicate your preference on the scale below.

(J) Judger ▰▰▰▰ ▲ ▰▰▰ **Perceiver (P)**

Great! At this point, we'd like you to go back and review your guess for each of the four preferences, and record them in the spaces below. And don't worry if you are still unsure about any of them. In fact, we encourage you to think of all your choices only as "best-guess estimates." In the next chapter, we will lead you through the "verification process," the system for accurately identifying your one true type.

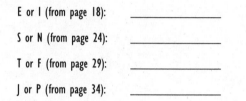

E or I (from page 18):   _____

S or N (from page 24):   _____

T or F (from page 29):   _____

J or P (from page 34):   _____

ALPHABET SOUP: USING LETTERS TO DESCRIBE TYPES

Because it is extremely cumbersome to constantly refer to a type by the full name of each preference, we use letters as shorthand. Thus, rather than say, "Introverted, Sensing, Thinking, Judging type," we say, "ISTJ." As you become more familiar with the letters, you will find using them becomes second nature. Please note that all the preferences are abbreviated by their first letter (E for Extravert, S for Sensor, etc.) *except* Intuitive, which is abbreviated by the letter N. This is because the letter I is used to abbreviate Introvert, and it would be too confusing to have two preferences abbreviated by the same letter.

SYNERGY: WHAT MAKES TYPE SO POWERFUL

One last point before moving on to Chapter 2. The word *synergy* is roughly defined to mean that the total of something is greater than just the sum of its parts. And this is certainly true of Type. From our experience, it is virtually impossible to understand Type without first learning about the individual components, or preferences, that make up a type. But keep in mind that as important as the individual preferences are, it is the whole type, the particular combination of preferences, and the way they interact with each other that enables Type to provide such incredibly useful insights about people.

For example, there are eight Extraverted types. But since no one is *just* an Extravert, each person's other three preferences play a huge role in influencing his or her behavior. In other words, people who are ISTJs and people who are INFPs are both Introverts, but since their other three letters are opposite, they are very different types of people. Even one letter, say, the difference between an ENFP and an ESFP, can be profound. While this may not seem terribly significant at this moment, it will soon become apparent how important it is in understanding the obvious and subtle differences between the sixteen types. And this understanding is essential if you are to learn how to SpeedRead people accurately.

So, on to Chapter 2 to determine your one and only personality type!

CHAPTER TWO

To Thine Own Self Be True: Verifying Profiles

Very shortly you will begin the process of "verifying" your type, that is, deciding which of the sixteen types describes you best. To help you do this, and to increase your basic understanding of Type, there is one more important concept you need to become familiar with — the "type hierarchy." Each type has its own pattern, which ranks the parts of that type which lead, are naturally favored, and are the most developed. Each type's pattern also identifies which parts of one's type are the least favored and least developed. (When we say naturally favored, we don't mean to imply that people make a conscious choice to lead with a certain preference. Remember, this is an unconscious, involuntary predisposition.)*

A type's hierarchy is really a blueprint of its natural strengths and weaknesses. And since all people of one type share the same hierarchy, once you know a person's type, you will have a very good idea as to his or her innate strengths and weaknesses.

For example, most Sensors are practical, realistic, and detail oriented. However, they are also often limited in their ability to see the big picture or see possibilities that don't currently exist (because their Intuition is not well developed). Conversely, most Intuitives easily see patterns, possibilities, and implications, but due to their less-developed Sensing, can be inaccurate with facts, impractical, and unrealistic.

*For a more thorough explanation and discussion of this aspect of Type theory, see *Do What You Are*.

While Thinkers are usually logical, analytical, and objective, their "inferior" Feeling can result in their inability to deal sensitively with others, or to be in touch with their own values. And Feelers, whose talents lie in understanding, empathizing, and communicating with others, may well lack objectivity and take things far too personally to make good decisions.

A few more things you need to know: *By definition*, there are four possible parts of each person's type that make up their hierarchy, and they are *always* only what are called the "functions": Sensing or Intuition, Thinking or Feeling. The hierarchy does not involve Extraversion or Introversion, Judging or Perceiving — which are called attitudes or orientations, and are represented by the first and last letters in a type.

The order of importance of these four functions is different for each type. In other words, for one type, Intuition may be the greatest strength. In another type, Sensing might be the strongest. Likewise, Thinking is the most important for some types, while Feeling is for others.

And each of the four functions has a different role to play. We call the first function the "Lead"* because it is the boss; the most developed and most trustworthy part of that type. The second in command or "Second," for short, is also reflected in the letters of a person's type. The important job of

the Second is to help the Lead by creating balance — either promoting sound decision making or encouraging accurate information gathering. There is also what we call the "Third" function, which, in most people, does not begin to develop in earnest until around midlife. In young people, because it is so undeveloped, it is often more of a weakness than a strength, but as people mature, it can become an important ally. Finally, there is the least-developed function (or "Least," for short). In each type's pattern, the Least is the opposite of the Lead. Since the Lead is the most developed, the most trusted of the functions, the Least is the least developed and least trustworthy. It is the person's Achilles' heel — that part which, when used, tends to cause the most frustration and stress. Unfortunately, many adults *never* adequately develop their Least. And for those who do, the process doesn't usually happen until late in one's fifties.

You may find the following metaphor useful; it is commonly used to help people understand the idea of the type hierarchy.

Picture a family of four taking a car trip. In the front seat there are two adults, and in the back are two children — one about ten years old, the other only three. Think of the Lead as the adult driving, and the Second as the other adult doing the navigating. Think of the ten-year-old as the Third, and the three-year-old as the Least. Clearly, you want the Lead to be in charge (somebody has to drive!), and the Second to help navigate. But you still have to pay attention to the kids (the third and Least) in the back seat — to break up fights, stop to go to the bathroom, etc.). We all operate at our best

THE MOST- TO LEAST-FAVORED FUNCTIONS

Organized by Temperament Groups

	Type	LEAD #1	Second #2	Third #3	LEAST #4
SJs	ESTJ	Thinking	Sensing	Intuition	Feeling
	ISTJ	Sensing	Thinking	Feeling	Intuition
	ESFJ	Feeling	Sensing	Intuition	Thinking
	ISFJ	Sensing	Feeling	Thinking	Intuition
SPs	ESTP	Sensing	Thinking	Feeling	Intuition
	ISTP	Thinking	Sensing	Intuition	Feeling
	ESFP	Sensing	Feeling	Thinking	Intuition
	ISFP	Feeling	Sensing	Intuition	Thinking
NTs	ENTJ	Thinking	Intuition	Sensing	Feeling
	INTJ	Intuition	Thinking	Feeling	Sensing
	ENTP	Intuition	Thinking	Feeling	Sensing
	INTP	Thinking	Intuition	Sensing	Feeling
NFs	ENFJ	Feeling	Intuition	Sensing	Thinking
	INFJ	Intuition	Feeling	Thinking	Sensing
	ENFP	Intuition	Feeling	Thinking	Sensing
	INFP	Feeling	Intuition	Sensing	Thinking

KEY

Thinking: making logical, objective decisions
Feeling: understanding and relating to people
Sensing: being in the moment; seeing things realistically
Intuition: seeing possibilities and implications

TEMPERAMENT GROUPS

(A thorough discussion of Temperament is presented in Chapter 4)

SJs: Sensing Judgers or "Traditionalists"
SPs: Sensing Perceivers or "Experiencers"
NTs: Intuitive Thinkers or "Conceptualizers"
NFs: Intuitive Feelers or "Idealists"

when we are using our Lead and Second functions. But occasionally, due to stress or other factors, we are forced to operate out of our less preferred functions. When this happens—especially when we use our Least—it's as if the three-year-old suddenly jumped over the seat and started driving the car, often with predictably disastrous results!*

So how do you know what the hierarchy is for each type? We have developed a chart that ranks the most- to least-favored functions and present it below. While you are welcome to look it over now, it will be most valuable as a tool for helping you verify your type, and, later on, as a reference for understanding other types in depth.

SO, WHAT'S MY TYPE?

From reading about and estimating your type preferences in Chapter 1, you probably have already identified your type. All you need to do now is to confirm, or "verify," it. Or you may be confident that you've identified two or three preferences that describe it but are still unclear about the remaining one(s). Or, perhaps, you are still unclear about any of your preferences, though this is very unlikely. But if you do fall in this last group, please don't worry about it! There are several good reasons why, for some people, it takes a little longer

*We first learned this metaphor from Mary McCaulley in 1980 and gratefully acknowledge her insight. An excellent book that deals in depth with the effects of Type dynamics, and specifically the role of the Least function, is *Beside Ourselves*, by Naomi L. Quenk, Consulting Psychologists Press, 1993.

to identify their type than for others. Ultimately, you will.

THE VERIFYING PROCESS

Verifying your type is really an exercise in the process of elimination. It's always best to start with those preferences you feel most sure about. For example, suppose you are quite sure you are an Extravert, Intuitive, and Thinker, but are unclear if you are a Judger or a Perceiver. You would begin by reading two profiles: ENTJ and ENTP. Although these two types share a lot in common, they are also very different in significant ways. In all likelihood, after reading these two profiles, you will decide that one is your "true" type. Does that mean that every word in the profile will sound exactly like you? No, because as we've said before, every person is unique. However, when you read "your" type profile, it should sound a lot like you; if you feel that about 80 percent of it describes you well, you've probably found your type.

Speaking of true types, people will often ask: "Do I have to be only ONE type? . . . It seems there are times when I'm more like this one, and other times I'm more like that one." While a few different types may describe you fairly well, we believe—based on helping thousands of people identify theirs—that everyone really does have *one and only one* true type, although in some people it is harder to identify than in others.

But back to the verifying process. Again, suppose you are clear about three preferences: say

Introversion, Thinking, and Judging, but are not clear if you are a Sensor or an Intuitive. You would begin by reading two profiles: ISTJ and INTJ. If you are still unclear, you might find that rereading the sections which describe Sensing and Intuition will clarify the issue for you.

Another way to help verify a type is by using the Most- to Least-Favored Functions chart. Suppose you are clear about your preferences for Extraversion, Intuition, and Judging, but unclear whether you're a Thinker or a Feeler. If you look at the chart, you will notice the Lead for ENTJ is Thinking (and the Least is Feeling), while the Lead for ENFJ is Feeling (and the Least is Thinking). Since these two types are so different, this may confirm for you which is your true type. At this point, you should probably reread the section on Thinking and Feeling (page 24) and then the ENFJ and ENTJ profiles. One profile will certainly sound a lot more like you.

An important thing to keep in mind while going through this verification process: you are trying to find the type that describes the way you *are*, not necessarily the way you might *want to be*. In our experience, the most common reason people have trouble verifying their type is that they believe it is better to be a different type or preference. Remembering that all types are equally valuable, and that no matter what type you turn out to be is fine, usually results in people saying: "You know, I guess if I'm really honest with myself, I really am a Thinker (or whatever!), but I sure would like to be a Feeler."

Let's consider one more example. Suppose you

are clear on only two preferences, say Extraversion and Judging. This would mean you are unsure of both middle letters. Beginning with those letters you are surest about, you would need to read the profiles for all four Extraverted Judging types: ESTJ, ESFJ, ENTJ, and ENFJ. And because these types are so different from each other, you will almost certainly be able to quickly eliminate one or two from consideration. Suppose after reading these four, you are convinced you are a Thinker, rather than a Feeler. Then you have reduced the potential types down to just two: ENTJ and ESTJ. And again, while these types have a lot in common (the Lead is Thinking, for example), they are also different in some significant ways.

What do you do if you've reread the appropriate sections and several profiles and *still* aren't sure of your type? First of all, don't panic! Let us assure you that you do have a type, and you will find it. But rather than be distracted by the fact that you haven't found it yet, we suggest you pick the closest one you can and consider that "a working hypothesis," recognizing that as you learn more about Type in the coming chapters, you are very likely either to confirm your hypothesis or to find your true type. It is important to remain open to the process and realize that your efforts will pay off eventually.

Reviewing the Profiles

The descriptions in the Verifying Profiles are, by necessity, somewhat generic. That is, they describe characteristics and behaviors which are true for most people of that type. Obviously, not every word in a profile will accurately describe you. For, as we've said before, every person is unique, and although ten people of the same type will have a tremendous amount in common, none will be identical. So you need to look for *patterns* of similarities.

Some people find a second opinion helpful and ask a spouse or close friend to read their profile, or a profile they think may fit them. This may be a good idea, especially if you can't decide between two or more types. After all, few of us are totally objective when it comes to ourselves.

One last point. The profiles discuss each type's natural strengths and potential blind spots. It is often easier to notice and acknowledge our strengths than our weaknesses. Therefore, if you find the strengths sound a lot like you, but the blind spots do not, then either you have not yet found your true type or you may be unwilling to own up to your potential weaknesses. If you fall into the latter group, we encourage you to allow yourself to honestly take stock of your weaknesses (recognizing that everyone has them!), and that once you are in touch with your own, you'll know where to start should you decide to engage in some self-improvement.

So on to verify your type!*

---

*For each type and temperament, we provide an estimate of the percentages found in the American population. These percentages were developed by Dr. Charles K. Martin of the Center for Applications of Psychological Type (CAPT), Gainesville, Florida.

ESTJ

Extraverted, Sensing, Thinking, Judging
Estimated to be between 12 and 15 percent of the American population

ESTJs are the consummate project managers. Regardless of the nature of the task to be accomplished or whether they do it as part of their job or for fun, these Lead Thinkers are talented at realistically sizing up a situation, setting goals, determining available resources, and organizing and supervising the personnel to make sure the job gets done correctly, always in the most efficient manner. Logical and analytical, ESTJs are natural leaders and quick decision makers. Their serious, no-nonsense approach to life inspires confidence and trust from the people they work and live with. Respected for their objectivity and fairness, ESTJs live by a code that includes working hard and behaving honorably and ethically. They are seldom accused of playing favorites or acting capriciously. Thoroughly committed to the organizations they belong to, they are willing to take on difficult assignments and make the tough decisions for the good of the organization.

Because ESTJs' Least function is Feeling, they may inadvertently act insensitively at times. But when they do, it is because they are not very tuned in to the emotional side of people, and, consequently, they may not consider how people feel about an issue particularly relevant to the decision-making process. Although they are often outgoing and friendly, ESTJs are highly competitive, have a strong need to be in control, and are also strong willed and very verbal. Therefore, by the sheer power of their personality, they may easily intimidate less assertive people.

Often drawn to work environments that are highly structured, ESTJs are most comfortable when everyone knows the ground rules, and where there are established operating procedures and clear expectations. They are loyal team players who are more interested in maintaining than challenging the status quo. They respect authority and expect others to do the same. Practical and realistic, ESTJs consider it important to be accurate with facts and to pay close attention to details. ESTJs are particularly good at maintaining existing systems and using resources wisely.

Traditional and often conservative, ESTJs have little interest in or enthusiasm for experimental, creative, or new approaches. Instead, they prefer to stick with familiar and tested ways of doing things. Nor do they adapt well or easily to change. As a result, they can be forceful and effective opponents, constantly challenging the necessity of change. They are rarely convinced by anything other than hard facts and logical reasoning.

Because they are so focused on the present, they may fail to appreciate how current actions may affect the future. And they are not particularly good at anticipating future needs or forecasting future trends. Because they tend to make quick decisions, they sometimes rush to judgment before they have carefully and thoroughly considered all their options. And once they have made up their minds, they are difficult to convince otherwise. When they slow down and take the extra time to listen patiently to suggestions, they may find the added perspective helps them make better choices for themselves and others.

ISTJ

Introverted, Sensing, Thinking, Judging
Estimated to be between 7 and 10 percent of the American population

ISTJs are responsible, reliable, hardworking people whose word is their bond. Literal, precise, and nononsense, they say what they mean and mean what they say. Led by their Sensing, ISTJs are especially attuned to the specifics and details of life. They are careful and accurate about facts, and plan and go about their work in a thoughtful, meticulous fashion. Extremely conscientious people, ISTJs have a strong work ethic and always choose to get their tasks done before they take the time to relax. ISTJs also have excellent memories for details, and can usually recall with impressive clarity seemingly unimportant events that occurred many years in the past. Quiet and serious, ISTJs are often happiest when they are left alone to work at their own pace, without interruption or unsolicited input from others. They know what they have to do and how to do it, and seldom need close, if any, supervision.

Even when they are relaxing, ISTJs are productive, and often enjoy using their hands to do crafts like woodworking, restoring antique autos, pottery, needlepoint, and so on. Many also enjoy reading and being a part of nature by hiking, fishing, or camping.

ISTJs are happiest and most productive doing things in familiar ways in familiar surroundings, and they can become uncomfortable and anxious when faced with a new challenge without being given proper guidance as to how it should be done. Because their Least function is Intuition, they are naturally distrustful of new, untested ways of doing things, especially those with which they have had no firsthand experience. Although they pride themselves on their efficiency, they can resist efforts to improve existing practices if they don't immediately see the practical benefit in doing so. And because they are not global thinkers who naturally think about the big picture and future implications, their skepticism can impede real and needed progress.

Logical and objective, ISTJs are impersonal decision makers, who may at times seem unsympathetic or uncaring. But they make decisions by weighing the pros and cons, and then decide based upon what makes the most sense, given the situation. They are not likely to be significantly influenced by how people will feel about, or be affected by, their decisions. And while they like to be helpful, they are usually comfortable making the tough calls, and don't become preoccupied with how they will be viewed by others. While appeals based solely on emotion may fall on deaf (or at least hard-of-hearing!) ears, ISTJs are eminently fair.

Usually possessing great powers of concentration, ISTJs are not easily diverted or distracted from the task at hand, which they approach in a systematic, step-by-step fashion. However, while their single-minded determination is one of their greatest assets, it can also make them stubborn and unyielding, and incapable of necessary flexibility when they are unexpectedly forced to change their plans or act spontaneously. Likewise, they are very conservative by nature, and are sometimes reluctant to take even reasonable risks. Usually, as they amass a great number of experiences, they become more willing to try new things.

ESFJ

Extraverted, Sensing, Feeling, Judging
Estimated to be between 11 and 14 percent of the American population

The saying "A friend in need is a friend indeed" could well have been inspired by an ESFJ, because ESFJs are often the first to volunteer their assistance. Friendly, outgoing, and sympathetic, these Lead Feelers are extremely sensitive, have a very strong need to please and an equally strong need to be liked and appreciated by others. Generous and loyal, ESFJs tend to be very traditional people who value their family and friends above all else. They give freely of themselves, often committing large amounts of time to work in programs sponsored by charity, community, or religious organizations that serve their communities. Conscientious and hardworking, ESFJs usually have a well-defined code of behavior—based upon the value system to which they subscribe—and wish others would as well. But sometimes it is not enough for them to be good people; they often feel compelled to try and instill their values in others.

Because ESFJs' Least function is Thinking, they are often unable to evaluate situations fairly and objectively. ESFJs are so sensitive, and take things so personally, they rarely see the logic in an argument or reason, and they may not consider objectivity a particularly admirable quality. They tend to personalize everything and have such a relatively thin skin that they are prone to having their feelings hurt easily and often. ESFJs who feel they have been wronged, especially if something they value has been maligned, may take drastic actions, such as ending the relationship with the person who offended them — even if it has been a long-standing friendship. But, more often, ESFJs get into trouble by becoming overly involved and assuming too much responsibility for the feelings of others. In their effort to be good friends, they sometimes run the risk of actually making themselves sick by overburdening themselves with others' problems.

ESFJs are down-to-earth, realistic, and practical people. To many of them, life is a serious business. Therefore, responsibilities and obligations come before relaxation and fun. Although they are not humorless, they may have a hard time taking a joke or being teased — especially if it is about them or something they care deeply about. Many ESFJs especially enjoy their physical possessions, are conscientious about maintaining them, and are very careful to keep their things neat and tidy. In their spare time, many ESFJs like to engage in physical activities — walking, biking, or playing sports. They also often enjoy working with their hands and doing crafts.

Usually very organized and productive, ESFJs are most comfortable following a familiar routine. And they often have difficulty shifting gears and doing things in new or different ways. This can apply equally to little things like taking an unfamiliar road on a car trip, and to big things like changing jobs or moving to a new town. In either case, they do not happily embrace change. ESFJs also tend to see the world in absolute terms; things are either good or bad, right or wrong. Fortunately, most ESFJs have plenty of balance to avoid this temptation, for if they don't, they run the risk of becoming opinionated and judgmental.

ISFJ

Introverted, Sensing, Feeling, Judging
Estimated to be between 7 and 10 percent of the American population

ISFJs have a strong need to belong, and the organizations or groups they choose are lucky to attract these thoughtful, hardworking, and devoted people. As Lead Sensors, ISFJs focus all their energy on the problem or issue that is before them at the moment. They are painstakingly accurate when working with facts, attentive to details, and methodical in applying both qualities in their work. ISFJs like gathering, analyzing, and applying data for some useful purpose, and documenting the results. They generally have excellent memories, and are especially good at remembering dates and events that pertain to people. Consequently, they often fill the role of unofficial family or office historian.

Quiet and reserved, ISFJs are loyal and devoted

family members, friends, and coworkers who take their responsibilities toward others very seriously. Sensitive and sympathetic, they are good listeners, eager to help people in real and practical ways, which they do best by drawing on their own personal experience. Because ISFJs don't like confrontation and are uncomfortable when people are unhappy with them or people close to them, they usually try hard to accommodate others and to avoid arguments. They are also often reluctant supervisors or managers, who disdain disciplining or evaluating subordinates, and may suffer great anxiety if they have to fire someone.

Because ISFJs' Least function is Intuition, they may have difficulty imagining possibilities or scenarios that don't yet exist. In problem solving, they are much more comfortable applying knowledge gained through direct experience than trying a new approach. ISFJs are so rooted in the present, and so trust the lessons of the past, that when they look to the future and its many unknowns, it is often with apprehension and a sense of dread. ISFJs may also have trouble appreciating the interconnectedness of things, since they naturally pay attention to the specifics, rather than to the big picture.

Because ISFJs are such nice, accommodating, and generous people, they run the risk of being taken advantage of. In fact, they often have trouble asserting themselves, and most avoid potential confrontational situations whenever possible. While they are warm and helpful, ISFJs are also very private, and are comfortable sharing their personal thoughts and feelings with very few people. In fact, they may consider information disclosed about them to others without their permission a serious

invasion of their privacy—even if the disclosure involves information that is innocuous and not very personal. For relaxation, ISFJs often prefer activities that engage their senses, such as cooking, gardening, painting, or making things with their hands. While they may occasionally enjoy the company of a close friend or two, they are comfortable spending much of their time alone. ISFJs tend not to like surprises, and are most at ease when they are in familiar surroundings, enjoying, uninterrupted, the things they have planned to do. But when it comes to holidays or other special events, ISFJs will plan them carefully and thoughtfully, and then participate with great gusto!

ESTP

Extraverted, Sensing, Thinking, Perceiving
Estimated to be between 6 and 8 percent of the American population

For ESTPs, life is full of one fun-packed adventure after another. Active, curious, and playful, these Lead Sensors notice everything around them and are active participants in every aspect of their physical life. Responsive and adaptable, ESTPs act first, rarely thinking through the consequences—especially any long-term implications of how their actions may affect other people. Realistic, yet impulsive, they immediately seize upon any exciting opportunity that presents itself. Superobservant, ESTPs are indiscriminate about the sensory impressions they notice, as they constantly scan the environment and people around them. They learn best when they are physically engaged in the process, talking through what they are doing, and commenting on the many details they see, feel, and hear.

Full of energy, ESTPs love all kinds of surprises, and willingly join in whatever is going on around them, as long as it doesn't get too involved, complicated, or intense. Because their Least function is Intuition, when conversations get too serious or discussions too theoretical, or when things are overly planned, they grow bored and restless. To try and lighten up the mood, they may act silly or treat issues with too much superficiality. Most ESTPs love the outdoors and are avid sports fans. Of all of the sixteen types, ESTPs are perhaps the most naturally athletic and coordinated, learning physical skills and tricks almost effortlessly. They typically have a host of interests and hobbies, which they are ready to plunge into at a moment's notice. This is good because they often have trouble sitting still or remaining inactive for any period of time.

Happiest when they are totally immersed at all times in the action of the moment, ESTPs are usually good at immediate problem solving, bringing logic and objectivity to their analysis. They are often quite pragmatic, and are poised to change directions quickly if they think there is a better or more expedient approach. As ESTPs age, most grow increasingly more conservative in their attitudes and political leanings, but they usually maintain a "forever young" attitude about themselves and their own lifestyles.

Friendly, talkative, and energetic, ESTPs love to laugh and joke around, and are naturally flirtatious. Easygoing and casual, they tend to know a lot of people and are popular, since they are so much fun to be around. The life of the party, they are also often the first to try physical feats of daring or risk. They can sometimes give the erroneous impression that they are more emotionally invested in an idea or a relationship than they really are. And they may have to work hard to overcome their tendency to move on to greener pastures once things become too familiar or predictable. ESTPs are often so eager for the next physical thrill or experience, they sometimes neglect to follow through on the projects they've already started and can wind up disappointing or letting people down who are counting on them. When they put their minds to something, however, they are usually able to pull it off with skill and style, even if it is at the last moment!

ISTP

Introverted, Sensing, Thinking, Perceiving
*Estimated to be between 4 and 7 percent of
the American population*

Independent, self-contained, and often aloof, ISTPs are the ultimate pragmatists. They are supremely cool and objective about all things, even-tempered and unflappable. In times of crisis or high anxiety, they are able to focus on the demands of the moment and apply their Lead Thinking to solving problems with skill and dispatch. They are at their best responding to challenges that arise spontaneously, preferring to get busy and skip a lot of discussion or preplanning. Once they "put out the fire," they have little energy for the follow-through and little need to reap praise.

Resourceful and adaptable, ISTPs seem to possess an innate understanding of how anything works—from toasters to computers. They are especially effective when they combine their keen powers of observation with their talent for logical analysis to solve problems. But since people rarely act with the same logical predictability that things do, ISTPs are generally less skilled or effective dealing with interpersonal conflicts. The inherent inconsistency and irrationality of human beings is both so confusing and frustrating to ISTPs that they will frequently just walk away from a personal conflict rather than be left feeling helpless and inept. Very private about personal matters, they rarely share their innermost feelings or fears, even with people they know well and trust.

Realistic and extremely practical, ISTPs are people of action and self-direction. They like to work alone or alongside other skilled and capable people, figuring things out for themselves without outside help or input. Although they seek fun and action in both their work and personal lives, ISTPs really feel the most alive when they are doing something independent, risky, or even dangerous. So strong is the allure of the adrenaline rush that they often seek occupations which place them in harm's way. And even those ISTPs whose jobs involve great risk, such as firefighters, police officers, or pilots, often seek additional thrills in their choice of recreational activities by racing cars, riding motorcycles, or skiing expert slopes.

Direct, honest, and down-to-earth, ISTPs tend to be literal and explicit and find pretentious people or those with hidden agendas annoying. But ISTPs are ever cool and unemotional, and so easygoing that they rarely try to control others. Above all, ISTPs want to be left alone to live their lives as they see fit, and have little interest or energy for trying to change others. The people in their lives may find it difficult to develop and maintain any deep level of intimacy with ISTPs, whose Least function is Feeling, since they are often so unwilling to let others in. Learning the skills necessary to maintain healthy relationships helps them become more invested in making them work.

ESFP

Extraverted, Sensing, Feeling, Perceiving
Estimated to be between 8 and 10 percent of the American population

ESFPs are natural performers who delight in surprising and entertaining people. Warm, outgoing, and friendly, they are usually vivacious and talkative. They know a lot of people and, as long as the people are nice, they seem to like everyone equally well. Animated and fun loving, ESFPs prefer to be at the center of the action, surrounded by other easygoing, optimistic, and considerate people, laughing, talking, or sharing a common interest or activity. Enthusiastic and high spirited, social and spontaneous, ESFPs can find it hard to settle down and finish their work because they are so easily distracted.

Down-to-earth and practical people, ESFPs are

so focused on whatever they are doing at the moment, they can sometimes be ambushed by their Least function, which is Intuition, since they do not naturally anticipate future events, or consider the effect their current choices may have on the future. Realistic and literal, they appreciate the simple pleasures of life and tend to notice beauty everywhere. ESFPs like to fill their homes, offices, and cars with objects from nature or sensory delights like soft fabrics, bright colors, and sweet smells. They take pride in their appearance and often spend time and energy keeping themselves fit and attractive. Their busy social lives and many active, physical interests and hobbies fill every free moment, and they are often rushing breathlessly from one experience to another. Since they live completely in the present moment, and do not like to plan ahead, they may find themselves overextended. And because they hate to miss out on anything, they leave so many options open that they may have real trouble making decisions, or focusing on only one project at a time. Often running late or forgetting appointments in the flurry of their busy lives, ESFPs feel very guilty when they unintentionally let people down.

Generous and eager to please, ESFPs are loyal friends and great companions. They are curious people, who accept life as it is, and rarely come to things with preconceived notions or agendas. Unpretentious and matter-of-fact, they also are very sensitive to other people's feelings, and tend to take criticism and rejection very personally. While they are generally open and expressive, they do tend to keep their most private feelings to themselves, and are selective about whom they share

them with. Since they find conflict and tension between people uncomfortable, they will rarely initiate a confrontation, and simply avoid overbearing and insensitive people. Eager to help others, they are most satisfied when they can make a tangible contribution, and are most gratified to see and hear that their efforts have made a real difference to someone in need.

Sympathetic and compassionate, they may be disappointed by people when they refuse to see anything but the most positive attributes of others. They may even become overly involved in other people's problems and have a hard time breaking free of unhealthy relationships. Since they rarely apply objective analysis to their decision making, instead relying solely on their personal feelings and values, they run the risk of becoming confused or being taken advantage of. Finding a balance between deciding with the head or the heart can be a lifelong, but worthwhile, challenge for many ESFPs.

ISFP

Introverted, Sensing, Feeling, Perceiving
Estimated to be between 5 and 7 percent of the American population

Gentle, sensitive, and compassionate, ISFPs are the most unassuming and down-to-earth of all types. Typically people of few words, they demonstrate their commitment and loyalty to their friends, families, and the few causes that are near to their hearts with actions, rather than words. Modest and reserved, under the surface these Lead Feelers nevertheless feel all things personally. ISFPs are deeply affected by the pain, unhappiness, or misfortune of others, but hide their vulnerability behind a veneer of detachment, appearing cool and removed. It can take a long time to really get to know an ISFP, for they are intensely private people, and highly selective about whom they take into their confidence. Only trusted friends are privy to their deepest thoughts and feelings.

ISFPs are so sensitive, they tend to take the worries of the world on their shoulders. Observant and curious, they are quick to notice what other people need. Since they want so much to help others, they can become overly involved. And because their Least function is Thinking, they often lose their objectivity in the process. Since they tend to be unassertive, they don't readily speak up in their own defense, and are sometimes taken advantage of by others who are less considerate and more assertive. In their desire to maintain harmony and please others, they also may be less than forthcoming about their true feelings of resentment, holding on to their hurt feelings and resentment for longer than is healthy for them. Some ISFPs are vulnerable to fast-talking, charismatic but unscrupulous people because they are so inherently trusting. It never occurs to them to look for anything but the best in others. Developing a bit of healthy skepticism will protect them from being disappointed by others.

Patient and flexible, ISFPs are especially tolerant and accepting of life. They rarely criticize the actions or beliefs of other people. They tend to follow the path of least resistance, accommodating and responding to change rather than trying to control or resist it. Focused and concerned with living life to the fullest in the present moment, they find beauty and joy in simple pleasures. Because they value an inner balance for themselves, they like to keep their lives as uncomplicated as possible, and rarely place a higher importance on their work than on their family or personal lives. And because they dislike preplanning, they sometimes find themselves taken by surprise by unpleasant situations that could have been avoided. Similarly, because they don't naturally or easily imagine what might be coming down the road, they may become pessimistic and discouraged when it looks as though they have no options. Along with their relaxed and easygoing style often comes great difficulty getting and staying organized. Trying to manage complicated or long-range projects can leave them feeling overwhelmed. They are usually much happier working quietly, behind the scenes, doing their best as part of a caring team.

ENTJ

Extraverted, Intuitive, Thinking, Judging
Estimated to be between 3 and 5 percent of the American population

ENTJs are natural leaders, whose competence and strength inspires confidence and respect in others. Their Lead Thinking enables them to analyze problems logically and objectively, weighing the pros and cons of an issue, and then make efficient, sensible, and often tough decisions. ENTJs value honesty and directness; they get right to the point and don't beat around the bush.

However, because their Least function is Feeling, ENTJs can be unaware of the impact their actions have on others. In fact, many ENTJs are rather removed from the world of emotions, so they may behave in ways that are insensitive to the needs or feelings of other people. While this is not intentional, they can be brusque, critical, and appear arrogant when they become impatient with people who may not grasp an issue as quickly as they do, or who take an opposing position. ENTJs also have the propensity to be overbearing and bossy, and may intimidate others into supporting their positions. And because they are often in a hurry to get things done and move ahead, they may fail to acknowledge or express their appreciation when others have helped them or done a good job.

Talented strategic planners, ENTJs are capable of both seeing the big picture and anticipating how current actions may affect future decisions. Creative and often innovative, ENTJs have great courage when it comes to making bold, sweeping changes, especially with respect to complex problems or issues. Not easily intimidated, they engender confidence in others and often have a commanding and even awe-inspiring presence. Great lovers of learning, ENTJs are always looking for ways to improve themselves and increase their expertise and power.

Typically friendly, outgoing, and energetic, ENTJs like to be where the action is, and are good at juggling several projects at the same time. They are often very articulate, think quickly on their feet, and can make very effective public speakers. ENTJs are usually not the least bit shy about sharing their ideas or expressing their strong opinions — which may pertain to any number of subjects. But because they are so eager to get one project completed and move on to the next, ENTJs may not spend enough time reflecting and thoughtfully considering the immediate and practical consequences of their actions. And they may be surprised to learn that their good ideas are not as enthusiastically accepted as they expected them to be.

ENTJs are often very career driven. Organized and productive, they like to work hard and eagerly take on difficult challenges — often the more complex the better. And as a result of their competence and resourcefulness, they are usually able to accomplish or even exceed their goals. But sometimes, once they have embarked upon a course of action, they may be unwilling or unable to modify their plans and pursue a new direction, even if such action is warranted. ENTJs sometimes have difficulty striking a healthy balance between their work and home life, becoming so preoccupied with furthering their careers that they sacrifice their family and personal life in the process. Not surprisingly, reevaluating their priorities in midlife is an activity many ENTJs find worthwhile.

INTJ

Introverted, Intuitive, Thinking, Judging
Estimated to be between 2 and 3 percent of the American population

INTJs are global thinkers with original minds. Their Lead Intuition enables them to clearly see connections, and to understand the long-range implications of current actions and events. Ingenious and innovative, INTJs have a unique talent for looking at almost anything and seeing how it can be improved. This is true of the smallest product or service or can involve envisioning how best to restructure and refine whole organizational systems. But, by far, their favorite subject for improvement is themselves. INTJs are on a constant quest to increase their knowledge and, by extension, their overall competence.

Creative and imaginative, INTJs are both intellectually curious and daring, even as they may be physically hesitant to try new things. Able to quickly grasp and analyze complex issues, INTJs are excellent strategic problem solvers, with highly developed critical thinking skills that allow them to perform incisive analyses. Constantly seeking new intellectual challenges, they set very high standards for themselves, and usually reach or exceed them.

However, because their Least function is Sensing, INTJs sometimes have difficulty operating in the real world. They tend to spend so much of their time and energy in the inner world of ideas and perceptions that they may be completely unaware of, or unconcerned with, the details of their physical surroundings. This can result in small consequences—such as bumping into the furniture or wearing mismatched socks—or large ones, such as failing to realistically assess the feasibility of a project because they are unaware of the cost of necessary resources. And sometimes, because they tend to be abstract and theoretical, they have trouble communicating clearly with people who are not as technically oriented, or being patient as they try to find common ground.

And because INTJs are most comfortable operating from an intellectual level, they are sometimes unaware of the emotional reactions or states of others. They may act in ways that are insensitive and neglectful of those close to them, and may need to be reminded to take time to appreciate and actively nurture those relationships. Perfectionists who set very high standards both for themselves and others, INTJs can be condescending and/or patronizing to those who fail to live up to their expectations, and parsimonious with their praise for those who do.

Given their powers of concentration, INTJs often prefer to work alone, or with a small group of equally competent colleagues. They are especially reticent to take the time and energy to explain themselves or their work to others they perceive to be less competent. Because they are so private, they are very difficult to get to know. They especially do not like to share their ideas or work until they feel it is perfect. Hard workers capable of persevering against great odds, INTJs have enviable focus and determination, and will not be deterred from reaching their goals. Their single-mindedness may come with a price, however, since it may result in their being stubborn and inflexible. And INTJs may have particular difficulty making transitions from one project to another. Usually, all it takes is an even more fascinating challenge to recapture their attention.

ENTP

Extraverted, Intuitive, Thinking, Perceiving

Estimated to be between 4 and 6 percent
of the American population

ENTPs usually make a great impression, and often have a natural gift for getting people excited about their ideas. Charming, outgoing, and friendly, they are extremely perceptive and skillful at communicating with all kinds of people. As Lead Intuitives, they possess the ability to see the big picture and anticipate trends, a willingness to take reasonable risks, and enormous confidence. Their enthusiasm is so infectious, and their negotiating skills so accomplished, they are often able to persuade others to join them in their always innovative, and often successful, ventures.

But ENTPs can sabotage their best inspirations by neglecting their Least function, which is Sensing. Many of their best ideas never come to fruition because they do not pay close attention to important details, grow bored after the initial, creative phase of the project has been completed, or tend to ignore the important follow-through on the many commitments they make. For many ENTPs, it is definitely the thrill of the chase, rather than having obtained the prize, that is most exciting, energizing, and satisfying.

Although they are Thinkers, ENTPs like to please people and have a strong need to be liked. Comfortable occupying center stage, they enjoy demonstrating their cleverness and sophisticated language skills—which usually include an impressive vocabulary and penchant for puns. Eager to entertain their many friends and acquaintances, they are often funny, witty, and engaging storytellers. ENTPs are also superb negotiators who know how to use their strategic thinking skills to get what they want. Despite their outward charm and facility with people, they are ultimately pragmatic decision makers, capable of analyzing situations objectively, weighing the pros and cons dispassionately, and making decisions that are politically expedient.

But because they are so personable, engaging, and apparently sincere, ENTPs may disappoint or even alienate their friends and supporters when they fail to follow through on their commitments or when they talk a better game than they actually play. People find this behavior inconsistent, confusing, and misleading, and can come to mistrust the ENTP.

ENTPs are very flexible and adaptable, and able to turn on a dime and go in the opposite direction if the situation calls for it. Neither particularly liberal or conservative by nature, ENTPs are aware of the rules of the game, and masters at bending them to suit their purposes. Curious and open-minded, they are extremely process oriented, preferring to continue collecting data and keeping their options open as long as possible. But because they so dislike closing off options, many ENTPs have difficulty making decisions or sticking with choices already made. For ENTPs who have this problem, there can be some serious consequences. They run the risk of becoming chronic procrastinators, squandering their inspiration, and never reaching their true potential. And they may develop a reputation for being indecisive and untrustworthy. Fortunately, most ENTPs who have these tendencies are smart enough to recognize their destructive potential, learn from their mistakes, and change their behavior. And, usually, when they focus even a bit of their considerable talents, they reap great rewards.

INTP

Introverted, Intuitive, Thinking, Perceiving

Estimated to be between 3 and 4 percent
of the American population

As Lead and Introverted Thinkers, INTPs are intensely logical, analytical people. They are at their best turning concepts, ideas, and problems over in their minds. Like the tumblers inside a lock rotating until they find the correct combination, INTPs search for the perfect solution or approach. Detached, intellectual, and complex people, INTPs are constantly on the lookout for increasingly difficult creative challenges.

Independent, skeptical, and often brilliant, INTPs are innately self-assured people. They possess an inner confidence that they can tackle any problem by logically working their way through it. In a crisis, they are generally unflappable, remaining amazingly calm and unperturbed, even when they are up against seemingly insurmountable odds. They are fascinated with power and are rarely intimidated by anyone or anything.

But INTPs are also easily bored with simple issues, and tend to pay little attention to mundane facts or details. They are especially intolerant of redundancy, in thought or discussion, and may simply ignore those things they see as trivial. This tendency can also give them a rather arrogant attitude, especially when they tune out people who may still be struggling to understand something the INTP has already figured out. Since Feeling is their Least function, they are less generally aware of, and often out of touch with, the needs, and especially the feelings, of others. So while they are usually patient with people who are genuinely eager and quick to learn, they may be demanding and condescending with those who need more hand-holding.

Creative and often ingenious, INTPs see possibilities where others do not. They have a global perspective and are quick to find subtle connections between things and imagine far-reaching implications. Intellectual risk takers, they are usually very curious and eager to learn new things, in an effort to become more competent. While they are especially capable at almost anything they deem worth the effort, they are often not nearly as competent in the area of interpersonal relationships, closing off those who love them from their most private reactions and feelings. And often, they are not even aware of their own or others' feelings about important issues. They do not understand that other people need more reassurance than they do, since they view their commitments as self-evident.

Because INTPs often spend so much time in the

world of ideas, they can become so complicated and removed that it is difficult for them to communicate simply and effectively with other people. And since they rarely focus their impressive powers of concentration on the details, they may miss important realities that could make their ideas more workable.

INTPs absorb new information with incredible speed, and can synthesize it almost immediately. They are good at seeing flaws in ideas and generating innovative solutions. But because they are really energized by the creative process and working out the problems, they often have more energy for starting projects than they do for finishing them. Although they usually resist it, when they occasionally allow others to help them implement their vision, the results can be impressive.

ENFJ

Extraverted, Intuitive, Feeling, Judging
Estimated to be between 3 and 5 percent
of the American population

To ENFJs, maintaining harmony in relationships is a lifelong goal as well as a natural, accomplished skill. Their Lead Feeling enables them to understand people's feelings and drives them to try to make them happy. Warm, compassionate, and friendly, ENFJs are so tuned in to others that they can often anticipate their needs — especially emotional ones. And they are excellent at helping people solve personal problems in creative ways.

Articulate, vivacious, and enthusiastic, ENFJs are often excellent public speakers who possess an innate sense of what their audience wants. Blessed with a rare gift for making personal connections, ENFJs are skillful communicators, both one-on-one and with groups. They are tactful and diplomatic, and pride themselves on being able to make people feel good. They go to great lengths to avoid offending others or hurting their feelings.

Because ENFJs' Least function is Thinking, they often suffer a serious lack of objectivity. They may be overly sensitive and take things personally that were not intended to be. They may also experience difficulty making decisions that are logical, because they find it hard to know whether a particular behavior or action is fair, or to trust themselves to make a just and impartial ruling. In an effort to please and impress others, they often take on more than they can comfortably manage, and sometimes end up feeling overwhelmed and unappreciated.

Because ENFJs are prone to idealize relationships, they can be deeply disappointed when people they believe in let them down. And because it is often more important for them to satisfy others' needs than their own, they run the risk of trading off honesty for harmony.

Most ENFJs are highly productive and organized people who run on high energy. Any social interaction further increases the energy level of these engaging conversationalists. They are often capable of juggling several thoughts and/or projects at the same time, giving each the necessary attention that it deserves. And they are happiest when they have a plan and can work cooperatively with others to realize their goals. They are most satisfied when they are helping others find ways to reach their full potential. Aware of and concerned with global issues, ENFJs usually have strong, value-based opinions that they generally feel free to share.

But sometimes ENFJs are in such a hurry to make a decision or complete a task that they can foreclose options prematurely. As a result, they can fail to consider important information, as well as miss experiencing the process as fully as they might. In their desire to get the job done as quickly as possible, and according to the way they feel it should be done, ENFJs can become inflexible and incapable of adapting or acting spontaneously, even when the situation calls for it. Once reassured about their worth and the value of their unique contribution, they can usually take a step back and regain their sense of balance.

INFJ

Introverted, Intuitive, Feeling, Judging

Estimated to be between 2 and 3 percent
of the American population

Two words that best describe most INFJs are integrity and originality. Their Lead Intuition provides them with vision and creativity, both of which they find great satisfaction using in the service of others. They are usually excellent listeners, patient and supportive. Extremely perceptive and empathetic, they are especially gifted at thinking up new and better ways to help people get their

needs met, and are usually eager to provide whatever support is necessary.

Typically gentle and soft-spoken, INFJs do not like to call attention to themselves, and often are content to work behind the scenes. Thoughtful, caring, and sensitive, INFJs will usually go the extra mile to maintain harmonious relationships. But they can also be fiercely independent — willing to subject themselves to skepticism or criticism in order to make their vision, which is driven by their strong values, a reality. They are so honest and earnest, they exude integrity, which causes people to immediately trust and respect them. For this reason, they often make inspiring leaders.

Because INFJs' Least function is Sensing, they may fail to take into account realities that might prevent their ideas or vision from working on a practical level. Preferring to focus on the big picture, they sometimes miss essential details or choose to ignore important facts that are not congruent with their ideas. Because they believe so deeply in the correctness of their position, they can be judgmental and dismissive of competing views.

INFJs' single-mindedness can become a liability if they are not flexible enough to modify their plans once they have embarked on a course of action . . . much like a person driving down a highway making great time but who, unfortunately, turns out to be going in the wrong direction! INFJs' perfectionism can also result in a tendency to be stubborn and unyielding. They usually find sharing their vision with someone they trust helps them see the flaws and gain a more realistic perspective.

INFJs are decisive, organized, and great planners. Combined with their single-mindedness and sometimes fierce determination, they are often extremely productive. They like to set goals, and can work tirelessly to achieve them. But sometimes, in their haste to come to a conclusion, they run the risk of missing out on experiencing the process. And they can become so preoccupied with achieving the goal that they lack the ability to act spontaneously.

Since INFJs are run by their values and deeply held convictions, they tend to take things personally, and may have their feelings hurt when no hurt was intended. And, unfortunately, their sensitivity can cause them to become defensive and write off a person or an idea. They may need a gentle reminder from a friend not to take themselves so seriously that they lose the ability to enjoy some of life's lighter, yet most pleasurable, moments.

ENFP

Extraverted, Intuitive, Feeling, Perceiving
Estimated to be between 6 and 7 percent
of the American population

ENFPs are driven by possibilities. Because their Lead function is Intuition, they are compelled to see beyond the present or obvious and to understand things, especially people. They have an almost insatiable curiosity, which they usually apply to a wide spectrum of interests. Enthusiastic, friendly, and energetic, ENFPs are generally fun-loving people, even as they seek to find meaning in all they do.

Unconventional and occasionally irreverent, ENFPs are seldom impressed by authority or rules. To the contrary! They pride themselves on their uniqueness and originality, and are talented at solving problems and overcoming obstacles, including finding creative ways to bend rules they consider unnecessary. One of ENFPs' greatest gifts is their belief that nothing is impossible! Brainstorming possibilities, and bouncing ideas off other creative people, is one of their favorite pastimes.

Because ENFPs' Least function is Sensing, they are often inattentive to details. They frequently are searching for some lost object, and tasks like proofreading that require them to focus all their attention on a single activity — especially for long periods of time — can be extremely draining. While ENFPs are usually capable of generating a torrent of new ideas, they can lack the realistic judgment to determine if any of them are practical and workable. And because they are driven by the *idea*, rather than by the reality, they can become easily bored and neglect to follow through on details once a project has moved past the fun and energizing inspiration stage.

ENFPs are usually well-connected people, counting among their legion of friends and associates people from many different walks of life. Because they hate to "close doors," they tend to maintain friendships for many years. They are enthusiastic and effective catalysts who derive great satisfaction from drawing on their huge network to put people together for their mutual benefit. Perceptive, insightful, and empathetic, they are often gifted at understanding others' motivations. And they are usually good talkers, capable of persuading people of the merits of their positions.

Because ENFPs enjoy keeping their options open, and not being tied down, they may experience great difficulty making decisions — especially important ones, which can result in a tendency toward procrastination. ENFPs generally don't work well alone, and can be easily distracted and diverted from the task at hand (especially if it is not something they are excited about). Because they are so sensitive, they tend to take things personally and avoid situations that involve interpersonal conflict. They may avoid confronting issues or people when it would really be in their best interest to do so.

Warm, caring, and concerned, ENFPs have strong personal values upon which they base most decisions, especially important ones. They are deeply committed to their many friends, and are usually eager and willing to help a friend at a moment's notice. While usually cheerful, ENFPs can become withdrawn and moody when they become frightened or overwhelmed. In the throes of their gloomier side, their usual perceptiveness can become badly flawed, and they may misjudge others' intentions and motives and generally feel pessimistic and alone. Being reassured by those they care about usually helps restore their natural optimism.

INFP

Introverted, Intuitive, Feeling, Perceiving
Estimated to be between 3 and 4 percent
of the American population

INFPs are on a lifelong quest for meaning and inner harmony. Their Lead function is Feeling, so they are driven by their deeply felt personal val-

ues, and are passionately committed to make sure their beliefs and actions are congruent. Their need for authenticity and personal integrity is so strong, they simply can't do something they don't believe in their heart is right. Sensitive and caring, INFPs have great empathy for people, and can be extremely nurturing and comforting to those they feel close to. However, because they are so selective about what and whom they allow to enter their private world, they may appear rather cool, aloof, and even uncaring to people who don't know them well. It can take a long time to really get to know an INFP.

Because INFPs' Least function is Thinking, and because they feel things so deeply, they have difficulty stepping back and considering things objectively. Since they take almost everything personally, they frequently get their feelings hurt quite easily. Even remarks that are not intended to be critical can cause them pain. And comments or actions that unintentionally offend INFPs' values are often experienced as a personal affront. Rather than confront the offender, INFPs are more likely to keep their feelings to themselves, allowing the resentment to fester. And they are often reluctant even to discuss the matter later, so sometimes INFPs will simply drop people from their lives, rather than make the effort to work it out. Ironically, because INFPs tend to idealize relationships, they are often disappointed when someone does not live up to their expectations.

Creative and imaginative, INFPs have a great curiosity about the world, and often have a passionate and lifelong love of the arts. They especially appreciate new and unusual forms of self-expression. Not bound by convention or traditional ways of doing things, INFPs do not follow the pack, and, in fact, often feel a little out of sync with the rest of the world. Open-minded, and adaptable in small things, they are usually supportive and tolerant of others with alternative lifestyles, as long as their behavior or customs don't have a personal impact on INFPs, or cause them to compromise their values. In those cases, the INFP can become rigid and unforgiving.

INFPs' primary focus is inward, and many have highly developed and deeply meaningful spiritual components to their lives. Sometimes their pre-occupation with self-awareness can keep them from noticing or participating in some of the more pedestrian activities of the outside world. While they naturally imagine possibilities and consider how things are related to one another, they don't tend to be especially realistic or practical. They may find the more mundane, day-to-day activities of life unfulfilling and may have to work hard to stay on top of them. INFPs often enjoy spending large periods of time alone, in quiet reflection, reading, or writing. They are happiest when they can totally immerse themselves in interesting and personally meaningful projects.

PART TWO

The System:
Learning How to
SpeedRead People

CHAPTER THREE

The Preferences as Clues

Using clues to identify certain type preferences when SpeedReading people is helpful because there are certain behaviors that people of the same preference commonly share. For example, there are numerous behaviors that Sensors are much more likely to engage in than Intuitives. Therefore, if we see this behavior often enough, we can assume the person is *probably* a Sensor. However, a word of caution is in order: Human beings are extremely complex. And because of the tremendous range of behaviors available to all people, and the uniqueness of every individual, there are few, if any, single behaviors that will automatically reveal a person's preference. Rather, accurate SpeedReading results when we observe a behavior that is repeated, and/or when we see a pattern emerge that is typical of a particular preference. And more often than not, it is a combination of factors that gives us the truest picture of a person's type.

As we discuss each of the type dimensions, it may appear we are describing behavior that belongs at the far edges of each continuum — in other words, generalizations about Thinkers, Feelers, Judgers, and Perceivers, and so on. In reality, many of the clues you will observe when you SpeedRead people will be more subtle than those presented here. But a demonstration of the most dramatic examples will give you a clear understanding of the differences between the preferences much more quickly.

EXTRAVERT OR INTROVERT?

We'll begin by looking at the clues that help differentiate Extraverts from Introverts. Since so much of this first type dimension has to do with energy — where people get it from, and where they direct it — Extraverts and Introverts frequently have very different energy levels, which show up in many ways.

Body Language/Energy Level

Perhaps the first thing you notice about people who are strongly Extraverted is their incredible energy. In conversations, Extraverts are usually much more animated and energetic than Introverts. They are more likely to express their thoughts and emphasize their points by using their bodies; waving their arms around, engaging in lots of hand movements, and displaying a wider range of facial expressions. As is consistent with their nature, Introverts are generally more reserved physically, as well as verbally. Their natural drive to conserve the energy they expend in the outside world directed at others often gives them a quieter, calmer, air. They seem to communicate the message: "What's your hurry? . . . We've got plenty of time."

These differences are particularly noticeable in group situations, where Extraverts gain energy from other people — much as a hurricane picks up strength out in the warm sea — and become louder and more boisterous. In contrast, for many Introverts the more people, the greater the energy drain, causing them to become even more quiet and withdrawn.

Communication Style

If you watch and listen carefully to an Extravert and an Introvert having a conversation, you may notice some very significant differences. First, you will probably notice that the Extravert is doing most of the talking. Because they think out loud, Extraverts are often guilty of monopolizing conversations. When asked a question, most Extraverts will immediately begin speaking. Conversely, when they are asked a question, most Introverts will pause and think about it before offering their response. Since Extraverts are uncomfortable with dead air, any gaps in the conversation are more likely to be filled by them. Introverts, who are generally comfortable being quiet, are less likely to speak just to end the silence.

Extraverts are generally noisier than Introverts, although this difference is sometimes easier to spot when people are in groups. Not only are Extraverts more vocal, they are often comfortable escalating their volume, especially when they are forced to compete for "air time." On the other hand, the members of the group who are more content to listen to the conversation, and not press to get their points made, are more often the Introverts.

While Extraverts generally talk a lot more than Introverts, there are exceptions. When Introverts are talking about something very important to *them*, they can easily monopolize a conversation, and may even seem oblivious to how they are being perceived by the people with whom they are speaking. For the same reason, some very strong Introverts may be unaware of the amount of physical space others need in order to feel comfortable, and may unknowingly violate that space by standing or talking too close.

This tendency *not* to focus on the people and things around them also contributes to Introverts' sometimes being socially awkward. Therefore, Extraverts are generally much more comfortable in social settings, and (although they may not *want* to do it) are usually able to make small talk fairly easily.

The actual language — vocabulary and syntax — of Introverts and Extraverts does not often provide very useful cues. The exception is that, because they are more self-focused than Extraverts, Introverts will sometimes use the pronoun "I" when an Extravert would use the pronoun "we." For example, an Introvert might say: "I'll be moving to Georgia next year," when describing a family move, whereas an Extravert is more likely to include his family in a statement that is about him, as in "We got a promotion."

In addition to talking more than Introverts, Extraverts also tend to talk faster. In contrast, the speech patterns of most Introverts are measured, constant, and the pace slower and more even. Whereas Extraverts often move quickly from one topic to the next, Introverts usually prefer to discuss one subject in depth before moving to the next.

Because Introverts prefer to devote their attention to one thing at a time, they will generally maintain good eye contact, while some Extraverts maintain less eye contact because they are easily distracted and are busy scanning their environment to see what's going on, in order to make sure they are not missing out on anything important.

Appearance

While not the strongest clue for this dimension, there are some differences that may be useful. Because Extraverts generally like to call attention to themselves more than Introverts, they are more likely to be considered flamboyant; they may wear brightly colored, highly fashionable, or sexy clothing, or drive flashy cars. Introverts may choose more subdued colors, since they are generally less comfortable in the spotlight.

Amount of Interaction Sought

Typically, Extraverts seek and enjoy much more social interaction than do Introverts. With strong Extraverts, this may be a great clue. Take, for example, the boyfriend who always wants to include others when he and his girlfriend go out, or the coworker who always insists the whole gang eat lunch together.

Strong Introverts can be often identified by the absence of great numbers of people in their lives. For example, the woman who eats lunch alone while she reads a book every day, or the coworker who never shows up for office parties or functions unless they are mandatory. In such extreme cases — on either side — people often have well-deserved reputations for being either Extraverts or Introverts. But since such extreme cases are not common, these clues will more often come from observing people engaging in their everyday interactions, where you will discover that Extraverts are more likely to engage strangers (or anyone else, for that matter) in conversations, while Introverts are more likely to keep their interpersonal transactions to a minimum. And Introverts almost always prefer conversation and interactions to be of a longer, more substantive nature.

Occupations

On occasion, occupational choice can provide a useful clue. However, making assumptions based solely on someone's occupation can be dangerously misleading, because most people have jobs that do not make use of their natural talents, and, consequently, are not very satisfying. So your SpeedReading will be more accurate if you can shed some of the stereotypes we've all accumulated over the years.

In many situations, you will get the chance to talk at length with people you are trying to Speed-Read. Your assessment, based on occupational clues, is likely to be infinitely more accurate if you are able to find out the answers to a few important questions, such as how they got into the particular line of work, whether they like their job, what they like most and least about it, and what is their ideal or fantasy job. Knowing this will help you discover whether you are looking at a satisfied accountant or an Extraverted stand-up comic desperately trying to burst out.

As we've already discussed, since many people are not really well suited for their jobs, it is extremely helpful if you can find out if that is the case for the person you are trying to SpeedRead. In the event you can find out, it is also important for you to know what does constitute job satisfaction for Extraverts and Introverts. In general, Extraverts tend to be happiest in jobs that allow them to have a lot of interaction with others, work on a variety of projects, and be able to talk about their ideas. Introverts tend to be happiest in jobs that allow them to concentrate on one project at a time, think things through carefully, and work at a steady pace.

Keeping in mind the warning not to jump to conclusions based solely on a job title, there are some jobs and careers that tend to attract large numbers of Extraverts and others that are more appealing to Introverts. Knowing about them can help you form a working hypothesis about someone while you collect more data.

Some jobs/careers with high percentages of Introverts include: artist, computer programmer, librarian, architect, college faculty member, bookkeeper and accountant, engineer, writer, researcher.*

*For comprehensive information regarding Type and occupational choice, see *The Type Atlas*, Center for Applications of Psychological Type (CAPT).

Some jobs/careers with high percentages of Extraverts include: marketer, public relations specialist, actor, salesperson, manager, social worker, and public speaker.

It is important to understand that most jobs allow people the flexibility to perform the work in their own style. For example, both Introverts and Extraverts may teach American history, but they will probably do it in very different ways. The Introvert may prefer to lecture, assign her students a lot of reading to be done individually, and offer to advise them one on one. The Extravert may suggest his students form study groups, and may enjoy dressing up as George Washington or encourage his students to act out important historical events such as the signing of the Declaration of Independence. Incidentally, this caution to not be misled solely by occupational stereotypes applies to all of the type preferences.

Interests and Hobbies

What people choose to do with their spare time can also sometimes provide useful clues about Extraversion and Introversion. But, as with occupations, the most important question is not *what* people do, but *how* they do it. Take fishing, for example. While both Extraverts and Introverts may enjoy this sport, they usually enjoy it in very different ways. While an Introvert may love nothing better than to spend an entire day fishing alone, or perhaps with one close friend, most Extraverts find this type of fishing too isolating, and would almost always prefer to have company.

Other activities that are generally done alone, such as reading, gardening, and sewing, or those that take time — like playing chess — may appeal more to Introverts. Extraverts usually prefer activities that involve a lot of action and interaction, such as group card games or charades.

When it comes to sports, Introverts are more likely to be attracted to individual sports, such as swimming, running, tennis, or golf. Extraverts typically gravitate to team sports, which allow for more social interaction.

There are clearly limitations in trying to determine a person's preference based solely on their interests and hobbies. For one thing, all people have a need for balance in their lives, and for many, this balance is achieved by using the opposite sides of their personalities that get less exercise. This is especially true for people approaching midlife. For example, Intuitives who spend most of their time and energy in more intellectual pursuits may find doing physical things, such as playing sports or cooking, very gratifying. Likewise, Sensors who operate in the physical world most of the time may enjoy engaging their Intuition by reading a good mystery or learning a new computer program.

For easy reference, we present the following list of major clues for this type dimension. While not every item will pertain to every person, both lists should nevertheless provide you with a good thumbnail sketch of Extraverts and Introverts.

SENSOR OR INTUITIVE?

Since perhaps the greatest differences exist between Sensors and Intuitives, there are some very

✔ QUICK RECAP
Extraversion / Introversion Clues

Extraverts
- Have enthusiastic demeanor
- Talk more
- Are usually more animated
- Think out loud
- Talk faster and usually louder
- Are easily distracted
- Change subjects quickly
- Like to be around people
- Often seek center stage
- Act first and think about it later
- Interrupt and finish sentences

Introverts
- Have calm, measured demeanor
- Talk less
- Are usually more reserved
- Think, then talk
- Talk slower and usually more quietly
- Are able to focus their attention
- Stay with one subject at a time
- Like to spend time alone
- Often shun the limelight
- Are more cautious and hesitant
- Start conversations without a preface

useful clues that can help us differentiate the two. But because perception is mostly an unconscious process, which goes undetected while it is occurring, many of these clues are more subtle than those involving other preferences, such as Extraversion and Introversion.

Percentage of Population

We believe that about 65 percent of the American population is comprised of Sensors, and only about 35 percent are Intuitives. Therefore, before you know *anything* about the person you are trying to SpeedRead, the flat odds are about two to one that person is a Sensor.

Communication Style

Since communication is in great part a reflection of how one thinks, some of the best clues involve language, including sentence structure and vocabulary. Sensors tend to communicate in an uncomplicated, straightforward manner, while Intuitives communicate in a more complicated, circuitous way. If you hand a Sensor an apple and ask: "Would you please tell me about this object?" she's likely to say something like this: "Well, this is a McIntosh apple. It's round, has a brown stem about an inch long and two green leaves coming out of the center. The skin is smooth. It's cold and smells ripe." She reports as accurately as she can what her senses tell her about the object. But if you ask the same question of an Intuitive, you could just as easily hear something like this: "Apples have been around a long time—probably since the Garden of Eden! They're very versatile—you can make pies, sauce, juice, and a lot of other stuff from them, and they're supposed to be good for you—you know: an apple a day, keeps the doctor away . . . kids used to bring them to their teachers . . . New York City is called the Big Apple, although I'm not sure why . . ." He doesn't report specifics about the object, but rather his associations with it.

Sensors also concentrate on facts and specifics, and talk sequentially, each thought naturally following the one before it. They start at point A and continue until point Z, without much diversion in between. Sensors also tend to be precise. The combination of these two characteristics can be seen in the example of a Sensor giving someone directions to a mutual friend's house: "Make a left out of the driveway and go about three hundred yards to the end of this block. Make a right turn. That is South Street. Continue on South Street for five blocks until you come to Chestnut Street. There is a large white church on the corner. Make a right turn onto Chestnut and continue until you get to the third light, which is Elm Street. You'll know it

because there is a Shell gas station on the northwest corner and a Burger King on the opposite one. Make a left onto Elm. Go about three-tenths of a mile—you will pass the high school on your right. Two blocks past the high school is number 37—a white colonial house with blue shutters. You'll recognize my red Toyota Camry in the driveway. You can park right behind it."

Because they don't naturally pay attention to details, and because they jump from idea to idea so quickly, an Intuitive attempting to give the same directions may sound more like this: "Let's see . . . I think I'll send you up South Street. Turn at the corner and drive until you come to Chestnut Street . . . or is it Walnut Street? . . . umm, I'm not sure, but you'll know it because the name of the street has a nut in it. Anyway, turn on that street and go until you come to Elm . . . I think it's a right turn. The house is a few minutes down on the right, and you'll see a lot of cars parked out front. If you get lost, I'm pretty sure there's a gas station when you first turn onto Elm where you can stop and ask directions. Oh, and if you reach the highway underpass, you've gone too far."

Sensors' sentences tend to be short, contain one thought, and end with a period. Intuitives' sentences tend to be long, compound, rambling, and often trail off unfinished. Because they mentally anticipate the point a speaker is making, they will frequently finish other people's sentences for them. And their assumptions are often correct (although this habit is not always appreciated). Those most likely to engage in this behavior are Intuitives who are also Extraverts (ENs).

Sensors tend to be literal and economical with regard to language. The character Joe Friday on the classic television show *Dragnet* expressed the Sensing attitude with his famous line "Just the facts, ma'am." Put another way, Sensors believe people should say what they mean and mean what they say. Intuitives are more figurative, and also more wordy. They enjoy and liberally use analogies and metaphors to communicate and repeat their thoughts (although they will usually say the same thing with a different spin or subtle interpretation). This is more likely to be true of Intuitives who are also Extraverts (ENs).

Language as an idea generally appeals to Intuitives. They often choose their words carefully and are aware of the power and nuance of vocabulary. They like words that are interesting, unusual, or even obscure, and appreciate turns of phrases, plays on words, double entendres, and puns. Intuitives enjoy finding novel ways of expressing thoughts both verbally and in writing. Sophisticated with regard to language, they consider it an art. Conversely, the more practical Sensors consider and use language as a tool. Its purpose is to convey thoughts in the most efficient manner possible. For *most* Sensors, language is about utility. Aesthetics may be a nice byproduct, but they are not its primary purpose.

The differences described above sometimes show up in what Sensors and Intuitives choose for recreational reading. Because Sensors value facts and realism, they tend to enjoy nonfiction, such as biography, history, or magazines for sports fans. Intuitives, with their appreciation of imagination, tend to prefer literary fiction, poetry, and plays (although this is certainly not always the case). Sensors also tend to be attracted to books and magazines that deal with real things that interest them, such as fishing, photography, doll collecting, or model building. For example, manuals that provide directions for assembling or repairing products are more appreciated and used by Sensors, while Intuitives often find the details too confusing or boring, and try to figure it out by themselves.

The types of humor that Sensors and Intuitives enjoy can sometimes also provide a useful clue. Intuitives often appreciate cerebral or intellectual humor that deals with language, politics, or current issues. The rambling, free-association rants of comedian Dennis Miller offer a terrific example of Intuitive humor at its best. Conversely, Sensors often appreciate physical, as well as slapstick, humor, the kind that comedian Lucille Ball perfected. (But this is certainly not to imply all Sensors find the Three Stooges hilarious, or that only Intuitives appreciate comedians like Mark Russell or George Carlin.)

Future or Present Orientation

Sensors typically have a strong orientation to the present and the past. They often have excellent memories for things they have experienced, and use this information to make decisions. They are more comfortable with things they have known, the tried and true, rather than experimenting on things yet untested. Intuitives, however, are generally intrigued with anything new or original. They have a more future orientation and, in fact, tend to spend more waking hours thinking ahead than they do in the moment or reliving the past. As a general rule, Intuitives are more trusting of the unknown than are Sensors.

Movement and Body Awareness

By definition, Sensors are often keenly aware of things, including their own bodies and their physical surroundings. (This is especially true of Sensors who are also Extraverts.) We describe their natural comfort with things physical as "being in their bodies." Combined with their propensity for living in the present moment, Sensors often have a natural gracefulness and ruggedness. This characteristic can sometimes be seen in natural athletic prowess, but is more often seen in the effortless way most Sensors move. They seem to be more closely in step with the natural world, and their smooth and graceful movements seem known, rather than learned.

The same cannot be said of most Intuitives, who experience much of life thinking about things as opposed to doing them. While certainly there are uncoordinated Sensors (especially Sensors who are also Judgers — SJs), as well as graceful Intuitives, they seem to be the exceptions, rather than the rule. It is far more likely, for example, for an Intuitive to misjudge the distance of an upcoming step, or bump into a door jamb, than it is for a Sensor.

Occupation

As is true of Extraverts and Introverts, Sensors and Intuitives are found in all kinds of jobs, but not with the same frequency. And they often perform the same jobs quite differently. Ideally, Sensors find work that allows them to work with real things, apply past experience to solving problems, have a clear understanding of expectations of them, and at the end of the day, see what they've accomplished. Intuitives are happiest when they choose work that allows them to focus on possibilities, to consider creative or innovative approaches to solving problems, and to take on new and constantly challenging projects.

Keeping in mind the cautions already expressed about SpeedReading people based solely on their job titles, there are some positions that attract more Sensors than Intuitives. Knowing about them can help you form a working hypothesis about someone while you collect more data. Some of these highly Sensing jobs/careers include: manager, banker, police officer, administrator, farmer, tradesperson, teacher (elementary school), nurse or other health care provider, bookkeeper, accountant, military person, real estate agent, secretary, and retail salesperson.

Some jobs and/or careers that reflect a higher percentage of Intuitives include: psychologist, counselor, the clergy, writer and journalist, social scientist, philosopher, artist, musician and composer, researcher, marketer, social worker, college faculty member (especially in the liberal arts), consultant, lawyer, computer programmer, and designer. While this does not mean that every writer you meet will be an Intuitive, or every pilot will be a Sensor, the odds are this will be his or her preference, if the person really finds the job satisfying.

Education

The subjects people choose to study in college and graduate school, and the level of education they achieve, can sometimes be useful clues for Sensing and Intuition. In general, Sensors are drawn to learn about real things that have practical utility. College courses and majors that most often appeal to them are science, math, engineering, and business. Intuitives are more naturally attracted to the courses that involve ideas, concepts, and theories, such as can be found in the arts, science, psychology, sociology, and political science.

In addition to the subject matter, another useful clue sometimes can be the highest educational level achieved. In the United States, there is an inherent bias in favor of Intuitives in higher education. Most of the standardized entrance examinations used to qualify candidates for colleges and graduate programs are designed so that Intuitives perform better than Sensors. This is because the tests are written by Intuitives, who, as we have seen earlier, learn and think differently than Sensors. In elementary and even in high school, the emphasis is on memorizing facts and mastering basic skills, all of which Sensors do quite naturally. And in those lower grades, the majority of teachers are themselves Sensors. But in college, the emphasis is on drawing inferences from facts and understanding theoretical concepts, activities Intuitives do naturally. To make it even more difficult for Sensors to succeed in college, there is a highly disproportionate percentage of Intuitive faculty members. Although Intuitives make up only about 35 percent of the general population, they represent about 65 percent of college faculty. So it is important to keep in mind that simply because Intuitives, as a group, achieve higher academic levels, they are not any more intelligent than Sensors. Rather, it is the result of an educational system that unwittingly makes it harder for Sensors to succeed in academia.

Knowing the subject of a person's graduate degree can also help reveal or confirm their preference for Sensing or Intuition. If someone has gone all the way through graduate school pursuing one course of study, the chances are he or she has a genuine affinity for the subject. In other words, it's more likely the person is an Intuitive if he has a graduate, rather than only an undergraduate, degree in psychology, since many students use their undergraduate education to experiment and learn about themselves. But this does not always hold up, as people will sometimes continue with a graduate course of study that is not a good match for a variety of understandable reasons, including parental pressure, fear of losing the time or money already invested, or because of a particularly bleak job market.

Appearance

Once again, appearance sometimes provides good clues to a person's natural preference for Sensing or Intuition, but is not as reliable a predictor as other areas like communication style, work, or hobbies. Generally, Sensors, with their heightened awareness of their bodies, tend to have a

✔ QUICK RECAP
Sensing / Intuition Clues

Sensors

■ Are about 65% of the American population

■ Have clear, straightforward speech pattern

■ Have sequential thoughts — one follows the next

■ Are more literal; use facts and real examples

■ Use language as a tool

■ Are more aware of their bodies

■ Are more attracted to jobs that require practicality

■ Are less likely to have graduate degree(s)

■ Often prefer nonfiction reading

■ Are direct and to the point

■ Include details and facts

■ Remember the past accurately

■ Tend to listen until others complete their whole thought

Intuitives

■ Are about 35% of the American population

■ Have complex speech pattern; use lots of compound sentences

■ Have roundabout thoughts — leap from one to the next

■ Are more figurative; use analogies and metaphors

■ Use language to express selves

■ Are more in their heads

■ Are more attracted to jobs that involve creativity

■ Are more likely to have graduate degree(s)

■ Often prefer fiction reading

■ Repeat themselves, recap, and rephrase

■ Talk about global issues, the big picture

■ Envision the future

■ Tend to finish others' sentences

more highly attuned fashion sense and notice what is fashionable. While Intuitives may tend to be the famous fashion designers and are the true trend-setters, it's the Sensors — in their larger numbers — who really decide what is fashionable or not. Sensors who are also Extraverts tend to wear bolder colors and patterns than Introverted Sensors. Intuitives may generally dress according to their own personal identity rather than from any fashion demand. And in general, Sensors are more likely to wear the right clothing item for the activity — whether it's hiking boots or an evening gown — than are Intuitives, who are less interested in and aware of the details of situations.

THINKER OR FEELER?

As with the first two type dimensions, there are some very good clues to help you identify a person as a Thinker or a Feeler. As we mentioned briefly in Chapter 1, men are more likely to be Thinkers (about 65% of American men are), while women are more likely to be Feelers (also 65%). This can constitute both an advantage and a danger when SpeedReading people. It is an advantage because it is usually easy to differentiate men from women, so the odds are if you are talking to a woman, she is probably a Feeler. Likewise, if you're talking to a man, he is probably a Thinker. The danger is that we all have been raised with many stereotypes about normal male and female behavior such as: men are tough and aggressive; women are soft and nurturing; men are logical and analytical; women are emotional and subjective; men are competitive; women are cooperative; men are brutally honest; women are sensitive and diplomatic, and so forth. The truth is, most, if not all, of the characteristics listed above are more related to type than to gender. And the danger in knowing more women are Feelers and more men are Thinkers is that novice SpeedReaders will be tempted to misread *all* men as Thinkers and *all* women as Feelers. Succumbing to this temptation will result in inaccurate SpeedReading, because a man and a woman who are both Thinkers are more similar in the way they make decisions than are two women when one is a Thinker and the other a Feeler. And the same thing goes for men. The goal is to identify one's true type. Remember that Thinking and Feeling are really about decision making.

Demeanor

Although other preferences, such as Introversion and Extraversion, can greatly influence a person's demeanor — generally defined as one's behavior towards others — several personal qualities are connected to a preference for Thinking or Feeling.

Typically (but not always) Thinkers act cooler towards people and Feelers act warmer. When SpeedReading someone, it is always important to consider the context of the interaction: Who is this person talking to . . . her child or her boss? Where is the conversation taking place . . . on the beach or at the office? What is her purpose . . . to get her child to eat his lunch or to ask for a raise? The point is that the specifics of her behaviors will be different depending on the situation, and unless the context is taken into account, you may easily misinterpret a clue.

What does a Feeler's warmth or a Thinker's coolness look like? First, Feelers generally act friendlier than Thinkers (this is especially true for Extraverted Feelers). They are often described as "nice." Because most Feelers are both naturally tuned in to people's feelings and like to please others, they will often go out of their way to help people — even strangers. They do this in big ways, like volunteering to hold crack-addicted babies in hospitals, and in small ways, like letting a person with a few items cut ahead of them in line at the grocery store. Although they seldom consider it a sacrifice, they often put the needs of others ahead of their own. Also, Feelers are more comfortable revealing information about their personal lives, from displaying photographs and artwork of their children to sharing their feelings with others. Most Thinkers are reluctant to share how they feel, even sometimes with those they know well, like family members and close friends. If someone is accurately described as being "all business," the likelihood is that person is a Thinker.

This is not to suggest that Thinkers won't help someone in need, but they do tend to be less likely to notice when someone needs their help (especially emotional support). And because they don't have the Feelers' natural drive to please people, they are less inclined to inconvenience themselves when they do notice.

Feelers' natural thoughtfulness is often seen in the importance they place on engaging in social niceties. For example, they usually put great thought into selecting just the right gift to give, and are much more likely to immediately write thank you notes acknowledging gifts they receive. They also tend to show genuine concern for the welfare of others, and often can be found doing things like visiting with older people or sick relatives or friends, listening to their problems and offering gentle support. Acts of kindness performed by Thinkers are usually more impersonal in nature, perhaps helping people solve a specific problem, such as resolving a disputed bill with a utility company or shopping for their groceries.

Feelers' sensitivity shows up in other observable ways. They are less likely to make jokes at others' expense or find situations in which people get hurt or embarrassed amusing. For this reason they usually don't enjoy TV shows or movies that involve a lot of violence — even when the situation involves fictional accounts. They are frequently sentimental, more likely to cry at movies, and may become nostalgic much more quickly and visibly than the usually emotionally contained Thinkers. Feelers are generally more able and willing to be caught up in the emotional element or be moved by the emotional drama of stories, plays, movies, and television.

For their part, Thinkers are usually much more assertive than Feelers, which tends to make them appear more confident. Feelers shun conflict and would almost always rather acquiesce than risk creating disharmony. Their deep aversion to hurting people's feelings creates in them a desire to cooperate rather than compete. Feelers often get their own feelings hurt by the insensitivity of others, and because they take almost everything personally. Therefore, they are more frequently, and aptly, described as having a thin skin, whereas Thinkers are naturally, and accurately, called thick-skinned, as a result of their natural inclination to remain objective. Therefore, Thinkers tend often to have a more emotionally even demeanor, while Feelers may exhibit more emotional highs and lows.

Perhaps surprisingly, while Feelers will go to great lengths to avoid conflict, they may become hostile or even aggressive if their values are violated. Because Feelers are run by their values, if someone's words or deeds trample them, they tend to be hurt deeply, and many Feelers may be unable or unwilling to just let it go. Instead, they can become angry and punishing. Such volatility is seldom seen in Thinkers, who are less inclined to take things personally, and therefore are less likely to become offended.

In normal interpersonal transactions, Feelers are usually very complimentary and express their appreciation to others easily. If you observe someone gushing over how great a job Sally did, or how terrific Jeffrey looks, you can be fairly certain that person is a Feeler (and probably an Extraverted Feeler). (Though, because of their socialization, women—even women Thinkers—are more likely to engage in this type of behavior than are men.) Thinkers, in contrast, are usually parsimonious with their compliments. As the Thinking boss said when asked if she ever tells her employees how much she appreciates their work: "They know I think they do good work, because if I didn't, they would have been fired a long time ago." Whereas Feelers are more affirming, Thinkers are generally quick to tell others where they need improvement. It's important to understand that Thinkers don't point out flaws to be mean, but to be helpful. For them, honest feedback is essential if people are to improve their performance, which is a goal most Thinkers have in common.

Another easily observable behavior has to do with the fact that Thinkers are more comfortable arguing, and may enjoy a heated debate. For them, it is an intellectual exercise and is not something they take personally. The same cannot be said of Feelers, who seldom engage in recreational arguing, because to them, it means people are unhappy or angry at each other.

Language

The language, and especially the vocabulary, that people use helps reveal their preference for either Thinking or Feeling. Feelers naturally look for points of agreement in conversations first and later work themselves around to discussing points of difference once some sense of harmony is established. Thinkers tend to first notice and deal with points of difference and, later, if there's time, address the points of agreement. This means that Feelers tend to do a lot of appreciating and complimenting up front and couch any criticism in careful and diplomatic terms. Thinkers, on the other hand, tend to be much more direct, critical, and totally truthful, even blunt, and they may occasionally forget to offer positive feedback.

Consistent with their more emotionally detached demeanor, Thinkers often use words that are precise and appropriate to the situation, but which don't shed any light on how they personally feel about an issue.

A Thinker describing a movie he just saw: "The two biggest problems with this movie were: first, the characters were too one-dimensional, and, second, it lacked a believable plot. The writer simply failed to convince me that the main character was capable of such evil behavior, since the film didn't provide sufficient background history. And the same could be said for all the main characters. With regard to the plot, it simply defied credulity. In my judgment, the characters, even ones as shallow as these, simply wouldn't have done what they did in this film."

A Feeler, commenting on the same movie, might sound more like this: "How offensive! What a waste of my money! And to think we waited forty-five minutes to get in! Everything about this movie stunk: the acting was pathetic, and the writing—if you could call it that—was atrocious. But what really got me was all the gratuitous violence. The whole plot was such a thinly veiled excuse to find even more novel and gruesome ways of killing people. This movie has absolutely no socially redeeming value. Needless to say, I won't be recommending this trash to any of my friends."

At the end of the second review, there would be little doubt as to the Feeler's opinion of the movie, since the words reflect deeply held values. Clearly, this Feeler's remarks are less an objective critique of the merits of the movie than they are an expression of how he felt about it. In contrast, the Thinker's comments reflect little about how he felt (subjectively) about the movie and more of what he thought (objectively) about it.

An effective SpeedReading technique is to ask a Thinker how he feels about something, like a movie, a news report, or a current event—almost anything that would not be considered personal. Most Thinkers won't relate to the word "feel" used in this context, and may pause or ask: "What do you mean, how do I *feel* about that? What's to feel about?" It's not that Thinkers don't have feelings. Rather feelings pertain only to something truly *personal*, as in: "How did you feel when your child got sick?" On the other hand, Feelers will often tell you how they feel about something, even if you don't ask. And you don't have to be concerned that they won't think you are asking for their feelings, because they consider most everything personal, and natural to have feelings about.

In addition to the choice of words used, Thinkers usually speak in a more calm, even, and dispassionate manner. Often their thoughts are highly organized, even in times of stress or conflict. In contrast, Feelers may get very involved, especially when discussing something important to them, and may become louder and more animated as well. Consequently, people who habitually demonstrate more passion when they speak are more likely to be Feelers than Thinkers. (Again, this is especially true of Extraverted Feelers.) During conflict, Feelers become nervous and anxious, which may become apparent by their wavering voices or shaking hands or knees.

Finally, another good clue involves the speaker's use of names. While this is not always the case, Feelers are more likely to use a person's name repeatedly when talking to him or her. But there is a caveat with regard to this clue: sophisticated communicators know that most of us like to hear our names spoken out loud, and many have learned to do this as a communication technique. This is similar to a tactic used by many politicians when they call supporters looking for contributions. Often they will ask the potential contributor about his family, referring to them by name: "Say, how's your daughter Lisa doing? She must be, what, about ten by now?" Of course, in all likelihood, the pol is looking at note cards with the names and other useful information about the potential contributor's family, but the potential contributor is still likely to be flattered and impressed that such an important person remembered something about his kids. People who frequently (and not consciously) use others' first names a lot when speaking with them are often trying to make a connection, and are more likely to be Feelers.

✔ **QUICK RECAP**

Thinking / Feeling Clues

Thinkers

- Act cooler, more distant toward others
- May seem insensitive
- May be blunt and tactless
- Often appear businesslike
- May argue or debate for fun
- Are more "thick-skinned"
- Get right to the point
- Seldom ask if timing is inconvenient
- Appear low-key and matter-of-fact
- Give praise sparingly
- Are usually very assertive
- Use impersonal language
- Use people's names sparingly
- Often are engaged in jobs of strategy
- Are more likely to be male (65% chance)

Feelers

- Act warmer, friendlier toward others
- Are very sensitive to others' feelings
- Are usually very gentle and diplomatic
- Engage in social niceties
- Avoid arguments, conflict, and confrontation
- Have their feelings hurt more easily
- Engage in small talk first
- Ask if timing is inconvenient
- May appear excited and emotional
- Are generous with praise
- May lack assertiveness
- Use lots of "value" words
- Use people's names frequently
- Are often involved in helping jobs
- Are more likely to be female (65% chance)

Body Language

Feelers generally, smile, frown, and employ more facial expressions than Thinkers. When they are happy or excited, Feelers are usually quick to smile, and when they are unhappy or frightened, their faces register their pain and discomfort. (This is especially true of Extraverted Feelers.) As a result of years of using their facial muscles in these ways, you may see more lines around Feelers' eyes and mouths than on the faces of Thinkers.

A Feeler's desire for closeness and intimacy will often result in physical expressions such as kisses, hugs, pats on the back, and arms draped around another's shoulder. While there are cultural forces at play here (for example, women are "allowed" to be more physical with each other than are men), Thinkers are usually much less comfortable with such public displays of affection.

There is an interesting gesture many Thinkers use when talking. They will announce the number of points they're about to make, and then number each point. "There's three reasons why we should act on this plan now: First, the timing couldn't be better. Second, the funds are available, and third, management is behind it." As they make each point, they count it off on their fingers, beginning with the index finger and adding as many others as are needed. Feelers rarely use this organizational system when talking.

Occupation

As you can imagine, both Thinkers and Feelers can be found performing most all jobs, but not with the same frequency or levels of satisfaction. Jobs that appeal most to Thinkers are those which capitalize on their natural abilities to analyze problems logically, weigh the pros and cons, and then make fair and objective decisions, often in a competitive environment. Feelers, on the other hand, usually prefer work that is personally meaningful, involved in helping others in some way, makes them feel appreciated, and is done in a friendly, cooperative, and supportive environment.

Occupations that attract a large percentage of Thinkers include: business, especially upper management, consultant, administrator in almost any field, school principal, scientist, engineer (all kinds), farmer, attorney, judge, accountant, pathologist, and computer specialist.

In contrast, the largest percentage of Feelers can be found in the clergy, all kinds of counseling, teaching of liberal arts, child care and health care, as family practice physician, psychologist, social worker, retail salesperson, real estate agent, and customer service representative.

JUDGER OR PERCEIVER?

According to the latest research, Judgers represent about 60 percent of the American population and Perceivers about 40 percent. Because this dimension has to do with the different ways people like to live their lives, there are many good, visual, behavioral cues that accentuate the differences. However, there is also a strong cultural bias in favor of Judging behavior, which makes a lot of Perceivers *appear* to prefer Judging. This is especially true of people in their work environments.

Demeanor

In general, Judgers tend to be more formal, conventional, and traditional, whereas Perceivers are usually more casual, unconventional, and nontraditional. As a result, Judgers often appear somewhat weighed down, and may come across as serious and no-nonsense. In contrast, Perceivers often seem lighter: more fun-loving, playful, and even irreverent.

Judgers are more likely to take charge and want to be in control (this is especially true of Extraverted Judgers), whereas Perceivers are usually more easygoing and seemingly compliant. This does not mean that Perceivers will automatically acquiesce to the requests or demands of Judgers, but they do tend to avoid public power struggles (especially Feeling Perceivers), and privately find ways to circumvent the Judger's rules and do what they wanted in the first place. If someone can be accurately described as being bossy, the likelihood is greater that he or she is a Judger, just as someone who has a reputation for being adaptable is most likely to be a Perceiver.

Because of the different ways these two types regard time, Judgers are often in a hurry, rushing from one appointment, meeting, or project to the next, with seldom a break in between. This is not to imply they are scurrying about helter-skelter, for they are typically well organized, and make the most efficient use of their time. Perceivers are very different: they often seem less harried, unhurried, and, occasionally, oblivious to time. And they may also appear (and in fact be) much less organized than Judgers. However, when they are under the pressure of a deadline that has finally come crashing in on them, Perceivers are usually very frazzled and frantic.

Appearance

Judgers often have a finished, buttoned-down, or at least pulled-together look. They make sure before they leave the house that everything is in order: shoes are shined, clothes are clean and pressed, hair is combed, appropriate jewelry and accessories are on and in place, and so forth. Of course, you must consider the context: you wouldn't expect a Judger who was preparing to paint his house on a Saturday morning to take the same care with his appearance that he normally does when he goes to work. But even if it's a trip to the paint store, the Judger will probably run a comb through his hair first. Because Judgers are time conscious, they know how long things take, and typically allocate the necessary amount of time to accomplish their preparation. They generally dislike being late or excessively early. They plan and use their time so efficiently that they usually arrive promptly to all appointments. And since they are typically well organized, they are often able to locate "lost" items — even things that belong to others in their families or offices.

Perceivers prefer a more casual or, sometimes, unfinished look. Getting out of the house in the morning for Perceivers can pose a serious challenge as they search for clothes that somehow never made it to the cleaners, jewelry they've misplaced, or scramble around to find the iron to press a wrinkled piece of clothing. More often than not, they run out of time to attend to "secondary" tasks like shining their shoes or really combing their hair (though this is certainly more true of Perceiving men than women).

Judgers' outfits are usually well pulled together — shirts and pants, blouses and skirts, and so on, all likely to match. And unless they are significantly overweight, their clothes are more likely to be more formfitting than baggy. In fact, their whole look is more formal. And for Judging men who wear ties, the top button will probably be closed, the knot pulled up tight and neatly tucked beneath the collar. At the extreme, people whom you would describe as meticulously well groomed are probably Judgers. (There are exceptions to this, which will be discussed in Chapter 5.)

Most Perceivers choose a more casual look, which usually includes wearing more comfortable, often loose-fitting, clothing. Men who must wear a tie will often leave the top button of their shirt open and pull the knot down to give them some room to breathe (symbolically as well as physically). When they think they can get away with it, perhaps when attending a conference or an informal meeting, Perceiving men will almost always choose more casual clothes, such as slacks and shirts or sweaters. Given the same situations, Judging men will more often opt for the suit and tie, or at least slacks and a sports jacket.

Judging women and men are similar in this regard. In this culture women are strongly encouraged to dress appropriately for the circumstances and to strive for a ladylike appearance at all times. Given this social pressure, all women tend to take more time and care with their appearance than men do, regardless of their preferences. But even within these confines, Judging women are more conformable being dressed appropriately and carefully, while Perceiving women are usually delighted to hear the dress code for a function is casual. And, typically, Perceivers are also less concerned than

Judgers with whether various items of clothing will match each other. So, at the extremes, people who are chronically rumpled or who border on being disheveled are probably Perceivers. (The same caveat about exceptions applies here as well. But more about that in Chapter 5.)

For both men and women, but especially for women, the attention Judgers pay to their hair may be a good clue. Judgers' hair is usually cut and styled to look its most flattering, and Judgers are more likely to carry combs, brushes, and other grooming implements with them to make sure it stays that way. On the other hand, the hair of Perceivers, particularly men, is often unkempt, even wild, as if it, too, has a mind of its own.

Another very useful clue is available to you if you get the chance to observe the inside of the person's car. Usually, Judgers' cars are neat and clean, consistent with their belief there should be a place for everything and everything in its place. Perceivers' cars are often a very different story. It's not unusual to find empty soda cans, half-eaten sandwiches, gym bags, clothing, books, toys, or a myriad of other items, which reflects their desire to keep their options open and be able to respond spontaneously to whatever opportunities may be presented. But an important caveat is necessary here, too. This clue is most useful if the car you are observing is driven *only* by the person you are SpeedReading. In cases in which two people share a car, you won't necessarily be seeing the way either person might naturally maintain the vehicle. Many people don't have as much control as they'd like over the condition their car is kept in. Consider, for example, the Judger who spends two hours a day chauffeuring her chronically messy teenagers and their friends. Or the Perceiver whose carpooling responsibilities involve driving others and thus has a need to keep his car neat.

Communication Style

One of the most noticeable things about Judgers is their decisiveness and deliberateness.. One of the best cues for Perceivers is their tentativeness and resistance to making decisions, or having options foreclosed on. Fortunately for those of us engaged in the art of SpeedReading, most people have to make dozens of decisions every day, often in plain sight of others. This affords us an excellent opportunity to observe this revealing behavior. One good indicator is how long it takes for someone to make a decision. When asked for their opinion, Judgers will typically answer quickly, often without asking any clarifying questions. (This is especially true of Extraverted Judgers.) Perceivers (especially Introverted Perceivers) are more likely to delay offering an opinion instantly, and will usually ask questions to try to find out more information. And Perceivers often answer questions with questions.

Another useful indicator can be how emphatic the person is when offering his or her opinion. Judgers are often so adamant about their positions that they communicate great confidence. On the other hand, Perceivers, who are more willing to modify their positions should new information

warrant it, may appear less sure of themselves. Therefore, the words used are less revealing of Judgers and Perceivers than the way they use them. Judgers tend to make declarative statements that end with an exclamation point! Many Perceivers' statements end in question marks (since they are naturally curious and driven to get more and more information before deciding), or they let their sentences trail off into ellipsis dots (. . .), indicating their perpetually open-ended approach to life.

At the outer extremes, people who have a well-deserved reputation for being opinionated and dogmatic are more likely to be Judgers, while people who are chronically "wishy-washy" and equivocal are much more likely to be Perceivers.

Some commonly used expressions of Judgers include: "Absolutely!" "Definitely!" "Positively!" and "Without a doubt!" Perceivers often express their tentativeness by using expressions such as: "As best as I can tell . . ." "Now, I could be wrong, but . . ." "Um, that's interesting. . . ." "I don't know . . ." Perceivers are also more likely to use less formal expressions such as "Yeah" or "Yup" for "Yes," "Nope" or "Nah" for "No," and "Huh?" rather than asking a more specific question like "What did you mean?"

Work Style

Many good clues can be found by examining the different work styles of Judgers and Perceivers. One of the greatest differences centers around the emphasis Judgers place on the product and Perceivers place on the process. Judgers are driven to complete one project before beginning another. But for Perceivers, it is the activities involved in achieving the goal, or the process, that is most important. Put another way, the most important thing to Judgers is *that* the job gets done. Once a Judger establishes a goal, it's "Full steam ahead!" They have great determination, focus, and energy for overcoming any obstacle that prevents them from reaching their goal. For Perceivers, the most important thing is *how* the job gets done, so they are more easily distracted and diverted, and are, in fact, liable to change the goals as the process unfolds and new information comes to light.

Because they are organized and driven to be productive, Judgers are naturally attracted to systems. Systems provide a source of direction and sense of comfort, so they make perfect sense to most Judgers. For Perceivers, most systems are seen as unnecessary and limiting. Consequently, Judgers spend lots of time and energy developing systems that Perceivers spend an equal amount of time and energy trying to circumvent. Not surprisingly, Judgers and Perceivers also often have opposite views about the importance of rules. Judgers generally embrace them, while Perceivers usually rail against them.

There are some particularly helpful clues that pertain to the use and management of time. Judgers are often driven by their calendars and schedules, striving to make the most of their valuable time. Judgers tend to buy and use date books and organizing systems to keep on schedule. They also tend to schedule appointments in small incre-

ments — say fifteen minutes at a time — and even write things in ink more often than pencil.

Many Perceivers, lamenting their lack of skill in this area, do go to great lengths to try and get organized. Some even develop elaborate systems to keep them on track. The problem is, creating the system is usually more satisfying than actually using it. Hence, these systems are often abandoned once the novelty runs out. Judgers are also more likely to make and use "to do" lists and take pleasure in crossing out completed items daily. But again, a caution: as a means of compensating for their normally poorly developed organization skills, many Perceivers will also create lists. However, since they will seldom complete all the items on the list, they will often transfer them onto a *second* list (presumably to be completed another day), or never look at the list again.

Some visual clues pertaining to one's work space can also be useful. Although by no means a failsafe indicator, one's preference for tidiness or clutter can be revealing. In general: Judgers are "filers" and Perceivers are "pilers." Judgers tend to like to put things away as soon as they are finished using them, while Perceivers tend to leave things out and around so they can easily get at them, if the occasion presents itself again. At the extremes: a person whose desk is perpetually tidy, with few, if any, papers, files, pictures, et cetera, adorning it, is much more likely to be a Judger, while a person whose desk is constantly cluttered with files, papers, and other works in progress is much more likely to be a Perceiver. If the person's office is *also* equipped with a variety of toys, such as waste-paper basketball hoops, magnetized perpetual motion machines, and other fun things that can be a diversion from work, the odds of the person being a Perceiver increase substantially.

While Judgers and Perceivers naturally have very different work styles, it is worth noting that in the American culture, work-style clues can sometimes be misleading. There is great pressure for everyone to act like a Judger, since hard work is valued and rewarded; people are expected to follow the rules, and be on time for their appointments. Therefore, most capable Perceivers develop some measure of Judging-like behavior on the job in order to succeed.

There are few body/movement clues that, considered in isolation, are definitive. However, as you become more familiar with Type, you will learn to quickly discover that Judgers and Perceivers have their own look. Although often very subtle, Judgers' and Perceivers' body language are physical manifestations of their many psychological qualities. For example, Judgers' movements are quite deliberate and purposeful, and they generally move from point A to point B quickly, and with intention. On the other hand, Perceivers often stroll, even when they are late going from one appointment to another. Whereas Judgers tend to walk briskly, even mechanically, Perceivers tend to amble and meander in a more fluid way.

Judgers' posture is often (but not always) more erect, while Perceivers may be more prone to slump and slouch. Perceivers are also more likely to do things like rock back in their chairs (which their mothers told them a million times not to do!), slouch down and prop their feet up on a desk, or swing one leg over the arm of a chair.

Occupation

Although Judgers and Perceivers can be found performing many of the same jobs, as we've discussed above, they will usually go about them in very different ways. And Judgers and Perceivers have different criteria for satisfaction. Judgers are best suited to work that allows them to make a lot of decisions, work in a predictable and stable environment, have specific goals and the resources to accomplish them, and exercise a lot of control over their projects. Perceivers most enjoy work that involves flexible and changing situations, allows them to respond to problems as they arise, has few rules and procedures, and is fun. Some jobs that attract a large percentage of Judgers are: manager, school principal, police officer, bank employee, consultant, engineer, dentist, accountant, judge, teacher (elementary through high school), family practice physician, and attorney.

Perceivers tend to gravitate in large numbers to the following occupations: journalist, writer, artist, entertainer, agent, carpenter, psychologist, and all kinds of independent consulting and counseling.

This chapter was designed to accomplish two goals: first, to deepen your understanding of Type and the preferences; and second, to teach you how to identify these preferences in others as part of the SpeedReading system. It's important to keep in mind that, as powerful as being able to identify

✔ **QUICK RECAP**

Judging / Perceiving Clues

Judgers

- Are more formal and conventional
- Are more serious
- Like to take charge and be in control
- Like to make decisions; decide quickly
- Are definitive and often express strong opinions
- Are often in a hurry; like rapid pace
- Have a "finished," neat appearance, clothes pressed, hair combed, etc.
- Dress more for appearance
- Probably have neat car interior
- Like to set and reach goals
- Are driven to finish projects
- Like rules, systems, and structure
- Are usually well organized
- Make lists and check off completed items
- Usually have neat and tidy work space
- Walk faster with deliberate movements
- May have straighter posture
- Seek jobs that give them lots of control

Perceivers

- Are more casual and unconventional
- Are more playful
- Are good at adapting
- May procrastinate; put off decisions
- May be tentative and more "wishy-washy"
- Prefer a more leisurely pace
- Often have "unfinished" look; clothes rumpled, unruly hair, etc.
- Dress more for comfort
- Probably have messy car interior
- Are liable to change goals
- Prefer to start projects
- Find rules, systems, and structure confining and limiting
- Are often disorganized
- May make lists, but seldom complete all items
- Usually have messy, cluttered work space
- May walk slower
- May slouch more
- Seek jobs that are fun

individual preferences is, it is only *one part* of the system. In Chapters 4 and 5, you will learn the next two parts, which, together, will enable you to master the SpeedReading techniques.

Just before we move on, it bears repeating that everyone learns at his or her own pace. You may have absorbed the information in this chapter after one read-through, or you might benefit from reviewing some or all of it again before proceeding. Either way is the right way, as long as it works for you. Think of this course as like a house: the exterior may look great, but in order for it to last a long time, it has to be built on a solid foundation. These early chapters are the foundation of this course, and the more time you take to really understand the concepts presented, the greater will be your ability to SpeedRead people. So . . . whenever you're ready, it's on to Chapter 4.

CHAPTER FOUR

Temperament:
Four Different Human Natures

In Chapter 3, you learned the clues for identifying type preferences — the first of the three components that make up the SpeedReading system. In this chapter, you will learn about the second component — how to identify temperaments.

As you've already seen, the individual type preferences provide some very useful SpeedReading clues. But as important as each preference is, certain combinations of preferences, and the way they interact with each other, are what make insights gained through Type so powerful. This is true because, for example, no one is just an Introvert, but rather an *Introverted, Sensing, Thinking, Judging* type (ISTJ), or an *Introverted, Intuitive, Feeling, Perceiving* type (INFP). And as you now appreciate, there is a huge difference between ISTJs and INFPs. We believe that one important combination of preferences forms the core of a person's type. It is called temperament and it essentially identifies a person's key values and drives. Learning about temperament will be beneficial in two ways: it will greatly enhance your understanding of behavior and Type, and it will provide you with a highly effective shorthand method for Speed-Reading people.

To illustrate what we mean, imagine you are standing outside a room. Behind the door, you know there is an animal, but you don't have any idea what kind. It could be an elephant, a mouse, or anything in between. Knowing a person's temperament is like knowing the animal's species — say, a dog. This is very useful information, because it gives you a pretty good idea of what awaits you as you walk through the door. However, you still don't know what kind of dog — a vicious pit bull, or a lovable Labrador retriever.

Knowing a person's type is like knowing the specific breed of dog — in this case, let's say the Labrador retriever. Once you know this, you have a much better idea of the traits typical for these kinds of dogs, and you can more accurately predict how the animal is likely to behave — and, therefore, how you should treat it.

Now certainly all individuals — whether they are dogs or people — are unique. But more often than not, people of the same type (like dogs of the same breed) can be expected to act in fairly predictable ways. And since people's temperaments remain constant throughout their lifetimes, temperament can provide reliable insights into understanding people.

We owe our knowledge and understanding of temperament to a California psychologist, Dr. David Keirsey, who discovered that throughout history (as far back as 450 B.C.!), philosophers, writers, psychologists, and others from a variety of times and cultures all observed four distinct natures into which all people seemed to fit. Keirsey realized that the four different groups — which he called temperaments — described remarkably similar characteristics. When Keirsey learned about Personality Type, he discovered that four combinations of type preferences also corresponded to the four temperaments. And within each of the four temperaments were four types similar to those described by Isabel Myers.* Over the years, leading

psychological researchers such as Dr. Linda Berens, director of the Temperament Research Institute in California, have studied temperament in depth, and their work has contributed greatly to our understanding.[†]

Many different labels have been used to identify the four temperaments. The names we use in this book, some borrowed and some original, were chosen because we feel they best describe each temperament's most central qualities and characteristics.

TRADITIONALISTS

Traditionalist is the name we use for people who prefer the Sensing and Judging combination. Their preference for *Sensing* (paying attention to facts and details, and living in the present moment), coupled with their preference for *Judging* (seeking closure and having a strong work ethic), combine to make them the most responsible of the four temperaments. They are also the most numerous — estimated to represent about 40 percent of the American population.

Values and Qualities

Among the things that Traditionalists value most are responsibility, duty, and service to society. These are the solid citizens who make sure every-

*For an excellent introduction to temperament, see *Please Understand Me*, David Keirsey and Marilyn Bates, Prometheus Nemesis, 1978.

[†] Information regarding the Temperament Research Institute can be found in Chapter 12.

thing that needs to get done, does. And because they appreciate structure, hierarchy, and organization, they are also the folks who manage most of our organizations and companies. Traditionalists are notoriously hard workers who pride themselves on being dependable, reliable, and thorough. They are absolutely trustworthy and their word is their bond. For most, "family values" is not a political slogan, but a way of life.

More than any of the other temperaments, Traditionalists trust and respect authority. They believe in the importance of having and following rules and laws, and support the people and organizations who enforce them. They play the important role of maintaining society's systems and traditions. Cautious by nature, Traditionalists are careful, practical, and realistic, and put great stock in the value of *common sense* and learning gained from real life experience.

TRADITIONALIST CLUES

As you review the following clues, you will no doubt recognize some overlap from the clue lists for specific preferences. This is because Traditionalists are Sensing-Judgers (SJs), and, therefore, many Sensing and many Judging clues will pertain to them. However, as you will see, a temperament is much more than just the sum of its parts, as many of these clues will reflect.

Please keep in mind that the following clues are, by necessity, presented as generalizations or extreme examples of each temperament. And since there are four types within each of the tempera-

ments, there will be some significant differences between those four types. So while most of the clues will apply to most Traditionalists, not all of them will apply to all Traditionalists.

Demeanor

Serious, responsible, straightforward, and consistent is how Traditionalists come across most of the time. They are usually rather formal, polite, well-mannered, and respectful—and may be deferential to their elders and people in authority. Although they like to be of service to others, they generally have rather rigid boundaries that define what the appropriate behavior is for various situations. And they don't deviate frequently or easily from the way they think things should be done.

Appearance

Appropriateness in all areas of life is a very important value to most Traditionalists, and it is commonly reflected in the clothes they wear. They tend to dress conservatively, with a preference for classic fashion, and tend to put function and practicality over style. They have a very "finished" look—their clothes are clean and pressed, shoes are shined, and their hair an appropriate length and style. In men who wear mustaches and beards, they are normally neatly trimmed and kept short. Men Traditionalists very seldom wear their hair exceptionally long, and when they do, it will usually be pulled back in a neat ponytail. In short,

S N A P S H O T
The Four Traditionalist Types

ESTJs are practical, realistic, and logical. Usually friendly and talkative as well, they are quick to notice just what needs to be done, and are adept at organizing tasks and people to accomplish their goals in the most efficient manner.

ISTJs are meticulous with details and accurate with facts. They excel at setting up and maintaining workable and efficient systems and procedures. More private and reserved, they are reliable and consistent people who exude calm and common sense.

ESFJs are outgoing, sociable, and talkative. Sensitive and sympathetic, they are extremely nurturing and derive great pleasure from helping others satisfy their needs in real, specific, and hands-on ways.

ISFJs are gentle, caring, thoughtful people. They are totally devoted to their families and friends and place their commitments ahead of self-serving interests. Careful and cautious about change, they take their responsibilities very seriously and tend to shy away from the spotlight.

Traditionalists' appearance often reflects the solid, stable, and no-nonsense people they are.

Communication Style

Traditionalists communicate in a direct, clear, and efficient manner. They prefer to talk about real things and experiences, using specific examples, and are less comfortable discussing theoretical or hypothetical situations. Neither are they terribly fond of activities like brainstorming. Extraverted Traditionalists may talk a lot, but they are generally direct and tell you exactly what's on their minds. Their conversation contains a lot of facts and details, and they are very precise and specific.

Body/Movement

Traditionalists are no slouches, behaviorally or physically. They tend to have good posture, sitting and standing up straight. They often walk deliberately and at a brisk pace, as if they always have something important to do (which, of course, they often do).

Occupation

Although Traditionalists are found in all jobs, they prefer to work in a stable and predictable environment, with a clear reporting hierarchy and steadily increasing levels of responsibility. The more structure and clarity, the better. They like to be evaluated, rewarded, and appreciated for their hard work and their ability to get things done in an efficient and organized way. They don't like a lot of change and prefer coworkers who take their responsibilities as seriously as they do. They are often found in large numbers in business, management, teaching, health care, and working in the judicial system.

Avocation

Traditionalists may have a wide range of interests, but their hobbies often involve some sort of physical activity, such as playing or coaching sports, jogging, walking, bird watching, fishing, carpentry or woodworking, or using their hands or bodies to make art or do crafts like needlepoint, pottery, and

so on. They may also enjoy collecting things, especially antiques. Traditionalists tend to volunteer in their communities and comprise a majority of the members of service organizations such as Kiwanis, Rotary, Junior Women's League, and the Shriners. Likewise, they are often active in churches and synagogues, hospitals, and other charitable organizations.

THE PERSONALITY TYPE PYRAMID

The Connection Between Type and Temperament

In a moment, we will describe the other three temperaments. But before we do, we want to intro-

**The Personality Type Pyramid:
Traditionalists***

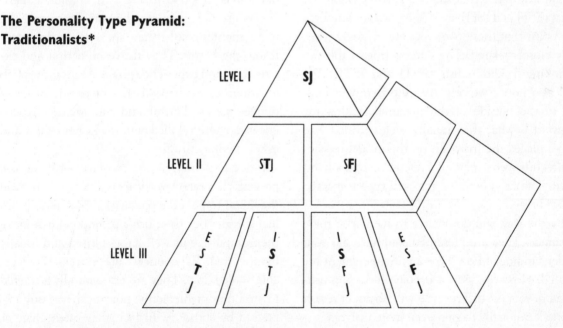

*The boldface letter in each full type identifies the Lead function.

duce you to the Personality Type Pyramid—a graphic we created to help you visualize how types are derived from and related to temperaments, and which can help clarify your understanding of both.

As you can see, the pyramid is divided into three levels. Level I identifies the Traditionalist, or SJ temperament. Level II divides the SJs into two groups: those who prefer Thinking (STJs) and those who prefer Feeling (SFJs). Having learned how different Thinkers and Feelers are, you can appreciate how useful it is to be able to make this distinction. Level III divides the Thinking and Feeling Traditionalists once again—this time into Extraverts and Introverts—creating whole four-letter types.

You will notice that the two Feeling Traditionalists (ESFJ and ISFJ) are side by side, to reinforce the point that these two types are, in some ways, very closely related. The same is true of the two Thinking Traditionalists (ESTJ and ISTJ). You will also notice we've placed the Extravert closest to the outside of the pyramid, for looking outward is what they usually prefer to do. And we've placed the Introvert on the inside, to symbolize Introverts' natural preference to look inward. The Lead function for each type is marked in bold type.

By the way, you don't have to memorize these pyramids. They are presented simply to aid your understanding of how Type and temperament are related. However, as you become more sophisticated in your use of Type, you will no doubt revisit them occasionally to gain even more insights.

EXPERIENCERS

We call people who prefer Sensing and Perceiving, Experiencers. Like Traditionalists, Experiencers prefer *Sensing* (realistic and practical), but their preference for *Perceiving*, with its more spontaneous, free-flowing lifestyle, makes them very different in significant ways. They are the most free-spirited of the four temperaments. They are also the second most numerous, representing about 30 percent of the American population.

Values and Qualities

Perhaps above all else, Experiencers value their freedom to respond to life as it unfolds. Experiencers are not planners, they are doers, and the more spontaneously they are able to do something, the better. They thrive on action and excitement, and experience physical sensations with an intensity far beyond that of people of other temperaments. Playful and fun loving, Experiencers are often skilled performers, who enjoy and excel at competition.

Since Experiencers are too busy enjoying the present, they rarely worry about the future. Instead they tend to be more pragmatic, short-term problem solvers. But their drive to respond can make them impulsive as well. Free-spirited and usually lighthearted, Experiencers are extremely adaptable and flexible. They are not naturally attracted to structure or hierarchy, nor are they easily impressed by authority. In fact, they often chafe at rules or laws, especially those that keep them from following their curiosity and impulses. Natural risk takers, some Experiencers become thrill seekers in their desire to experience as much of life as they can.

EXPERIENCER CLUES

Demeanor

Experiencers generally have an easygoing, carefree, and sometimes even happy-go-lucky, attitude. They are easy to be around, since they have an inherently relaxed style and like to have fun. They usually smile a lot, laugh easily, and rarely take things too seriously for too long. While they are neither harried nor hurried, Experiencers are perpetually eager and ready to respond to the next experience—whatever it may be or whenever it occurs. Totally in the present moment, Experiencers are able to remain completely aware of what they are experiencing at all times.

Appearance

In contrast to the more formal Traditionalists, Experiencers usually have a more casual, sometimes even irreverent, appearance. Whenever possible, they opt for comfortable, sporty clothes and accessories. For example, they may prefer a knapsack to a briefcase, a sports coat to a suit, and a running or sweat suit to a pair of pants and a shirt. While they prefer the casual, they are keenly aware of the look, texture, and color of their clothes and often enjoy looking good. Above all, however, their clothing must not hinder or restrict them. Depending on the situation, they may have a rather unfinished, or even messy, look.

Communication Style

Like much of what they do, Experiencers communicate with an easy and informal style. Their language tends to be simple and uncomplicated, and they may frequently omit the final letter or sound on words ("goin'" instead of "going"), giving their language a more relaxed and casual sound. Their sentence structure is generally free-flowing, containing references to their or others' real-life experiences. Since many Experiencers are involved in sports, they frequently use sports metaphors. For example, congratulating a coworker on a successful presentation, an Experiencer is likely to say: "Boy, you really hit that one out of the park!"

Because they prefer recreation to conversation, most Experiencers' idea of a good time is not to sit around talking about the meaning of life, but to get out and enjoy it. This is especially true of ISTPs and ESTPs, who would much rather be doing something active, like playing a game. And when they do get involved (or roped into) conversation, they would prefer to talk about real things, rather than ponder philosophical questions or debate the burning political issues of the day.

SNAPSHOT
The Four Experiencer Types

ESTPs are active, impulsive, and playful. Outgoing and talkative, they are realistic, observant, and pragmatic. They are adaptable, resilient, and resourceful when solving immediate problems. Free-spirited and popular, they like to stay busy and are content to take life one moment at a time.

ISTPs are independent, curious, and logical. They are private and calm, always the keen observer of their surroundings. Skillful and capable with things in the physical world, they have a special affinity for things mechanical and usually are especially gifted using tools of all kinds.

ESFPs are warm, friendly, and cheerful. Active, eager, and usually surrounded by a variety of people, the party seems to follow them wherever they go. Realistic, practical, and caring, they are spontaneous and easygoing.

ISFPs are gentle, modest, and compassionate. While initially reserved and quiet, they care deeply about people and animals and are devoted, loyal, and ready to help at a moment's notice. Practical and observant, they live fully in the present, enjoying the beauty of life around them.

Body / Movement

Of the four temperaments, Experiencers usually have the greatest body awareness. They are almost always conscious of how they feel physically, or are aware of what their bodies are doing. Their physical senses are generally so acute that they tend to be highly agile and coordinated. They even tend to learn physical tasks quicker than other temperaments. They innately know how much energy is required to perform a physical act efficiently, and may expend no more energy than is necessary. As a result, their movements are generally so fluid and graceful that they can make almost every physical skill look easy. Many can elevate the most ordinary movement—such as hammering nails into wood—into an art. Most Experiencers seem supremely comfortable within their own skin and tend to move with confidence and grace.

Occupation

While found in all jobs, Experiencers tend to derive satisfaction from work that includes a great deal of variety and change, where each day is different and presents fresh challenges. They like flexible, relaxed work environments without a lot of bureaucracy and rules, and which allow them to have plenty of fun on the job. They want to be evaluated on their skillfulness and capability to get the job done without a lot of help from others. And they like working with real things, often excelling with tools, crafts, or artisanship. Experiencers are usually at their best in a crisis and make great "firefighters," both the kind who put out real fires and those who work for companies to immediately solve important problems as they arise. Jobs that attract a large number of Experiencers include: law enforcement officer, restaurant worker, pilot, and emergency medical technician and various careers in sports and entertainment.

Avocation

Perhaps the single most popular hobby of Experiencers is sports. While not all Experiencers are jocks, a high percentage either participate in or follow sports closely, often well into their golden years. Experiencers also like to play games, and while they may enjoy more passive games like checkers, cards, and Scrabble, they usually prefer more physical ones. They like to use their bodies and work with their hands, and since they are often exceptionally skilled with tools, they frequently like woodworking, gardening, and restoring old houses and automobiles. Activities that require serious risk taking such as car and motorcycle racing, "extreme" sports like bungee jumping, hang gliding, snowboarding, scuba diving, and skydiving are most heavily populated by Experiencers.

As with the Traditionalists' Pyramid, Level I identifies the SP temperament, Level II divides SPs into Thinkers and Feelers, and Level III divides them, once again, into Extraverts and Introverts, to create whole types. You will notice the two Thinking Experiencers (ESTP and ISTP) are next to each other because they are so closely

The Personality Type Pyramid: Experiencers

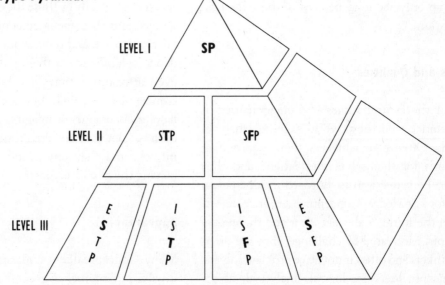

LEVEL I   SP

LEVEL II   STP   SFP

LEVEL III   ESTP   ISTP   ISFP   ESFP

related, as are the two Feeling Experiencers (ESFP and ISFP).

CONCEPTUALIZERS

We use the name Conceptualizer to describe people who prefer Intuition and Thinking. Conceptualizers are very different from both Experiencers and Traditionalists in significant ways. The first major difference is that Conceptualizers prefer *Intuition* rather than Sensing, so their focus is not on the specifics, but on the big picture, and not on the present, but on the future. The second big difference is that Conceptualizers prefer *Thinking,* which makes them logical and objective decision makers. This combination of Intuition and Thinking makes them the most independent of the four temperaments. Additionally, there are significantly fewer Conceptualizers, estimated to make up only about 15 percent of the American population.

Values and Qualities

One of the central values of Conceptualizers is competence, and the drive to excel at whatever they do. Often superachievers, they set very high standards for themselves and others, and they tend to be perfectionists. Engaged in a perpetual quest for knowledge, Conceptualizers are comfortable in the world of abstract ideas and theoretical concepts. Motivated by challenge, they are original thinkers and often innovative problem solvers.

Conceptualizers are logical, analytical, objective, and usually fair-minded. Strategic planners who often possess great vision, they enjoy applying their ingenuity to deal with complex issues. Conceptualizers are skeptical by nature and often need scientific or impartial proof to be convinced. They are fiercely independent, and demand, and usually command, respect. More than other temperaments, Conceptualizers understand, appreciate, and are usually skillful at gaining and leveraging power.

CONCEPTUALIZER CLUES

Demeanor

Conceptualizers tend to inspire trust and admiration from others, in part because they value their own competence so highly that they seem totally sure of themselves. They want very much to be respected, especially by those they respect. They may occasionally become argumentative when they are challenged, and their characteristic overconfidence can also make them seem dismissive, and even arrogant at times. Nothing is simple with Conceptualizers, and they are skilled at seeing flaws in arguments or imagining alternatives others miss. But they are also prone to overanalyze or nitpick, and they enjoy, and are very good at, playing the devil's advocate.

Appearance

Many Conceptualizers understand the subtleties involved in interpersonal communication, and use

SNAPSHOT
The Four Conceptualizer Types

ENTJs are natural leaders—strategic, organized, and decisive. Forceful, strong, and committed, they are usually able to mobilize whatever resources or people are necessary in order to get the job done in a way that meets their high and creative standards.

INTJs are excellent creative strategists. Complex and often brilliant visionaries, their logical analysis and single-minded determination often enable them to see with laser accuracy well beyond what others see. They are fiercely independent and strong-willed perfectionists.

ENTPs are enthusiastic, persuasive, and often charismatic. Their perceptiveness and their ability to understand and connect with people and anticipate societal trends make them natural entrepreneurs and politicians.

INTPs are very complex, independent, and creative people. They are fascinated with the most abstract and complicated of challenges and can argue any logical position with fairness and conviction.

their appearance to demonstrate their status and personal power. This can include a variety of behaviors, such as wearing designer clothing, driving luxury or exotic cars, surrounding themselves with important people, owning lavish houses, and belonging to exclusive clubs or organizations. These accoutrements are the tangible symbols of their success, and this tendency is more common with *Extraverted* Conceptualizers, ENTJs and ENTPs, and especially ENTPs.

It can be a wholly different story with Introverted Conceptualizers. INTJs, and especially INTPs, may be so absorbed in their inner world, and/or so independent, that they neither pay much attention to nor are concerned about their appearance at all. As a result, they may have a very unconventional, eclectic, or even rumpled look,

not unlike the stereotype of the brilliant, but eccentric, college professor.

Communication Style

Conceptualizers often love language and enjoy learning and using unusual and sophisticated words; many have impressive vocabularies. But since their thought processes are so complex, they frequently use compound sentences that may contain several different ideas and which can sometimes be difficult for others to follow. They really enjoy talking about the big picture in any issue, and are prone to using diagrams, models, or matrixes to illustrate their points.

As long as they work to keep it simple,

Conceptualizers can be skillful communicators, although Extraverted Conceptualizers (ENTJs and ENTPs) are usually better verbally, whereas Introverted Conceptualizers (INTJs and INTPs) may be more effective with the written word. Both Introverted and Extraverted Conceptualizers enjoy, and frequently use, metaphors and analogies to make their points. People who use lots of novel words or expressions, delight in puns, double entendres, and plays on words, and who enjoy a reputation for being clever and witty are probably Conceptualizers.

The following clue applies to many Conceptualizers, but certainly not to all. Depending on their age, station in life, and degree of self-esteem, some Conceptualizers seem to have a strong need to make others aware of how successful they are. This may manifest itself in a tendency to engage in one-upsmanship, name-dropping, showing off their awards or possessions, or simply bragging about their achievements.

Occupation

Conceptualizers, like the other three temperaments, are found in all jobs. However, they are most satisfied in environments that support high intellectual pursuits and achievements. They enjoy mastering new technologies and like using creativity to solve complex or theoretical problems. Naturally ambitious, they need to work with other people whose competence they respect, especially those to whom they report. Above all, Conceptualizers need constant challenge in the form of a steep learning curve and many opportunities for intellectual growth. Since they like working on new and original projects, they are best at perfecting flawed systems in ingenious ways and then moving on to their next creative challenge. Some jobs to which Conceptualizers gravitate include: high-level manager, independent consultant, computer professional, scientist, lawyer, strategic planner, financial analyst, and psychiatrist. Many college professors, especially those in the liberal arts and science, are Conceptualizers.

Avocation

Conceptualizers are often interested in self-improvement, especially in the form of advancing their education, learning a new language or skill, or studying the lives of other successful people. Many find pleasure listening to audiotapes or reading self-improvement books. Since they are typically career driven, it makes sense that most of their free time involves learning ways to get ahead professionally or improving themselves in some way. Many are virtual wizards on the computer and Internet. Games of skill and strategy and individual sports and hobbies are also popular with Conceptualizers, especially those with high degrees of personal challenge like golf, chess, or singles tennis.

As with the other pyramids, Level I of the Conceptualizer Pyramid identifies the NT temperament. But since by definition, *all* Conceptualizers are Thinkers, Level II divides them into Judgers

The Personality Type Pyramid:
Conceptualizers

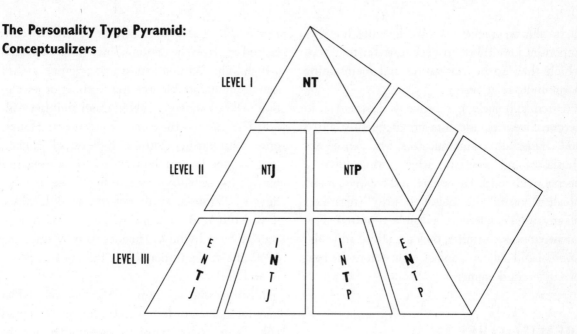

and Perceivers. Level III divides them, once again, into Extraverts and Introverts, to create whole types. You will notice the two Judging Conceptualizers (ENTJ and INTJ) are next to each other because they are so closely related, as are the two Perceiving Conceptualizers (ENTP and INTP).

IDEALISTS

The final temperament group are Idealists, people who prefer Intuition and Feeling. Like Conceptualizers, Idealists prefer Intuition, which means they focus on the big picture and on the future. But unlike Conceptualizers, Idealists prefer Feeling, so they make decisions based primarily on their own

values and how their actions will affect others. This combination makes them the most empathetic of the four temperaments. Like Conceptualizers, Idealists represent only about 15 percent of the American population.

Values and Qualities

For the philosophical Idealists, life is a journey of self-discovery—a perpetual search for meaning. Their mission is to understand as much about themselves and others as they can, in order to achieve their potential. Having personal integrity and being true to one's beliefs are not optional for Idealists; they are prized life goals. They place a high value on uniqueness and originality. It is very important for Idealists to feel connected to others, which they do by cultivating and maintaining harmonious relationships.

Often extremely perceptive and sensitive to people's feelings, Idealists are frequently gifted and charismatic communicators, who can be enthusiastic and persuasive when acting out of a deeply held belief. Passionate and creative, many Idealists possess "the soul of an artist" (regardless of any innate talent or possible training). Frequently nonconformists, they are attracted to the unusual and different, and often march to the beat of a different drummer.

IDEALIST CLUES

Demeanor

Idealists are often described as being "artsy." Many, especially the Introverted Idealists (INFJ and INFP) have an ethereal quality about them, perpetually detached and preoccupied with things of a spiritual nature. Since most Idealists spend many of their waking hours thinking or talking about issues of great global concern, especially those that affect people, they often look as though they have a lot on their minds, which they do.

Appearance

Many Idealists have an unconventional look about them. This is especially true of Perceiving Ideal-

ists, ENFPs and INFPs, who are even less concerned or driven by custom. Since they place such a high value on uniqueness and originality, they are most comfortable wearing clothing or jewelry that makes a statement about them and their values. This can run the gamut from choosing funky, often loose-fitting, clothing, Birkenstock sandals, long or free-flowing hair styles, to wearing ribbons, pins, or buttons espousing a cause they believe in. While certainly not true of *all* Idealists, if you run into someone who looks as though they've been living in Haight-Ashbury since the 1960s, he or she is more likely than not an ENFP or an INFP!

Idealists who are Judgers (ENFJs and INFJs) may look different from those who are Perceivers (ENFPs and INFPs), since they are both more conventional and more concerned about how they appear to others. In addition to having the more finished look common to all Judgers, they are also likely to dress with an eye toward appropriateness. This is especially true of ENFJ women, who usually go to great lengths to make sure their outfits are well coordinated and right for the occasion. But their overarching goal is to be true to their own sense of themselves, whatever form or fashion that requires.

Communication Style

Since the central value of Idealists is to understand themselves, others, and the meaning of life, their communication usually centers on personal concerns, especially relationships. They ask more

SNAPSHOT
The Four Idealist Types

ENFJs are enthusiastic, vivacious, and usually possess excellent public relations skills, which they like to use to help people reach their highest potential. Creative, energetic, and organized, they throw themselves fully into every activity and task.

INFJs are the most conceptual of the Idealists. Creative, original, and complex, they are rather formal and reserved, but hold deep personal convictions that rule their actions and decisions. They can be extremely focused and have great drive to accomplish their goals.

ENFPs see opportunities everywhere and live for exploring possibilities and helping other people to make changes or improve their lives. They are friendly, spontaneous, creative, and playful people who care deeply for their families and many friends.

INFPs are the most idealistic of the Idealists, and are driven by their deep personal values and unique view of the world. They are gentle, reserved and even cool to those they do not know and trust, but warm, passionate, and committed to the people and things they care deeply about.

personal questions, reveal personal information to others, and have an intimate communication style. They stand close, look people deeply in the eyes, and respond genuinely to others, offering words and gestures of empathy and concern. In essence, Idealists are the true heart-to-heart conversationalists and are much more interested in that type of discussion than in those of a less personal nature. Therefore, they become more engaged and animated when the conversation deals with things of a personal nature. And since they are so strongly ruled by their own values, they can be offended more easily than other temperaments when people are insensitive or cruel or when jokes are made that belittle or demean others.

Body / Movement

Just as Experiencers seen naturally graceful because they are so keenly aware of their bodies, Idealists seem mostly to inhabit the world of feelings and imagination. So they often (but not always) are less graceful, less *naturally* skillful with mechanical things. While Idealists may achieve a high level of athletic prowess, it is often more a learned skill than an inherent one.

At the extreme, Idealists (especially Introverted ones, INFPs and INFJs) are even a bit awkward. This is primarily due to their lack of attention to the physical world around them. Hence, they tend not to notice the edge of a table or the beginning of a flight of stairs. Since they have their minds on other things, they are often at greater risk of stumbling or looking clumsy.

Occupation

Idealists, like people of the other temperaments, are found in all fields, although not in nearly the same numbers. Remember that Idealists only make up about 15 percent of the general population. However, the most satisfying work for Idealists is that which they find personally meaningful and rewarding. They need to believe in their work and to be able to see the positive impact it has on the greater good. Idealists like their work environment to be as tension free as possible, working among caring people where they feel appreciated and liked. Solving problems with global or far-reaching implications in creative ways is especially enjoyable to Idealists, as it allows them and others to develop their greatest individual potential. Occupations that attract large numbers of Idealists are: the artist, psychologist, counselor, social worker, teacher of the humanities, trainer, and human resources worker.

As with the other Personality Type Pyramids, Level I identifies the NF temperament. But since *all* Idealists — by definition — are *Feelers,* Level II divides them into Judgers and Perceivers. Level III divides them, once again, into Extraverts and In-

The Personality Type Pyramid: Idealists

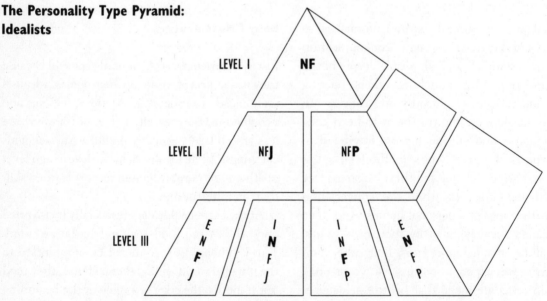

LEVEL I   NF

LEVEL II   NF**J**   NF**P**

LEVEL III   E N F J   I N F J   I N F P   E N F P

troverts, to create whole types. You will notice the two Judging Idealists (ENFJ and INFJ) next to each other because they are most closely related, as are the two Perceiving Idealists (ENFP and INFP).

In addition to the main purpose it serves in this course, Temperament can also be very helpful to those who may still be unsure of their own four-letter type. For example, suppose you are uncertain if your type is ENTJ or ENFJ. Beyond the obvious difference that one is a Thinker and the other is a Feeler, they are also different temperaments. ENTJs are Conceptualizers, while ENFJs are Idealists. If you reread the sections that describe these two temperaments, you should find that one describes you much more accurately than the other. Or perhaps you aren't sure if you are an ISTP or an ISTJ. Besides the fact that one is a Judger and the other a Perceiver, ISTPs are Experiencers, while ISTJs are Traditionalists. Again, reviewing these two different temperaments will likely confirm your true type.

TEMPERAMENT SKILL-BUILDING EXERCISE

This exercise is designed to test your ability to recognize temperaments based on a very limited amount of information. In the scenario that follows, you will briefly meet four people of different temperaments. Your assignment is to determine each person's temperament and identify three clues that led you to your conclusion. The exercise will be more beneficial if you don't refer back to the pages that list clues, but rather find the clues within the scenario. You will find the answers on page 105. Good luck!

A round of recent layoffs and a difficult local economy have sparked rumors that a family-owned manufacturing company might be relocating to another state. Because this has caused serious morale problems, the president of the company has invited four employees from different departments to a breakfast meeting to discuss the problems from the employees' perspective and to brainstorm ways of improving morale and productivity.

Alex, a forty-year-old human resource specialist, was the first to speak: "I hate to say it, but the problem in a nutshell is that people no longer feel connected to the company. It used to be that we were like a family. And sure, there were problems, but people cared about each other and felt appreciated—like they belonged here. Part of the problem is that we've gotten so big and impersonal that we've lost touch with each other. And I think it's clear that when people don't feel invested in the company—and by that I mean *emotionally* invested—they're simply not going to do their best work. We have to look for creative ways of meeting our employees' needs. For example, finding affordable, quality child care is a big problem for many of us in this town. We could explore the possibility of setting up a company-sponsored child care center, which might have an employee committee to oversee and direct its operation. Or we could look into instituting flexible hours, which would give workers greater flexibility in their lives outside of work.

Creative ideas like that, which meet people's needs, would be a *huge* goodwill effort on the part of management and would yield rich rewards for the company, not only at this moment, but for a long time to come."

Lillian, a fifty-five-year-old shipping and receiving manager, spoke up next. "I don't know, it may sound silly, but this place used to be a lot more fun. There were lots of activities that brought people together—like the softball and bowling leagues, the annual employee/family picnic up at Tobin Lake, and many other informal gatherings. And I remember, we were always running some crazy contest or other, with the winners announced in the cafeteria at lunchtime. The whole place just used to be looser—not that we didn't break our necks to get the work out! But after we worked hard, we enjoyed partying together. It also seems like the jobs today are too routinized—I hear people on the line constantly complain they feel like they're just an extension of their machine! And it seems now that every time you turn around, there's another new rule or procedure to follow, and, of course, endless paperwork to document that you followed it. All these excessive rules means it takes too long to make anything happen. I just think that if you could make this place less rigid and more fun again, people would relax and be more willing to really be here!"

Maureen, forty-seven, from accounting was next. "Not surprisingly, I don't agree with much of what Lillian had to say. She's putting the cart before the horse by suggesting recreational activities will motivate people. I think you reward people with something fun if, and only after, they do a good job, not

before it. And, if anything, I think we've gotten a little *too loose* around here. The left hand never seems to know what the right hand is doing. It's not that we have too many rules or procedures, it's that they are far too ambiguous, and inconsistently enforced when people don't follow them, which is quite often, in my opinion. We have policies for a reason, and they should be spelled out in detail, printed in a handbook, and distributed to all employees when they start working here. That way, everyone would know precisely what was expected of them. Maybe if we started posting individual productivity ratings, the people who aren't pulling their weight might work harder. The long and short of it is, if we were more efficient around here, people would take more pride in their work and the whole company would benefit."

The last to speak was fifty-year-old Charlie, who ran Computer Services. "I've been listening with great interest and, frankly, I think you are all missing the boat by concentrating on short-term problems and solutions. What we should be thinking about is the *future* . . . what can we do to ensure that the company will be competitive and profitable into the next century! And we should start by analyzing our needs with respect to our computers, and immediately upgrade our systems. Theoretically, anyway, people will work harder if they are invested in the company, so management should implement a profit-sharing plan—the more money the company makes, the more the employee makes. That is the way to get them really invested. I recommend we implement more autonomous teams to handle the various phases of product development. That would address both Lillian's concerns about more variety and Alex's desire to have people work more closely together. And, finally, I believe it would pay big dividends down the road if we were to offer advanced computer classes for all our employees. After all, computers are the future, and the more competent we all are, the more successful we will all be."

Directions

Identify the temperament for each employee and provide three clues that support your answer.

a. Alex's temperament: _____

    Clue #1: _____

    Clue #2: _____

    Clue #3: _____

b. Lillian's temperament: _____

    Clue #1: _____

    Clue #2: _____

    Clue #3: _____

c. Maureen's temperament: _____

    Clue #1: _____

    Clue #2: _____

    Clue #3: _____

d. Charlie's temperament: _____

    Clue #1: _____

    Clue #2: _____

    Clue #3: _____

Answers on page 106

Answers for Temperament Skill-building Exercise

Along with the answers, here are some of the many clues embedded in each of the temperament Skill-building examples. You may have noticed others not listed here.

a. Alex's temperament: Idealist (NF)
    Clue #1: Primary concern is for people and their needs, for their feelings of being emotionally invested, connected, and appreciated.
    Clue #2: Occupation in human resources.
    Clue #3: Recommendations of flex time and child care center address personal needs of employees.

b. Lillian's temperament: Experiencer (SP)
    Clue #1: Laments the lack of fun and activity at work and recommends reinstituting games, contests, and informal gatherings.
    Clue #2: Recommends jobs be less routinized and reducing the number of excessive rules and the time it takes to make things happen.

Clue #3: Generally wants the workplace to be more fun.

c. Maureen's temperament: Traditionalist (SJ)
    Clue #1: Disapproves of fun and games unless work is done first.
    Clue #2: Recommends detailed, written policies.
    Clue #3: Strives for productivity and efficiency.

d. Charlie's temperament: Conceptualizer (NT)
    Clue #1: Focuses on long-term problem solving, into the next century.
    Clue #2: Recommends autonomous teams and high-tech computer training.
    Clue #3: Suggests major company-wide overhauls rather than specific changes.

So, how did you do? If you did not fare as well as you hoped, you might want to read the earlier section again to see what you missed. If you aced this exercise, it's time to move on to Chapter 5, where you will learn the third component in the Speed-Reading system.

Why What You See . . .
Is Not Always
What You Get

Andrew's palms were sweating as he rang the doorbell of the impressive Georgian colonial. The only time he could remember being this nervous was four years ago, when he filled in at the last minute for the lead in his high school play, who had been rushed to the hospital for an emergency appendectomy. Andrew worried because tonight he was facing a more critical audience. He had come to meet Elissa's father. Elissa was the new love of his life, and someone whom he could easily imagine marrying one day. (He had met Elissa's mother briefly once before and they seemed to hit it off well.)

Despite reassurances from Elissa that her father would be "crazy about him," Andrew had his doubts. What, he wondered, would a senior art history major whose greatest lament was that he has missed out on the radical 60s and the lead scientist of a major pharmaceutical company have to talk about? The answer soon became painfully apparent: not much. The palpable awkwardness throughout the evening felt excruciating at times to Andrew, Elissa, and her mother but seemed to go completely unnoticed by her father. The conversation basically consisted of a handful of general, but probing, questions tossed at Andrew by his host, and Andrew's self-conscious, rambling replies.

Walking to his car after saying good night, Andrew was completely convinced he had bombed with Elissa's father, and might have slipped in her mother's estimation as well. After all, Andrew was an artist and an insightful judge of people. Elissa's father had not demonstrated the slightest bit of warmth toward him, hadn't engaged him in the usual small talk; he hadn't even looked Andrew in the eye more than a half dozen times throughout the whole dinner. And he certainly hadn't put his arm around Andrew's shoulder or told him how much he enjoyed meeting him, as Andrew had fantasized he might.

But the next morning, Andrew was flabbergasted when Elissa told him how much her father liked him. "He said you were intelligent, had depth, were a good listener, and seemed to have the strength of your convictions — qualities he really admires and rarely encounters in people our age." While very pleased, if not wholly convinced she might not be sugarcoating the truth a bit, Andrew wondered how he could have so badly misread Elissa's father.

It turns out that the old warning "You can't judge a book by its cover" has new meaning with regard to the study of SpeedReading people. We've all known people who have boundless energy. Enthusiastic about everything, they wear their feelings and emotions prominently for all to see. They are usually so excited and animated when they talk to you that their eyes actually seem to sparkle. We've also all known people whose demeanor is just the opposite — people who are painfully reserved and wear a perpetual deadpan expression that reveals little, if anything, about how they really feel about things. Granted, the two people described above represent opposite ends of the spectrum. And, clearly, most people fall somewhere between these two extremes. But whether people express their feelings publicly or hold them back tells us a lot

about them and can provide one of the most powerful clues for determining their type.

FEELINGS

Showing the world or keeping them to yourself

You will remember that people perceive (or take in information) in one of two ways — through their Sensing or through their Intuition. Sensors focus on the facts and specifics, and Intuitives focus on the possibilities and implications. For this discussion, it is helpful to think of the perceiving process as "input" — that is, information coming into the brain. You will also recall that people judge, or decide, in one of two ways — as Thinkers, employing logical and impersonal analysis, or as Feelers — relying on their personal values. It is helpful to think of the judging process as "output" — that is, doing something with the information.

Since the act of perceiving is primarily an internal process, it is hard to observe whether someone relies more on Sensing or Intuition. In other words, if a woman smells a flower, it's impossible for anyone to know — just from watching her — if she is primarily experiencing the flower through her Sensing or through her Intuition. If she used her Sensing, she might just be pleased by how wonderful it smells, or notice the subtle spice tones of the fragrance. But if she used her Intuition, the same experience might make her sad if the flower's fragrance reminds her of the perfume of the great-aunt who recently passed away.

However, since the act of judging (or deciding something) usually involves some behavior, it is often easier to observe whether a person is using Thinking or Feeling. For example, suppose a man tells a joke that his coworker finds offensive. The man telling the joke has no way of knowing how the information is going in (the input) and being processed in the other man's brain. But suppose the man hearing the joke says to his coworker: "Gee, I don't mean to hurt your feelings, but I've gotta tell you that I find jokes that perpetuate negative stereotypes about people very offensive, and I'd prefer not to hear any more of them." The joke teller can observe the behavior, or the "output." And if he's learned the SpeedReading techniques taught in this section, he can quickly and reasonably conclude that the man is probably a Feeling type (exactly how he could conclude this will become evident very soon).

In trying to identify someone's type, it would obviously be very helpful to be able to look at his behavior, determine that it reflects his Feeling values, and therefore eliminate all eight Thinking types from consideration. Likewise, if we could quickly identify the person as a Thinker, we could eliminate all eight Feeling types. Unfortunately, this is not always easy to do for two reasons: first, people of all types use both Thinking and Feeling *sometimes*. But, of course, since they prefer Thinking, Thinkers tend to be better at it and use it more consistently, just as Feelers prefer, and therefore use, their Feeling more often and with greater skill. The second reason it is sometimes tricky to quickly distinguish Thinking and Feeling from

one another is that some types naturally use their Feeling side out in public, and others naturally keep their Feeling side to themselves, even if it's not their "true" preference.

When people direct their feelings at others, and make public value judgments, it is called *Extraverting Feeling*. The man who throws his arms around a friend he hasn't seen for years, looks him in the eye, and with a big grin says: "Man! it's great to see you!" is Extraverting Feeling. Also Extraverting Feeling is the woman who watches a TV commercial for toilet bowl cleaner that she considers demeaning to women and exclaims: "That does it! I am never going to buy another product made by those sleazy, sexist morons again!"

When people apply their feelings inwardly, toward themselves, and/or keep their value-based opinions private, we say they are *Introverting Feeling*. The woman who is comfortable quietly contemplating how she feels about something, rather than being compelled to announce it to the world, is Introverting Feeling. So is the man who looks inward, blames himself, and feels guilty for something that went wrong, rather than seeking to pin the blame on someone else.

Using the words "extraverting" and "introverting" to describe how people express their feeling side can be confusing. However, be assured that as you become more familiar with the concept, you will appreciate that there is a dramatic difference in the affect, or outward behavior, of people who Extravert Feeling and those who Introvert it. This is such a powerful clue because once you master identifying it, you can reduce the possible types a person may be from sixteen down to four—often in a matter of seconds!

When we discuss this particular personality dynamic, we use the shorthand *E/I-Feeling Pattern.**

EXTRAVERTED FEELING

There are eight types that Extravert feeling. Four of these are natural Feelers, and four are really Thinkers. (Remember, *all* types—Thinkers and Feelers—are capable of using both functions.)

The four Feeling types that
Extravert Feeling are:
ENFJ
INFJ
ESFJ
ISFJ

You will notice that each of these types shares the same last two letters, F and J, because they are all Feeling Judgers. Therefore, by definition, *all* **FJs** Extravert Feeling.

The four Thinking types that
Extravert Feeling are:
ENTP
INTP
ESTP
ISTP

*Some of the most significant work in the area of Extraverted and Introverted Feeling has been done by Psychological Type researcher, writer, and counselor Terry Duniho, 104 Rankin Avenue, Providence, RI 02908.

You will notice that each of these types shares the same two letters, T and P, because they are all Thinking Perceivers. So, by definition, *all* **TPs** also Extravert Feeling.

Now you're probably wondering: "If FJs and TPs both Extravert Feeling, then aren't they really similar, and, if so, then what difference does it make how I deal with them?" The answer is no, they are not similar, but they can *look* similar, and that's precisely why it is important to be able to tell "real" Feelers from Thinkers who just look like Feelers.

To demonstrate this point, consider an experience common to most of us—buying a car or making another major purchase. Many effective salespeople, especially people in retail sales, Extravert Feeling. While some are really Feeling types, many are in fact Thinkers, which makes them TPs. (And most are also E_TPs (Extraverted Thinker Perceivers.) Now one of the things that make salespeople successful is their ability to make you like and trust them. They do this by creating a relationship with you. They usually smile a lot, compliment you freely, use your first name often, and try to be responsive to your questions and concerns. In other words, they try to make you feel that you are important to them—their new best friend, if you will. The question is, are they acting this way because you suddenly have developed a close relationship and they want the two of you to start hanging out together? Probably not. More likely, they are using their natural Extraverted Feeling in service of their real preference—Thinking— because they know, consciously or not, that if you like them, they are more likely to make the sale. We often describe TPs as "connectors," because they have a natural ability to connect with others.

Lest we leave the wrong impression: we don't mean to suggest that all connectors, or even all salespeople, are manipulative or not genuine. The point is, this is their natural way of behaving. They are not being phony, nor is this just an act—in fact, behaving in any other way would feel unnatural and dishonest, just as it would be equally difficult for a person who does not naturally connect to act as if he or she does, for any length of time.

This business of Extraverting Feeling is so important because, if you didn't understand and appreciate this dynamic and weren't able to tell the TPs from the FJs, you might assume that everyone you met who seemed friendly, engaging, or who smiled at you was a Feeler, just as you might assume that anyone who seemed distant, cool, or impersonal must be a Thinker. Your assessment would be wrong on both counts, and as a result, your ability to communicate effectively—the goal in learning to SpeedRead people in the first place—would be greatly diminished.

So now that we have established the importance of being able to differentiate between Thinkers and Feelers who both Extravert Feeling, let's take a closer look at what Extraverted Feeling really looks like. We'll start with the general characteristics that all people who Extravert Feeling exhibit, both the TPs and the FJs. Then we'll present the specific clues for FJs, followed by those for TPs.

General Clues for Identifying Extraverted Feeling

Typically, people who Extravert Feeling (both FJs and TPs):

1. Strive to connect with others
They naturally pay attention to other people, are good at reading feelings and knowing what others want and need, and are motivated to provide it.

2. Try to please others and seek approval
(Especially true of FJs)
They often will go to great lengths to promote harmony.

3. Can be charming and charismatic
(Especially true of Extraverts)
They are "people" people—good talkers who are usually good at convincing others to trust and follow them.

4. Are physically expressive
(Especially true of Extraverts)
When talking with others, their faces are usually very expressive—they often have twinkling eyes, tend to laugh easily, and exhibit a wide variety of facial expressions, from smiling to frowning, from beaming to grimacing. Their reactions are often dramatic and immediate, and they are able to shift from one emotion to another quite quickly.

Extraverted Feelers usually engage with others physically, lean into conversations, sit or stand close to the person, nod their heads in approval, touch, hug, pat shoulders, rub backs, engage in extended handshakes, and show other more public displays of affection.

They also give lots of supportive feedback and commiserate easily with people, using expressions such as "That must have been very hard on you" or "I understand how you feel."

5. Tend to praise and blame others

While they can be very complimentary, they can also direct their Extraverted Feeling toward others in negative ways, by deflecting blame from themselves and punishing others who may not be at fault.

6. Tend to be appearance conscious

They are generally very aware of and concerned about how they will be perceived by others, and often feel it is more important to look good or dress appropriately to the situation than it is to be comfortable. In other words, they frequently dress for others first, and themselves second. In this way, they tend to put appearance over function. This results in wearing coordinated outfits (this is especially true for women), and both women and men usually have a "pulled-together" look.

Specific Clues for Identifying Feeling Judgers (FJs)

Now that we've reviewed the general clues for all types that Extravert Feeling, here are the specific clues for the four Feeling Judging (FJ) types — ENFJ, INFJ, ESFJ, and ISFJ. Typically they:

1. Really do make decisions based on their own personal values, unlike TPs, whose decisions are more dictated by logic and impersonal principles.
2. Are usually comfortable with feelings, their own and others', understanding them, talking about them, and sharing them.
3. Are genuinely motivated to help people, and find great fulfillment in doing so. They are so eager to be helpful, they often put other people's needs before their own.
4. Use language that reflects their values. They tend to describe things using words like: "wonderful," "horrible," "beautiful," "terrific," "outrageous," "ridiculous," etc.
5. Have strong opinions and express them; they like giving advice, and it often includes words like "should," as in "What you *should* do, is march right down there and demand a refund! I know I would!"
6. Express their approval and disapproval with their facial expressions. Often they will raise their eyebrows and tilt their heads to one side as if to say, "Oh, really?" to demonstrate their displeasure.

Specific Clues for Identifying Thinking Perceivers (TPs)

In contrast, the four TP types, ENTP, INTP, ESTP, and ISTP:

1. Make decisions based upon impersonal analysis, rather than according to their own values or concerns about how others will be affected.

2. Often use their Feeling side strategically—that is, as a device to connect with others to accomplish their objectives.

3. Are good at seeing both, or even several sides, of an issue, and usually enjoy debating or arguing the merits of different sides. (This is in sharp contrast to FJs, who have such a strong need for harmony they will seldom risk confrontation and the tension or ill will an argument may create between people.)

4. Can be very dramatic with emotions (especially ENTPs and ESTPs). They have a wide repertoire of behavior and are comfortable moving from one behavioral extreme to another.

5. Are pragmatic: unlike FJs, they can usually change positions easily to accommodate new information or if they decide a different strategy is more effective. Also unlike FJs, they tend not to lock themselves into moral, or value-based, positions, so they tend to be able and willing to retreat from their original position as the situation warrants.

6. Are generally less serious, and more easygoing; they have a "lighter," more casual demeanor that usually makes them fun to be around.

Muddying the Waters: How Gender Affects Extraverted Feeling

Although people's types predispose them to either naturally Extravert or Introvert Feeling, there are also other factors that can greatly influence whether one Extraverts or Introverts Feeling, as well. Chief among these are gender roles. In the American culture, females are socialized to Extravert Feeling, are expected to be comfortable with feelings, and are encouraged to show emotions freely. Males, on the other hand, are socialized to Introvert Feeling, to play it cool, and to keep their feelings and emotions in check. Since none of us is immune to this conditioning, the result is that Thinking women who naturally Introvert Feeling (TJs) often learn to be more public with their feelings or use them to meet social expectations. Therefore, they can *appear* to be Extraverting Feeling, when in fact they are not. Similarly, Feeling type men who naturally Extravert Feeling (FJs), may learn to unconsciously tone down their reactions, since that is what is expected of them. Consequently, they may not *appear* to be Extraverting Feeling, when in fact they are. This may be especially true of older men with more years of conditioning, who were raised in more emotionally repressed times, or who spent a good deal of time in the military. Understanding this subtle, yet pervasive, cultural dynamic can help you SpeedRead people much more accurately by making you more savvy to the genuine clues people give and alerting you to the adaptive behavior many of us display.

At this point, you should have a pretty good picture of what Extraverted Feeling looks like, and how it is different in Thinkers (TPs) and Feelers (FJs). In individuals who have very clear type preferences, it is often easy to recognize. But in others, it may be much more subtle and difficult to discern. For this reason, it will take you time, and lots of practice before you will be able to spot it quickly in others. In either case, it is a very powerful tool, which, although a little complex and tricky to grasp at first, is worth the time to master, since it will enable you to SpeedRead people much more quickly.

INTRODUCTED FEELING

Since eight of the sixteen types Extravert Feeling, there are also eight types that Introvert Feeling. Four of these are really Feelers, and four are really Thinkers. (Remember, *all* types — Thinkers and Feelers — are capable of using both functions.)

The four Feeling types that
Introvert Feeling are:
ENFP
INFP
ESFP
ISFP

You will notice that each of these types shares the same last two letters, FP, because they are all Feeling Perceivers. Therefore, by definition, *all* FPs Introvert Feeling.

The four Thinking types that
Introvert Feeling are:
ENTJ
INTJ
ESTJ
ISTJ

And you will notice that each of these types shares the same two last letters, TJ, because they are all Thinking Judgers. And, once again, by definition, *all* **TJs** Introvert Feeling.

Two sides of the same coin:
Introverted Feeling and Extraverted Thinking

By definition, people who Introvert Feeling also Extravert Thinking, since people don't Extravert and Introvert the same function. And it is almost always easier to see what a person is Extraverting (or showing to the world), than what they are Introverting (keeping to themselves).

General Clues for Identifying Introverted Feeling

Typically, people who Introvert Feeling (both FPs and TJs):

1. Can appear rather impersonal and dispassionate.
2. Are more concerned with pleasing themselves than they are with pleasing others. That is, they are generally more concerned about how they feel or what they think about a given issue than about what others may feel or think about it.
3. Are not usually physically or emotionally expressive, except with people very close to them or in private. (This is especially true of TJs). In fact, they often have a blank expression, even while discussing emotional issues, which can belie the passionate feelings they may be experiencing inside (especially FPs).

4. In contrast to people who Extravert Feeling and who often have sparkly eyes, FPs and TJs often have what can best be described as sad eyes.

Specific Clues for Identifying Feeling Perceivers (FPs)

Now that you've reviewed the general clues for all types that Introvert Feeling, we'll look at the specific cues for the four Feeling Perceiver (FP) types: ENFP, INFP, ESFP, and ISFP. Typically, FPs:

1. Have a gentle and even mellow persona. They prefer cooperation to competition and have an easygoing attitude.
2. Have deep feelings, but are very private about them, and do not share them easily, except with people with whom they are very close. However, at the same time, they can be extremely sentimental.
3. Are extremely sensitive. Outwardly friendly, they can also become suddenly moody. (This is especially true of INFPs and ENFPs.)
4. When things go wrong, they tend to look inward and blame themselves rather than to look outside and blame others.
5. Are flexible when dealing with little, everyday matters but can be tenacious, stubborn, and even inflexible when it comes to dealing with matters that involve their values or something very important to them. This can result in a tendency to hold grudges when they have been deeply offended.

6. Often communicate their values more through their actions than through their words.
7. Are not overly conscious of appearance and generally dress to please themselves, not others. They can often have an unfinished, casual look about them.
8. Can be self-deprecating and humble and are often uncomfortable or embarrassed receiving public compliments or praise.

Specific Clues For Identifying Thinking Judgers (TJs)

As we've discussed, four Thinking types also Introvert Feeling. They are ENTJs, INTJs, ESTJs, and ISTJs.

Although TJs Introvert Feeling, they are *very* different from FPs! This is because, as Thinkers, they make their decisions based on impersonal logic. And, as Judgers, they seek closure, structure, and finality. This combination can make them among the toughest of all the types. For consistency's sake, we'll refer to TJs as people who Introvert Feeling, which they do. But what is far easier to see in TJs is not their Introverted Feeling, but their Extraverted Thinking. Typically, TJs:

1. Are no-nonsense and businesslike. They like to get right to the point and not waste time. They don't willingly engage in excessive social niceties, and may be somewhat awkward when engaging in small talk, for which they see little need and have little patience (especially Introverts).

2. Usually have and express strong opinions and can appear insensitive and unfeeling, since they give honest, truthful feedback, even if it is blunt or brutally frank.
3. Show little emotion. They keep their feelings in check and seldom let them influence their logical decision making.
4. Are not physically demonstrative and seldom touch people with whom they are interacting. (This is especially true of ISTJs and INTJs.)
5. Usually have a tidy, more formal professional appearance. They usually dress in a conventional, traditional manner.

By comparing the list of clues for TJs and the one for FPs, it is quickly apparent how very different they are and, consequently, how important it is to be able to tell them apart, because they can look so similar. It may be especially important to be able to accurately distinguish between a TJ and an FP to avoid the risk of hurting or offending an FP.

SKILL-BUILDING EXERCISE

To help you determine how well you were able to absorb and integrate the material presented in this chapter, and to help reinforce these principles, we've developed the following skill-building exercise. Read one scenario and try to answer the questions that follow it before moving on to the next. You will get more benefit from this exercise

if you don't refer back to the text until after you've answered all the questions pertaining to each scenario. You'll find the correct answers on page 119. Good luck!

Scenario #1: Tom

Tom, a fortyish real estate developer, confidently strolled into the bagel shop dressed in an expensive designer-label suit. As he made his way to the counter, he scanned the store and, taking inventory of the customers, stopped to chat with several of the regulars. When he reached Greg, he broke into a big smile, threw his arm around Greg's shoulders, and pulled him close. He then began to tease Greg unmercifully about the beating Greg's favorite basketball team had taken the night before. Although it was a good-natured exchange, Tom clearly took great pleasure in making Greg painfully concede his team had blown its chances to make the playoffs. At the counter, Tom flirted with the two young college students filling orders, the same way he did every day. After gobbling down his bagel and coffee, Tom "made the rounds," said good-bye to his buddies, jumped into his late-model Camaro convertible, and zoomed off to work.

1. From the brief information presented, Tom:
   a. appears to:
      ☐ Extravert Feeling
      ☐ Introvert Feeling
   b. is more likely a:
      ☐ TP
      ☐ TJ

☐ FP
☐ FJ

c. is also probably an:
☐ Introvert
☐ Extravert

d. is probably one of two types:

_____ or _____

e. Is *most* probably this one type:

_____

Scenario #2: Diane

After closing her door so she wouldn't be interrupted, Diane was not pleased to hear a knock a minute later. Julie, a new staff person recently assigned to work for Diane, apologized for the intrusion and pulled a chair up to the large wooden desk, which was bare except for one file folder, a legal pad, and a pen. Before Diane could say a word, Julie burst into tears, and began to unload what seemed to Diane to be a lifetime's worth of personal problems. Not wanting to appear insensitive, but clearly uncomfortable discussing such intimate matters with someone she barely knew, Diane offered the woman a box of tissues she kept in a drawer, and said: "Julie, I'm really very sorry you're having these problems, but I don't think that I can help you. First of all, I have a major presentation in two days that I have to get back to work on. And second, I'm just not very good at this sort of thing." Trying to be helpful in a practical way, Diane pulled out the employee manual and suggested Julie might want to take a personal day to pull herself together.

She also suggested Julie consult with a counselor in their employee assistance program.

2. From the brief information presented, Diane:
   a. appears to:
   ☐ Extravert Feeling
   ☐ Introvert Feeling
   b. is more likely a:
   ☐ TP
   ☐ TJ
   ☐ FP
   ☐ FJ
   c. is also probably an:
   ☐ Introvert
   ☐ Extravert
   d. is probably one of two types:

   _____ or _____

   e. Is *most* probably this one type:

   _____

Scenario #3: Carl

Carl was entering his senior year as a fine arts major at the university. His roommate, Alan, thought he was doing Carl a favor when he invited an art dealer friend of his parents' to their apartment to see some of Carl's work. Since Carl wasn't home at the time, Alan went into Carl's room and brought out several pieces Carl was working on. A half hour later, when Carl came home, Alan introduced him to the art dealer and told him what they had been doing. At first, Carl was unsure of how he felt about it. But he became much clearer as the art dealer, believing he was being helpful, began to critique Carl's work; first praising his talent and then telling him how he could make his paintings more commercially appealing. Suddenly Carl knew exactly how he felt! Gathering up his pictures, he hastily thanked the dealer and re-treated to his room. When a confused Alan knocked on Carl's door a few minutes later, Carl let him have it: "First of all, you have no right entering my room without my permission for *any* reason. Second, these paintings are not even finished, and when I want someone to see them — let alone criticize them — *I'll* decide who and when that will be!" Only several hours later, when he had cooled off a little, did he tell Alan: "I know you thought you were doing me a favor, but you were way out of line. Please don't ever do anything like that again."

3. From the brief information presented, Carl:
   a. appears to:
      ☐ Extravert Feeling
      ☐ Introvert Feeling
   b. is more likely a:
      ☐ TP
      ☐ TJ
      ☐ FP
      ☐ FJ
   c. is also probably an:
      ☐ Introvert
      ☐ Extravert
   d. is probably one of two types:

   _____ or _____
   e. Is *most* probably this one type:

   _____

Scenario # 4: Jamie

Jamie arrived at the cocktail party impeccably dressed. Her outfit was tastefully coordinated and totally appropriate for the occasion. Not a hair out of place, everything about her matched: dress, shoes, makeup, jewelry, and accessories. She greeted old friends and new acquaintances with the same poise, warmth, and enthusiasm. Giving new meaning to the phrase "good eye contact," she locked her gaze on each person she spoke with and never let it stray until the conversation was over. She had an easy smile and frequently touched the arm or shoulder of the person stand-ing next to her to emphasize a point. Talking in a small group, Jamie effortlessly moved from one subject to the next, sharing opinions that obviously reflected some deeply held beliefs. Yet she was not the least bit strident; rather, she found some-thing to agree with in most of the other people's opinions, and had a talent for making everyone feel at ease and important.

4. From the brief information presented, Jamie:
   a. appears to:
      ☐ Extravert Feeling
      ☐ Introvert Feeling
   b. is more likely a:
      ☐ TP
      ☐ TJ
      ☐ FP
      ☐ FJ
   c. is also probably an:
      ☐ Introvert
      ☐ Extravert

d. is probably one of two types:

_____ or _____

e. Is *most* probably this one type:

_____

Now check your answers below.

ANSWERS TO SKILL-BUILDING EXERCISE FOR E/I-FEELING PATTERN

1. Scenario #1: Tom
  a. appears to: Extravert Feeling
  b. is more likely a: TP
  c. is also probably an: Extravert
  d. is probably one of two types: ENTP or ESTP
  e. Is *most* probably this one type: ENTP

2. Scenario #2: Diane
  a. appears to: Introvert Feeling
  b. is more likely a: TJ
  c. is also probably an: Introvert
  d. is probably one of two types: INTJ or ISTJ
  e. Is *most* probably this one type: ISTJ

3. Scenario #3: Carl
  a. appears to: Introvert Feeling
  b. is more likely a: FP
  c. is also probably an: Introvert
  d. is probably one of two types: ISFP or INFP
  e. Is *most* probably this one type: INFP

4. Scenario #4: Jamie
  a. appears to: Extravert Feeling
  b. is more likely a: FJ
  c. is also probably an: Extravert
  d. is probably one of two types: ESFJ or ENFJ
  e. Is *most* probably this one type: ENFJ

How did you do? Hopefully, you were able to identify whether Tom, Diane, Carl, and Jamie Extraverted Feeling or Introverted Feeling. If so, then you are well on your way to mastering this critical SpeedReading skill. If you were able to take it to the next level and identify whether each person was a TP, FJ, TJ, or FP, so much the better. And if you could correctly determine the one or two probable types for each person, you are well ahead of the game!

This exercise should make it clear how powerful a tool being able to identify a person's E/I-Feeling pattern is. If, however, you had difficulty with it, don't despair. It is by far the most complex part of the process and takes some people longer to master than others. If you find yourself in this position, we strongly advise you to reread this chapter before moving on to Part 3, since the ability to be able to recognize the E/I-Feeling Pattern is a critically important component in the SpeedReading system.

CHAPTER SIX

Putting the System to Work

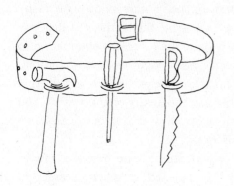

In the preceding chapters, you've learned about Personality Type and the components comprising the SpeedReading system. In this chapter, you will learn how they work together to enable you to SpeedRead people quickly and accurately.

The SpeedReading system is built around the three components presented — individual preferences, temperament, and a person's E/I-Feeling pattern — because these three provide the most valuable clues. As you become a more experienced SpeedReader, you will discover other combinations of preferences that can also help you identify people's types.

Just as many paths lead to the same destination, there are many different ways you can use these tools to determine a person's type. In fact, some types will naturally be better than others at spotting certain clues. For example, because Sensors naturally notice details, they may pick up on a small clue that an Intuitive might miss. On the other hand, while Intuitives may miss the details, they are better at interpreting the *meaning* of some subtle behavior, and extrapolating a pattern. It's not important *how* you arrive at an accurate assessment, as long as you ultimately do. But what about your goals and expectations about your newly acquired skills? Remember, it's always important to keep in mind the *ultimate* goal in mastering the SpeedReading system: to enable you to communicate more effectively with everyone you come in contact with. Obviously, the better you understand someone, the more likely this is to occur. Consequently, it is most helpful when you can identify a person's full four-letter type. But, for a variety of reasons, including an inadequate opportunity to observe a person, the presence of some psychological abnormality, or a misleading context or situation, this is not always possible, nor is it always necessary.

In some instances, you will be able to determine only a person's temperament, or perhaps one or two of his or her preferences. But in many cases, this is more than enough to accomplish your major goal of significantly improving communication. For example, suppose you are an Extravert, and you meet someone and determine she is an Introvert, but you are unclear about the rest of her type preferences. With all you've learned about the differences between Extraverts and Introverts, you would still know a great deal more about her, and how to communicate with her, than if you didn't understand Introverts, or couldn't identify her as one.

There is no right order in which the three components need to be used to work effectively. With one subject, you may first identify the temperament, then a particular preference, then his E/I-Feeling pattern. With another person, you may find her E/I-Feeling pattern jumps out at you. Frequently, one person will find one component provides the best clues and another person will find a different component more useful.

The act of SpeedReading People involves a process of elimination. Before you know anything about a subject, he or she might be one of sixteen types. As you gather more data, you begin to eliminate possible types from contention. Incidentally, after you have really mastered the techniques,

on occasion you will be able to identify a person's whole type, almost instantly, just by looking at him! This is because people of the same type often have a particular "look" which you will begin to recognize after extensive interaction with many people of the same type. But in the vast majority of cases, you will use the process of elimination to go from sixteen types to eight types, down to four, to two, and finally to one — the person's full type. Using the three components of the system, you will be able to accomplish this, in most cases, in a matter of minutes.

Shortly, we will demonstrate how the various components can be used in different order to SpeedRead a person. Before we do, we offer the following tried and true, practical tips to effective SpeedReading:

1. Always begin with what you are most sure about.
Regardless of whether it is the subject's temperament, one or more preferences, or his or her E/I-Feeling pattern, identify what you think is most clear, then eliminate those things you can most easily. For example, suppose you are certain the subject is an Extravert. Then you can automatically eliminate all eight of the Introverted types.

2. Don't rush to judgment.
Keep the door open and consider uncertain guesses as working hypotheses subject to change as you collect more data. This can present a particular challenge to Judgers, who, in their haste for closure, may not take in enough information before mak-

ing a decision. Remember, you can always modify your guess as you pick up new clues.

3. Be aware of your own biases.

We all filter our perceptions through our own biases and prejudices. With regard to Type, it is particularly easy to fall into the trap of stereotyping people based on our personal opinion of various type preferences or temperaments. For example, you may mistakenly believe all people who are friendly must be Feelers. But what you may really be seeing is Extraversion. Conversely, Feelers who Introvert Feeling may look cool and initially unfriendly and you may misread them as Thinkers.

WHEN YOU'RE NOT FACE-TO-FACE

Some tips for SpeedReading people over the phone

While it is always preferable to be able to look the person you are trying to SpeedRead in the eye, it is not always possible. Nor is it always necessary in order to get a good sense of his or her personality type. For once you have mastered the SpeedReading techniques, you will be able to identify most, and sometimes all, of a person's type preferences from a relatively brief telephone conversation. Your accuracy will depend, in addition to your SpeedReading prowess, on several factors, including the purpose, length, and context of the conversation, and, in some cases, the person's type as well.

The more open-ended and spontaneous the conversation, the greater opportunity to accurately SpeedRead the person. For example, people calling you to inquire if you have a job opening will be motivated to let you get to know them, and will generally make themselves available to talk as long as you want to. With such a scenario, you get the chance to ask them open-ended questions and hear how quickly or slowly they respond, which words they use, how warm or cool they are, and so on. Contrast this with a call you make to try and secure an informational interview with someone you have to convince to spare you a half hour of her time. She is much less likely to volunteer information freely, and therefore you will have much less information upon which to SpeedRead her.

The location of the call can even influence how much information you are able to glean. For example, someone calling from his office within earshot of coworkers or his boss may (depending on the purpose and content of the call) act and speak very differently than if he were calling from the privacy of his home. Similarly, the purpose for the call and the role of the caller can affect what you are able to learn. For example, an attorney for a collections company is likely to act tougher and more intimidating than she might normally be, or prefer to be, because she considers that approach helpful or necessary to perform her job. Although, in reality, few Feeling types choose this line of work, it is not hard to imagine one coming across much more like a Thinker. And it is therefore easy to see how someone trying to SpeedRead her might easily misinterpret her behavior and misread her type.

Although in some situations, there will be little you can do to improve your chances of accurately

SpeedReading the person, in most others you can do quite a lot. For example: always ask open-ended questions. Remember, the longer a person talks, the more you know about him or her. For example, in a job interview situation, you might ask: "How did you get along with your last boss?" To which the person is likely to answer: "Fine." But suppose you asked a series of open-ended questions, instead, such as: "Tell me about your last boss. What was she like?... What did you like best about her? ... What areas of conflicts did you two have?... How would you characterize your relationship with her?... What do you think she would say about you?" You would learn much more about the person's own values, perceptiveness, confidence, intelligence, not to mention key personality characteristics.

Sometimes, even when you ask an open-ended question, the person will give a very brief one-word or one-line reply (which in and of itself can be very revealing). You may need to encourage the person to expand her answer by asking: "Could you say a little more about that?" or "Could you give me an example?" or "I'm curious why you would think that."

Obviously, in the vast majority of cases, Speed-Reading someone by phone is not as effective as dealing face-to-face. However, there may be rare occasions when it is *easier* to type someone by phone than in person. One such situation might be when the person is freer to be himself on the phone than he might be at work, or in a group. And sometimes, SpeedReading people by phone can reduce unwanted distractions, which can in-hibit your ability to really focus your attention on certain clues.

Finally, it might be helpful to keep in mind that even if you are able to identify only a few preferences or the person's temperament over the phone, based upon your understanding of Type, you are still likely to have learned more about what motivates him than people who have known him for years! As always, we caution you to avoid jumping to conclusions based on limited information, and encourage you to think of an unsure guess as a "working hypothesis" subject to refinement with more information.

DIFFERENT APPROACHES FOR USING THE SPEEDREADING COMPONENTS

Imagine a carpenter who has three tools on his belt: a hammer, a saw, and a screwdriver. For one job, he may need only the hammer; for another, he might need only the saw; and for a third, he might only need the screwdriver. But for some jobs, he might need two, or even all three, tools. Which tools he uses depends on the situation and the specific requirements of that job.

Think of the three components of the Speed-Reading system as your three tools. In order to get your job done, that is, to SpeedRead someone accurately, you may need one, two, or all three tools. And just as the carpenter must decide which tools to use, and in which order to use them, you must decide which components will be most helpful and how to use them in a given situation.

Approach #1

In this first example, we'll assume that you use the preference cues as your primary source of data. Once you have a working hypothesis as to the person's full type, you will then use the other two clues—temperament and their E/I-Feeling pattern—as confirmation that your assessment was right.

Read this scenario carefully. Search for clues to Jane's true type by identifying each of her four preferences.

Jane is a thirty-five-year-old customer service representative working for a local savings and loan company. You have arrived to try and straighten out a discrepancy in your account that you believe has occurred as a result of a bank error. Your objective is to convince her that the bank should waive the $20 service fee you've been charged, since it was the bank, and not you, who made the mistake.

Jane is dressed in a neatly pressed business suit. Her long hair is put up in a French twist, and the few pieces of jewelry she is wearing (necklace, earrings, and rings) all go well with each other. On her desk are several photographs of her family and a paperweight that is a plaster impression of a small child's hand with an inscription: "I love you, Mommy. Love, Jessica." Her desk is very neat, with few items on it, and all seem to be in their appointed places. There are no piles of folders, and the only things in the center of her desk are a blank pad, a pen holder, and a clock.

As she greets you, Jane apologizes for making you wait for the few minutes it took her to end a phone call, asks you to sit, and politely inquires if you think this matter will take more than a half hour, because she has a meeting then and wants to make sure you get all the time you need with her.

Jane is friendly, energetic, yet attentive as you explain the situation, even as she occasionally glances up at customers entering or leaving the bank. She takes the time to hear you out completely and does not seem the least bit defensive. She frequently nods in agreement, and twice politely interrupts your explanation to clarify a detail of the story and to look over the paperwork you've brought with you. As she explains the steps she will go through to investigate the problem and try to resolve it, she uses her hands to gesture. Overall, you get the clear impression that she is genuinely concerned about your inconvenience and that she is trying to keep you as a happy customer of the bank.

QUESTION #1

Does Jane seem more like an Extravert or an Introvert?

Clues: Jane has lots of energy, appears to think out loud, is very animated with her hands and facial gestures, and seems very comfortable dealing with people. And although she is attentive, she seems to be aware of all the activity that is going on around her.

Answer: Jane seems like an Extravert.

By determining that she is an Extravert, you have eliminated all eight of the Introverted types, reducing the number of possible types from sixteen to eight.

QUESTION #2
Does Jane seem like more of a Sensor or an Intuitive?

Clues: Jane is very specific and precise, asking you to recite the details of the problem and stopping for clarification when needed. She is clearly interested in reviewing your documentation, and while she does look around the room from time to time, she is paying close attention to you and the events of the present moment, rather than daydreaming or being distracted by her own private thoughts.

Answer: Jane seems like a Sensor.

By determining that she is a Sensor, you have eliminated all eight of the Intuitive types, reducing her type possibilities down to only four types: those that share both E and S: ESTJ, ESFJ, ESTP, and ESFP.

QUESTION #3
Does Jane seem like a Thinker or a Feeler?

Clues: She is attentive and friendly, and communicates through her words and body language her concern for you and her desire to be of help. On her desk are several photographs of her family as well as a piece of her daughter's artwork.

Answer: Jane seems like a Feeler.

By determining that she is a Feeler, you have once again eliminated all the Thinking types, reducing the possibilities down to only two types: ESFJ and ESFP.

QUESTION #4
Does Jane seem like a Judger or a Perceiver?

Clues: Her appearance has a very "finished look"—her outfit reflects care and planning. Her desk is neat and orderly—there are no piles of folders or other works in progress on her desk. She seems very time conscious by virtue of the fact that she makes sure she has enough time for you and that one of the few items on her desk is a clock. If you could sneak a peek at her calendar, you would no doubt notice how neat her handwriting is, and that her appointments may be written in ink. She seems very much in control of the situation; her actions are deliberate and not the least bit tentative.

Answer: Jane seems like a Judger.

Since you are pretty sure she is a Judger, and if you were right on your other guesses, then her type should be ESFJ.

But to confirm your hunch, you use the other tools—the E/I-Feeling pattern and temperament.

QUESTION #5
Does Jane appear to Extravert Feeling?

Clues: Jane's appearance suggests she is very conscious of and concerned about the impression she makes on others. She is very expressive, both verbally and in her body language, frequently nodding her head in agreement and shaking her head while pursing her lips to communicate displeasure. She gives you the feeling that she is really hearing you, is concerned you've been inconvenienced, and will do everything to make the situation right.

Answer: Yes, Jane Extraverts Feeling.

This confirms the FJ part, since you have already decided that she is a Feeler.

QUESTION #6
Does Jane seem like a Traditionalist?

Clues: She is polite and respectful. And although she is friendly, she does not joke around and clearly considers this serious business. She is dressed conservatively and appropriately for her work environment and position. And she conveys a sense of stability and sincerity — you never get the impression she is just telling you what you want to hear, but rather that she takes her responsibilities to you as a customer very seriously.

Answer: Yes, Jane does seem like a Traditionalist.

This clue confirms both the S and J parts, since Traditionalists by definition are SJs.

By this process, you have come to a reasonable conclusion that Jane is an ESFJ. And while it is always possible that you were wrong about one, or even two, of her letters, the odds are very good that she is an ESFJ.

Approach #2

In this second example, you'll take a different approach. First, you will identify the subject's temperament and his E/F-Feeling pattern, then one final preference.

After a long and tiring business trip, you've arrived at your hotel eager to get a good night's sleep so you will be fresh for a big meeting with an important client in the morning. You approach the front-desk clerk, a man who looks about fifty-five, whose badge says his name is Gordon. Giving you a perfunctory nod, Gordon then looks down at his computer and asks: "Name?"— a greeting you consider mechanical and rather impersonal.

After providing your name, you try to engage him in some small talk, to which he doesn't really respond. You spend the next three or four minutes in silence as he checks his computer, finally reporting matter-of-factly that he has no record of your reservation. When you tell him the reservation was made weeks ago, he asks for the confirmation number, which you have, unfortunately, forgotten. Gordon's body language conveys skepticism and doubt, as if to say: "Yeah, I've heard that one before." Rather than recognize your dilemma or figure out a way to help you, he attempts to explain why the computer could not be responsible for the mix-up. Unfortunately, his explanation is so technical, you find it too confusing to follow. In any event, it is not helping you solve your problem. Mildly, you express your displeasure at his apparent lack of sensitivity to your situation, which only makes him dig in his heels and reiterate that you, rather than he or the hotel, must be responsible for the mistake. Although you are obviously becoming very anxious and frustrated about the situation, he seems indifferent to your plight. Finally, in desperation, you ask to speak to the manager. Much to your chagrin, Gordon replies: "You are." When you ask if he could call another hotel to see if there are available rooms, he mulls it over before responding. Just when you think the situation is hopeless, he announces that he has used an interhotel program on his computer and located a vacancy at a hotel a mile down the road.

QUESTION #1
What temperament best fits Gordon?

Clues: Gordon has a very independent, confident style, which, in his case, borders on arrogance. He becomes defensive and argumentative when you question his competence (his company's really, but by extension his) by suggesting the hotel made a mistake. His explanation of why the computer could not cause the problem is very convoluted, complex, and difficult for you to understand. Additionally, he clearly seems to be aware of and enjoy the fact that he is the person in power in this situation.

Answer: Gordon seems like a Conceptualizer.

By determining he is probably a Conceptualizer, you have reduced the type possibilities from sixteen to just four: ENTJ, INTJ, ENTP, or INTP.

QUESTION #2
Does Gordon appear to Extravert or Introvert Feeling?

Clues: Perhaps the strongest clue is that he makes no attempt to connect with you — either in his actions or his words. He is basically expressionless, shows no emotion, and reveals nothing about how he might feel about you or your situation. Neither does he seem aware of, or sensitive to, your emotional state. It is obvious he is not really motivated by pleasing others. He does try to solve the problem by using his technical know-how.

Answer: Gordon appears to Introvert Feeling (which means he also Extraverts Thinking).

By deciding he Extraverts thinking, you know he must be either a TJ or an FP. Since you have already determined he is a Thinker (part of the NT Conceptualizer temperament), then he must be a TJ. By this analysis, you have further reduced the type possibilities from four to just two: ENTJ or INTJ.

QUESTION #3
Does Gordon appear to be an Extravert or an Introvert?

Clues: His energy is very reserved. He is comfortable with the "dead air time" while he checks the computer, and is uncomfortable making small talk. He doesn't seek or sustain eye contact with you, and clearly he prefers to think things through before responding.

Answer: Gordon seems like an Introvert.

By determining he is an Introvert, you have identified his type as INTJ.

Approach #3

In this third example, the subject's E/I-Feeling pattern provides the first clue, followed by her temperament and preferences.

Forced to drop out of college in your senior year to care for an ailing parent, you have finally re-enrolled, now that your young children are in school. With an important research paper due, and finding it extremely difficult to meet family obligations and complete your work on time, you've come to ask your professor, Dr. Hoffman, for an extension or an "incomplete" so you can finish the work over the summer.

Based on your observations of her in class, you've always found her soft-spoken, articulate, and intelligent, but not particularly warm. As you enter Professor Hoffman's office, you are surprised by the instant sense of comfort. Rather than harsh fluorescent lighting, two antique floor lamps bathe the room in a warm glow. With a small Oriental rug, paintings on the walls, and a round oak table for a desk, it seems more like a cozy parlor than a faculty office. While it is tastefully decorated, it is also extremely cluttered, with files, books, and stacks of papers everywhere, including her desk and the floor surrounding it.

Although it is aesthetically appealing, the office is clearly designed to make her comfortable. It appears that everything in the room has some special meaning to her. After inviting you to sit in a large, comfortable chair across from her and offering you a cup of tea, Dr. Hoffman listens intently as you tell her your story. She seems genuinely concerned by the circumstances that forced you to leave college originally, and about the conflicts you are currently facing. She shares her strong belief in the importance of people being able to come back to school, and how colleges have a moral obligation to figure out creative ways to make it easier to do.

While you didn't anticipate she would deny your request, you were unsure about how approachable she would be. You are grateful when she tells you that she admires you for coming back to school and encourages you to take all the time you need to complete the paper.

QUESTION #1
Does Professor Hoffman appear to Extravert or Introvert Feeling?

Clues: While she doesn't appear to connect in any public way in class, she clearly seems like a Feeler. As you spend time with her one-on-one and get to know her, she begins to "let you in," and you discover how sensitive and sympathetic she really is. Also, her office is filled with objects that have special, emotional meaning to her. She seems highly influenced by her internal values—such as the importance of nontraditional students being given opportunities to succeed.

Answer: Professor Hoffman seems to Introvert Feeling.

By deciding she Introverts Feeling, you determine she must be either a TJ or an FP. And since all the evidence points to her being a Feeler, she is an FP, which reduces the type possibilities to four: ENFP, INFP, ESFP, or ISFP.

QUESTION #2
What temperament best fits Professor Hoffman?

Clues: Given her choice to teach English literature and her obvious love of language, you suspect she is either an Idealist or a Conceptualizer. Her genuine curiosity about you and her sensitive and empathetic nature, as well as her willingness to embrace unique situations such as yours, make you lean toward Idealist. Finally, the artistic and original way her office is decorated is added evidence for Idealist.

Answer: The professor is an Idealist.

By deciding she is an Idealist, you have further narrowed down the possibilities to just two types: ENFP and INFP.

QUESTION #3
Does Professor Hoffman seem like an Extravert or an Introvert?

Clues: Her quiet energy, thoughtfulness, and good listening skills, plus the focused concentration

necessary to achieve a doctoral degree, point to Introversion, as do her love of books and reading. It occurs to you she has tried to create a kind of sanctuary in her office — a private place to work and have quiet one-on-one conversations — a very Introverted place.

Answer: Your professor is most probably an INFP.

The preceding examples demonstrate some of the many different ways to use the SpeedReading tools. As you become more proficient with these skills, you will find that some clues will be more useful than others. The following exercise is designed to help you increase your ability to use each of the tools more effectively.

Below are several brief case studies. After reading each one, you will be asked to determine the subject's type. Once again, this exercise will be most beneficial if you do not look ahead to the answers and analysis that follow until after you've completed each case study. When you're ready, you will find the answers beginning on page 135.

SKILL-BUILDING EXERCISE

Case #1: The New Boss

Your company has just been purchased by a larger one, and your boss of twelve years has been forced to take early retirement. You are about to meet his replacement, who held a similar position at the acquiring company. She has asked you to come by her office at 6:00 P.M. She explained during her brief phone call to you that she needs the extra time to finish up some work before your meeting. She glances up and notices you through the open office door as you approach, takes a quick look at her watch, and gestures for you to take a seat.

As you enter what was your former boss's office, you are immediately struck by how different it looks. The once casual and informal furnishings have been replaced by an imposing wooden desk with two leather club chairs positioned in front of it and a bookcase filled with reference books and policy manuals. On the walls are several diplomas and certificates of achievement, one for manager of the month, and framed letters of commendation from the Chamber of Commerce and Girl Scouts of America formally recognizing her volunteer contributions.

After a minute or two of friendly small talk, she opens your personnel file, which has been sitting on her desk in preparation for this meeting. Her tone is formal and all business as she outlines her agenda in detail. Her language is clipped and precise, and she makes it clear from the start that she is in control of this meeting. In a clear voice, she reviews key points from your performance appraisals for the past several years, referring to a few entries that were not very positive. Next she talks about the tremendous responsibilities she has to the company as a result of the acquisition and personnel changes, and how difficult change is in any organization. She then lists several specific policy changes she wants to make and outlines a timetable for their implementation. Looking at her watch again, she asks if you have any

questions, thanks you for coming in, and picks up the phone to make a call.

What is your new boss's type? _____

Case #2: The Home Buyer

You are an experienced real estate broker with a 10:00 A.M. appointment with a woman you consider a good prospect for a sale. Her family will be moving into town in a few weeks as a result of her husband's new job. When she finally arrives at 10:35, you watch her slowly get out of her car, toss her sweater and the directions you faxed her into the backseat, and amble into your office. She sheepishly apologizes for keeping you waiting, but offers no explanation other than to say she is "running late."

She is still wearing her tennis whites, although you know she has several appointments with others besides you today, including a bank officer or two. She has a pleasant but quiet demeanor and seems sincerely grateful you could make yourself available to her on such short notice. When you ask what she wants most in a new home, she takes a few moments, considering your question carefully, and answers: "A neighborhood with lots of nice kids for my sons to play with, near a playground would be great. Aaron will be seven in February, and Ethan was just five in June. I hope they will be able to develop some close friendships here. We'd also like a house with a rec room and a yard for our two dogs. Oh, and we need at least two bathrooms." As you continue to talk, she becomes quite specific about other amenities she would find attractive.

She seems perfectly comfortable putting herself in your hands and appears to have no need to be in control of the meeting. And she is extremely flexible and amenable to changing plans as circumstances necessitate. As you learn from walking through several houses that day, she has a great eye for color and design. She also has an amazing memory, remembering small details you didn't even notice.

As you spend more time together and get to know each other better, she gradually shares more and more personal information about her life. In fact, the only negative thing about the whole day turns out that you may have done your job too well! She liked all of the houses you showed her, and seems daunted by the prospect of narrowing down her options to just one without having the benefit of more time and information.

What is the home buyer's type? _____

Case #3: The Soccer Coach

The parent of a ten-year-old, you have come to talk with his soccer coach about a problem your son is experiencing. Since the coaching job is a volunteer position, you are meeting the man at the car dealership where he works. As you walk into his office, you immediately notice the strong sports theme: in a glass case are several trophies, and on three of the walls are photographs of him with various teams he has played on or coached over a period of many years. Looking around, he proudly volunteers the stats on some teams he has coached, commenting in detail on the successes of many of his favorite former players.

The coach is very friendly and has a hearty handshake and big smile. You notice he is dressed casually and comfortably, and after offering you a seat, he leans back in his chair, props one foot up on the corner of the desk, and asks: "So, what can I do for you?" As you explain that this is your son's first experience with soccer and, in fact, his first foray into team sports, the coach seems fully attentive, making good eye contact with you as you speak. But you tell him that your sensitive and somewhat shy son wants to quit the team after only three weeks. You explain that he feels pressured to play well, even though he is new to the game, and that he takes a lot of teasing from some of the older players. You confide that your son has told you that the coach seems to be either unaware of what is going on or unconcerned about it. You explain that you don't expect him to coddle your son, but at the same time, this isn't the pros, and your main objective is for him to have fun.

All the while you are speaking, the coach is smiling, nodding, and shifting in his seat. After you finish, he immediately assures you that he knows *everything* that goes on at practice, and he is fully aware of how his kids get along with each other. Through his words and his body language, he communicates a very easygoing attitude, as if he sees this as no big deal. In fact, he goes so far as to suggest that this is probably just what your son needs to "toughen him up" a bit. While he agrees that he wants the kids to have fun, and that winning isn't everything, learning to be a tough competitor is an important life skill for anyone to gain, especially sensitive kids. At your insistence, he promises to keep a closer eye on the situation, but leaves you with the clear impression that you are making a mountain out of a molehill, and that if you lighten up a little about this, your son probably will also.

What is the coach's type? _____

Case #4: The Headhunter's Candidate

As a headhunter, your job is to find talented people who are working for one company, and convince them that they should move to another company. You are paid a commission by the company seeking to hire the employee. Your client, a new company that develops electronic marketing solutions to be used over the Internet, is looking for a computer whiz with a substantial marketing background. Having been given a lead on a woman who, at least on paper, seems like the perfect candidate, you are having your first face-to-face meeting to discuss her qualifications and interest in the position.

Her greeting is friendly but reserved. She admits she is curious about the possibility of changing jobs; her current job is manager of computer services in the marketing department of a large insurance company, but in assuming this position, she was promoted out of doing the kind of creative, challenging work that she really likes to do. The idea of working for a new small but growing company appeals to her.

She immediately strikes you as highly intelligent—perhaps even brilliant! In talking about her present position, she admits that she is frustrated by what she views as a lack of creativity, an overly structured environment, general resistance to new and innovative ideas, and the snail's pace at which those few ideas that are accepted are carried out. She clearly considers her marketing background to be unappreciated and grossly underutilized by her current employer. She reveals she is most energized by creative problem solving and considers herself an excellent troubleshooter; the more complicated and challenging the problem, the better she likes it. When you ask her for an example, she cites a recent restructuring project but explains it in such a roundabout and confusing fashion you, frankly, find it too technical to follow.

You are impressed to learn that her considerable skills with computers have been mostly self-taught. And, in fact, learning new things is one of her greatest pleasures in life! She reveals that she listens for hours at a time to audiotapes and has even taught herself to speak Japanese with the thought she may someday want to be an international consultant.

When queried about her weaknesses, she reluctantly admits that she is better on the start-up than on the follow-through, often becoming bored once the creative bugs are worked out of a program. And she readily admits that she feels stymied working in a large, bureaucratic organization because of the general resistance to considering innovative approaches, the lack of spontaneity, the endless number of stupid rules and regulations, and the high percentage of incompetent managers. While not admitting that she is a poor manager herself, she does suggest that dealing with people's problems is not her favorite pastime.

What is the headhunter's candidate's type? _____

Case #5: The Dissatisfied Customer

As the manager of a small family-owned clothing store, one day you are approached by a man returning a pair of expensive name-brand hiking boots. The boots were guaranteed to be waterproof and have begun to leak. While the customer admits he bought the boots almost a year ago, he explains he has only worn them a half a dozen times. Your inspection confirms they appear almost new.

The customer, who is neatly dressed in casual but functional clothes, smiles upon greeting you, and speaks in a polite and articulate manner. He is neither pushy nor belligerent. In fact, he seems rather uncomfortable raising the issue at all, and almost apologizes for taking your time. But he goes on to explain that he believes very strongly in the survival of small stores such as yours—so much so that he is willing to pay more for their merchandise in order to help keep them in business. However, he also feels that the additional cost entitles him to extra-good service.

You express your appreciation for his position and then explain to him the realities of small business in the nineties. The problem, you tell him, is that you know from past experience that this manufacturer will not take the boots back—under any circumstances. So, if you replace the boots, your store will lose not only the profit, but the money you originally paid the manufacturer for the boots. And, you

acknowledge, the problem is compounded by the fact that the large chains that have become your biggest competitors allow customers to return any product they aren't happy with, for any reason, with no time limitations. They are simply so big, they can afford to absorb the occasional loss, unlike a small store like yours.

The customer listens thoughtfully to your explanation, occasionally nodding in sympathetic agreement with your plight. But he still seems convinced that you should replace the boots at your cost. As he explains, "The issue goes way beyond satisfying one little customer. Rather, you need to look at the larger picture and see how a policy like this affects your store's reputation and integrity. What's most important is that you do the right thing, which means standing behind your merchandise, even if the manufacturer doesn't." He looks at you in silence for a few moments, and then he announces that he needs some time to think this through a little more and will return after he's completed his other shopping.

What is the customer's type? _____

After you have reviewed the answers to these cases, you will be ready to proceed to the next chapter. Up until this point, the emphasis has been on teaching you the skills necessary to SpeedRead people. In the next chapter, you will learn a new set of skills that will enable you to quickly and effectively communicate with all types of people. We refer to the results of using these techniques as Speed*Reaching* people.

The answers to this exercise follow.

ANSWERS TO SKILL-BUILDING EXERCISE

CASE #1: THE NEW BOSS

TYPE: ESTJ
Supporting Evidence

1. Preference Clues:

She seems like an *Extravert*, because she is outgoing, energetic, talkative, and appears to think out loud. Notice she also has displayed several pictures and letters that call attention to herself and her accomplishments. You know she is a *Sensor* because she is so factual and detail oriented, referring to several specific items in your personnel folder. And her language is simple, direct, and no-nonsense. She seems like a *Thinker* because of her brusque, impersonal style and apparent comfort at calling attention to negative notes in your file after having only just met you. And you think she might be a *Judger*, because of her clear work ethic, her attention to time, both in the short run — by referring to her watch twice — and in the long run by setting a timetable for implementing policy changes.

2. Temperament Clues:

She appears to be a *Traditionalist* because of her serious nature, her conservative appearance (both in terms of her office and her person), her apparently strong work ethic, and her volunteerism in traditional, service-oriented organizations. Once you see several clues indicating a preference for Sensing, including attention to details and direct language style, you can then rule out the Conceptualizer temperament (NT).

3. E/I-Feeling Pattern Clues:

She appears to *Introvert Feeling*, which means she also Extraverts Thinking. In her case, it is apparent she is a **TJ.** Neither her eyes, words, nor physical expressions suggest a desire for closeness. And she is impersonal and objective in her observations. Her reputation for toughness as a businesswoman, which preceded her, as well as her lack of stereotypically feminine behavior, all support this observation. You are also aware that the overwhelming majority of high-level managers are, in fact, TJs.

CASE #2: THE HOME BUYER

TYPE: ISFP

1. Preference Clues:

Her quiet demeanor, thoughtfulness before answering questions, and the fact that she needed time to get to know you before sharing much about herself suggest to you she is an *Introvert*. She appears to be a *Sensor* because she provides lots of specifics and details, such as the names and ages of her children, and because she notices and remembers many small details in each of the houses you show her. You believe she is a *Feeler* because she is friendly and seems comfortable and sincere when she expresses her gratitude for your help, and she has a gentle demeanor. There are several clues that convince you she is a *Perceiver*, including her lateness (which, from her casual reference to "running late" makes you suspect this may be normal for her), her flexibility and willingness to let you be in charge, her comfort just going with the flow of the process, and the fact that she is reluctant to make a decision without plenty of information.

2. Temperament Clues:

A variety of clues suggest she is an *Experiencer*. Among them are her casual appearance, including the fact that she seems not to mind going to appointments in her tennis clothes. Her clothes also tell you she is involved in sports. And she has stressed a desire to find a house near a playground with features that enhance an active lifestyle like a recreation room and large yard for the family's pets.

3. E/I-Feeling Pattern Clues:

The dominant clue that she *Introverts Feeling* is her rather gentle nature. She waits to express her values and feeling-based reactions until after you have spent time with her. She is not highly opinionated, and instead expresses what is important to her in less direct ways — like looking for features that will please her family and meet their needs.

CASE #3: THE COACH

TYPE: ESTP

1. Preference Clues:

The coach's outgoing, talkative, and expansive demeanor is a clue that he is an *Extravert*. The volume of evidence of his active, busy lifestyle surrounds him in the photographs of his many years of involvement with sports teams, which he obviously enjoys since he does so in a volunteer capacity. Whether or not his claim that he notices everything going on at practice is true, he obviously is constantly scanning the environment to discover what's happening at all times, which is further evidence of his preference for Extraversion and his preference for *Sensing*. He is generally more interested in the immediate action and results of playing sports, of the team's winning, and having fun, than with any long-range or larger implications of lessons they might learn. The coach's unaffected and impersonal reaction to your concerns about your son's emotional experience — the fact that he expresses his belief that learning to be tough is a virtue — is evidence of his preference for *Thinking*. Finally, his casual, even irreverent attitude and body language, and his rather vague promise to keep an eye on things rather than any firm commitment to action, are all clues to his preference for *Perceiving*.

2. Temperament Clues:

In addition to the coach's longtime love of and involvement in sports, other evidence of his *Experiencer* temperament is his extremely casual demeanor and the fact he never seems to stop moving. He proudly claims he is keenly aware of everything going on at practice at all times. Also, he values teaching the team to play hard and become tough competitors much more than discovering and adjusting to the individual needs of one child. He clearly thinks the parent is making too much of the situation, and seems to take this — as he takes most things in life — lightly.

3. E/I-Feeling Pattern Clues:

It may seem odd to discover that this coach does indeed *Extravert Feeling*, even though he is not a Feeling type. His big smile, hearty and friendly welcome, and eagerness to know what he can do for the visiting parent, are all clear clues of his Extraverted Feeling. He nods his head, encouraging the person speaking to continue and to express his understanding, even while he does not agree with the content of what is being said. Beware of demeanor that may say Feeling; the truth lies in words that reveal a true preference for Thinking.

CASE #4: THE HEADHUNTER'S CANDIDATE

TYPE: INTP

1. Temperament Clues:

The first impression you get of this candidate is the number of clues that she is a strong *Conceptualizer*. She speaks of creativity, innovation, and challenge as the most important aspects of satisfying work. Her obvious love of learning and mastering new skills (the self-taught Japanese, for example) and her affinity for and prowess with computers and technology are also good clues. She is most interested in the job opportunity you are discussing because of the creative challenge it offers.

2. Preference Clues:

Her generally reserved demeanor is the first clue that she is probably an *Introvert*. She tends to speak only about herself and her own experiences and skills. She admits to working best in an independent capacity, and is intrigued with moving out of the large, bureaucratic organization. Your assessment that she is a *Conceptualizer* is confirmed by you seeing and hearing plenty of clues for her preferences for *Intuition* and *Thinking*. She does *not* talk about a lot of specifics, nor does she express many personal values in her language, both confirmation that she does not have a preference for either Sensing or Feeling. In fact, she reveals more than once that she prefers working with other competent people and finds managing other people's problems tedious and boring. Finally, she admits that she is better on the start-up of projects than the follow-through and finds the lack of spontaneity frustrating within a large company. You are convinced that she prefers *Perceiving*.

3. E/I-Feeling Pattern Clues:

This case provides an example of how a person can technically **Extravert Feeling,** but in fact reveal very few clues to confirm it. The fact that the headhunter's client is an INTP contributes to this dynamic, since Extraverted Feeling is almost always harder to spot in an Introvert than in an Extravert. This case also demonstrates that sometimes you can SpeedRead people accurately just on the basis of two, or sometimes even only one, of the three SpeedReading components.

CASE #5: THE DISSATISFIED CUSTOMER

TYPE: INFJ

1. Preference Clues:

Chief among the clues that this customer is an *Introvert* are his unassuming demeanor, quiet voice, and need to think through what he wants to do before acting. His focus on the larger issue at stake in the disagreement, rather than on any immediate or short-term satisfaction, is evidence of his preference for *Intuition*. The strongest clue you get that he prefers *Feeling* is that his actions are governed by his strong personal values and his assertion that others should stand behind their products with integrity. His neat appearance, strong opinions, and comfort telling others what they should do are all evidence of his preference for *Judging*.

2. Temperament Clues:

The strongest clue that this customer's temperament is *Idealist* is his expressed clear and strong personal values, which guide and rule his behavior. He not only believes he ought to live by them, but believes in them so strongly that he feels free and even compelled to tell others to live by them as well.

3. E/I-Feeling Pattern Clues:

Again, the customer's reluctant willingness to tell a stranger what he holds dear is evidence of his preference for **Extraverted Feeling.** While he is neither pushy nor aggressive, he is also not shy with his opinions and beliefs. As with any Introvert, his demeanor is gentle, even while he expresses passionately held convictions.

How did you do?

If you were able to guess most of the types correctly, congratulations!

But even if you weren't able to identify most of the letters of each type, don't be discouraged! SpeedReading people is a sophisticated skill that takes time and patience. If you found it particularly hard to identify one set of clues—perhaps the E/I-Feeling pattern—you may wish to review that section before proceeding.

This chapter has been designed to sharpen your SpeedReading skills. Now it is time to learn how to use these skills to communicate with people of all types. We call this process, which you will learn in Chapter 7, Speed*Reaching* people.

CHAPTER SEVEN

SpeedReaching People: How to Communicate with All Types

REWRITING THE GOLDEN RULE

We've all been taught the Golden Rule: "Do unto others as you would have done unto you." However, when it comes to communicating effectively, this really should be modified to read: "Do unto others as *they* would like done unto *them*." In other words, to be effective with others, you need to speak *their* language—to deliver your message in the way *they* want, and will hear it.

Rewriting the Golden Rule means giving up our more egocentric approach to communicating for a more altruistic or responsive approach—one that is more concerned with the other person than with ourselves.

People who communicate egocentrically essentially communicate the same way with everyone, requiring others to adapt to their style. If you think about it, this really makes very little sense. For example, you wouldn't speak the same way to a child of three as you would to an adult with a Ph.D. in philosophy. You would use a different vocabulary and pace, and greatly alter your message so that each person would understand it. Or if you were trying to communicate with someone who was very hard of hearing, you might speak slower and louder to ensure that the person could hear you. Perhaps the clearest example is the change you must make to speak with someone from a foreign country. In order to really communicate well, you would have to speak their language.

Personality Type is such an effective tool for enhancing communication because people of different types prefer to communicate in profoundly (and predictably!) different ways. By understanding a person's preferred communication style, you significantly increase your chances of reaching that person. For example, we know that Sensors naturally focus on the facts and details rather than on the big picture and possibilities. Therefore, when trying to connect with a Sensor, it only makes sense to emphasize what they themselves will think is most important.

Comfort and Communication

Simply put, the more similar people are to us, the more comfortable we are with them. Unconsciously, we all want others to be like us, because when they are, we understand them better and are less threatened by them. Evidence of this abounds. For example, most people are uncomfortable with others who have physical or mental disabilities because they are different. And although American culture, legally, is racially integrated, when it comes to socializing most Caucasians choose to be with other Caucasians, just as most African Americans have more closer friendships with other African Americans. Similarly, people from very different social classes seldom socialize together.

Most of us tend to surround ourselves with others very much like us. A look at most American companies provides good examples of this: everyone looks pretty much the same. There are clear, if mostly unwritten, rules or norms for everything from the way people dress, wear their hair, speak, and walk, to which hobbies and interests they have.

Norms even extend to the size and shape of our bodies: most of our coworkers are neither extremely tall or short, very heavy or very thin. Aside from the fact that there are admittedly fewer of these individuals in the general population, those that are often don't make it through the interview process for two reasons: most interviewers are personally uncomfortable with them and are concerned they won't fit in.

So what does all this have to do with Speed-Reaching People? Quite simply, the more type preferences we have in common with someone, the more similar we are. And the more similar, usually, the easier the communication. (The exception occurs sometimes when people are *too* alike, and recognize in someone else a quality they don't like about themselves — not unlike looking in the mirror and seeing a flaw.)

Perhaps you've had the experience where you've met someone and just seemed to "click" with them; although they are strangers, you feel comfortable with them, as if you've known them for a long time. And with other people, perhaps certain family members or coworkers whom you know well, no matter how hard you try, you always seem to be at odds. More than likely, the explanation for both situations has a lot to do with your personality type similarities and differences.

Theoretically, then, communication between two people of the same type should be pretty easy. And it usually is. But what happens when the other person is our type *opposite*, or different on two or three preferences? Although we pay lip service to the notion that differences are good, in reality, most of us tend to see types that are different in negative terms. Recognizing our potential biases is an essential first step in eliminating them. For example:

Extraverts may see *Introverts* as:
- secretive; too private
- impersonal and unfriendly
- withholding and self-absorbed
- slow and uncooperative
- socially awkward

While Introverts may see *Extraverts* as:
- too talkative; apt to shoot from the lip
- intrusive and pushy
- superficial and disingenuous
- hyperactive and overwhelming
- rude and bossy

These are not always conscious perceptions. Often, they are reflex reactions based on past experience, without the benefit of understanding these fundamental differences in people.

Sensors may see *Intuitives* as:
- flighty and erratic
- unrealistic
- impractical
- having their heads in the clouds
- too complicated and theoretical

While Intuitives may see *Sensors* as:
- unimaginative and uncreative
- boring; resistant to new things
- stodgy: sticks-in-the-mud
- lacking vision
- simplistic

These are particularly powerful filters, since our preference for Sensing or Intuition reflects the way each of us sees the world. And common sense dictates that if we devalue so central an attribute in someone, it is highly unlikely we will want to identify with them or they with us.

Thinkers may see *Feelers* as:
- illogical
- overemotional
- weak
- hysterical
- irrational

While Feelers may see *Thinkers* as:
- cold
- insensitive
- uncaring
- inhumane
- hard-hearted

As we touched on earlier, but is worth repeating at this point: many people erroneously assume that all men are Thinkers and all women are Feelers. (Or at least that they *should* be!) Given that mind-set, such people are often uncomfortable with Feeling men and with Thinking women, which can present a particularly difficult obstacle to communication.

Finally, Judgers may see *Perceivers* as:
- lazy and/or unproductive
- chronically late; apt to miss important deadlines
- not serious enough
- irresponsible and unreliable
- procrastinators; incapable of making decisions

While Perceivers may see *Judgers* as:
- rigid and unyielding
- inflexible and stubborn
- controlling
- apt to regard things as too black and white
- apt to make decisions too quickly

Given the vast number of people in the world, and the fact that there are sixteen distinctly different types, the one thing you can count on is that most of your communications will *not* be with people of your same type. Therefore, the key to communicating effectively lies in your ability to recognize and transcend type differences between you and others. You can do this by learning how to maximize similarities and minimize differences between you.

There are three basic techniques that will help you begin to use your newly acquired understanding of Type to reach people who are different from you.

1. Pay attention to others' motivations, values, strengths, and weaknesses, and *follow the rewritten Golden Rule*. Temperament will tell you what they value, their Lead function will identify their greatest strength, and their Least function will generally reveal their greatest weaknesses.
2. *Pay attention to their preferred communication style*, which is greatly influenced by the individual's type preferences as summarized in the box on the opposite page.

    For example, suppose you are an ENFP salesperson and the person you are dealing with is an ISTJ — your opposite type. In this case, you would do well to resist your natural ENFP inclination to be clever, funny, and maybe a little irreverent. Remember, her lead is Sensing, so you should pay close attention to the facts and specifics, base your pitch on the logical consequences rather than how important the issue is to you, and make sure to honor any deadlines or schedules that you agree upon.
3. *Use the "bridging" technique to seek common ground*. "Bridging" is the process of using the type preferences you have in common with someone else to create a connection. Think of a wooden footbridge built over a raging river to enable people to get from one side to the other. The narrower and weaker the bridge, the more difficult and dangerous the passage. The wider and stronger the bridge, the easier and safer the crossing. In our metaphor, the more preferences people have in common, the wider and stronger the bridge, and the greater likelihood that the message will get across. Here are a few examples of how bridging works:

EXAMPLE #1: ESTJ AND ISTJ

Remember that the more preferences people have in common, the easier the communication process usually is, because there is a wide bridge between these two types. Put another way, there are also several different paths by which these two types might connect — through their shared Sensing, Thinking, and Judging preferences.

E		I
S	———	S
T	———	T
J	———	J

With Extraverts

- Let them talk, and think out loud
- Include a variety of topics
- Communicate verbally
- Expect immediate action
- Keep the conversation moving

With Sensors

- State topic clearly
- Prepare facts and examples
- Present information step-by-step
- Stress practical applications
- Finish your sentences
- Draw on past, real experiences

With Thinkers

- Be organized and logical
- Consider the cause and effect
- Focus on consequences
- Don't ask how they "feel"; ask what they "think"
- Appeal to their sense of fairness
- Don't repeat yourself

With Judgers

- Be on time and be prepared
- Come to conclusions; don't leave issues unresolved
- Be decisive and definitive
- Allow them to make decisions
- Be organized and efficient; don't waste their time
- Stick with plans made

With Introverts

- Ask, then listen carefully
- Talk about one thing at a time
- Communicate in writing, if possible
- Give them adequate time to reflect
- Don't finish their sentences

With Intuitives

- Talk about the "big picture" and its implications
- Talk about possibilities
- Use analogies and metaphors
- Brainstorm options
- Engage their imaginations
- Don't overwhelm them with details

With Feelers

- First mention points of agreement
- Appreciate their efforts and contributions
- Recognize legitimacy of feelings
- Talk about "people" concerns
- Smile and maintain good eye contact
- Be friendly and considerate

With Perceivers

- Expect many questions
- Don't force them to decide prematurely
- Provide opportunities to discuss options and change plans
- Focus on the process, not product
- Give them choices
- Be open to new information

In reality, these two types generally do communicate very well because they see the world in the same way (through Sensing), make decisions using similar criteria (through Thinking), and prefer to live in a decisive, organized way (through Judging). But in addition to having three preferences in common, these two types also share the Traditionalist temperament, which means they have similar core values, making communication even smoother.

EXAMPLE #2: ENTJ AND INTP

These two types relate to each other as Intuitives, as Thinkers, and as Lead Thinkers. And since NTs are Conceptualizers, they share the same temperament as well. This illustrates how types that are similar on only two preferences can still have a significant communication bridge.

```
E                    I
N  ―――――――――  N
T  ―――――――――  T
J                    P
```

These two people will do best to focus on common values of creativity, competence, and independence. They will best understand one another when they use language that appeals to them both, look at the big picture, and describe things in logical, impersonal terms.

EXAMPLE #3: ENFP AND INTJ

Having only one preference in common, you might assume these two types would form a very narrow, even shaky, bridge. While it's true these two types are very different in many ways, and they share only a preference for Intuition in common, that preference happens to be the lead for both. As a result, they both seek and see possibilities, look for the implications and meaning in things, are creative and open to new ways of doing things. And although they may not agree on everything, the chances are very good they will understand each other. Hence, just their lead Intuition, if used correctly, can be a powerful communication bridge.

```
E              I
N  ―――――――  N
F              T
P              J
```

But, as we all have experienced, there are certainly times when you share *no* preferences in common with another person. The key to success here is to start by following the rewritten Golden Rule, working to understand what the other person is all about, and then trying to speak his or her language. Next, look for other, non-type-related, connections. Of course, all human beings share lots of things in common. You may both have children, or work at the same company, belong to the same church, or live in the same town . . . or you may both love photography. There are many more things we have in common that connect us than that separate us. And while they are seldom enough to ensure good communication, these common experiences can form powerful bridges that help the effort.

SKILL-BUILDING EXERCISE

This exercise is designed to help you develop and practice your SpeedReaching skills. To do this, we will be referring back to the same cases used in the skill-building exercise in Chapter 6. You can find these beginning on page 130.

The directions are simple: first reread each case to refresh your memory, then answer the questions that follow below. Once again, you will get the most benefit from trying to answer the questions without referring ahead to our recommendations until you have finished. And you will also find it most helpful to complete the questions and check the answers for each case before proceeding on to the next. You will find the answers on page 148.

To SpeedReach the various people in each of these cases, you will first need to know two things: what is his or her type, and what is your objective in SpeedReaching him or her. Because it's always easier to get someplace if you know where you're going, this information will be provided for you at the start of each case.

To show you how it's done, we've completed the exercise for the first case, "The New Boss," as an example.

CASE #1: THE NEW BOSS (BEGINNING ON PAGE 130)

HER TYPE: ESTJ
Your objective: to impress her with your abilities and to keep your job

Questions to answer:

1. What drives her? Based on her temperament, what are the things she values most that relate to your employment and will help you meet your objective?

As a Traditionalist, the boss values hard work, taking responsibility, and dedication to the job. I need to make her aware of all the times I have willingly taken on extra assignments with great results, and to quantify the ways those successes benefited my department and the company. I might suggest she form a transition committee and volunteer to serve on it.

2. Using what you know about her preferred communication style (based on her type preferences), what specific strategies would you use to connect with her?

Appeal to her Extraversion: Make sure I'm prepared to spontaneously discuss any current projects when I run into her. Also, whenever feasible, I should prepare executive summaries for her (rather than give her long, involved reports to read); both appeal to her natural tendency to act first and think about it later.

Appeal to her Sensing: Make sure I am specific with regard to the facts and details of my projects, and stress that schedules and projections are realistic, based on my past experience.

Appeal to her Thinking: Focus on the bottom line, and provide information on how we can objectively evaluate the progress and success of the project.

Appeal to her Judging: Establish workable plans with achievable goals, and make sure I adhere to plans and comply with all deadlines. Also make sure I'm not late for meetings and hand in all work when it is due.

Now that you get the gist of it, complete the exercise for the next four cases.

CASE #2: THE HOME BUYER (BEGINNING ON PAGE 131)

HER TYPE: ISFP
Your objective: to establish a trusting relationship and make the sale

Questions to answer:

1. What motivates her? Based on her temperament, what are the things she values most that will help you meet your objective?

_____

_____

_____

2. Using what you know about her preferred communication style (based on her type preferences), what specific strategies would you use to connect with her?

_____

_____

_____

_____

_____

CASE #3: THE SOCCER COACH (BEGINNING ON PAGE 132)

HIS TYPE: ESTP
Your objective: for the coach to be more sensitive with your son

Questions to answer:

1. What drives him? Based on his temperament, what are the things he values most that relate to your problem and will help you meet your objective?

_____

_____

_____

_____

2. Using what you know about his preferred communication style (based on his type prefer-

ences), what specific strategies would you use to connect with him?

_____

_____

_____

_____

_____

2. Using what you know about her preferred communication style (based on her type preferences), what specific strategies would you use to connect with her?

_____

_____

_____

_____

_____

_____

_____

CASE #4: THE HEADHUNTER'S CANDIDATE (BEGINNING ON PAGE 133)

HER TYPE: INTP
Your objective: to convince the candidate to switch companies

Questions to answer:

1. What drives her? Based on her temperament, what are the things she values most that relate to a possible job switch and will help you meet your objective?

_____

CASE #5: THE DISSATISFIED CUSTOMER (BEGINNING ON PAGE 134)

HIS TYPE: INFJ
Your objective: to resolve his complaint and keep him as a customer

Questions to answer:

1. What drives him? Based on his temperament, what are the things he values most that relate to his concern and your interaction and will help you meet your objective?

_____

_____

_____

2. Using what you know about his preferred communication style (based on his type preferences), what specific strategies would you use to connect with him?

_____

_____

_____

_____

_____

_____

Answers to Case Studies

CASE #2: THE HOME BUYER (PAGE 146)

HER TYPE: ISFP
Your objective: to establish a trusting relationship and make the sale

Questions to answer:

1. **What drives her? Based on her temperament, what are the things she values most that will help you meet your objective?**

As an Experiencer, she is driven by her desire for freedom to enjoy her life, free from the hassles and stresses involved in moving her family across the country. By virtue of your expertise and experience, you are in a perfect position to reduce many of the hassles, thereby alleviating some of the stresses.

2. **Using what you know about her preferred communication style (based on her type preferences), what specific strategies would you use to connect with her?**

Appeal to her Introversion: I would let her know I am there to help her in any way I can, but I would not be pushy. I would listen patiently and carefully to her, try not interrupt her train of thought, and give her plenty of time to think about any suggestions I make.

Appeal to her Sensing: I would make sure to have

all my facts straight, and when telling her about new listings, try to remember all of the little details that I know she considers important, such as the size of the yard, the distance from school, and the ages and genders of children who live in the neighborhood.

Appeal to her Feeling: I would continue to be friendly and helpful in whatever ways I could. Yet I would not be intrusive; I would let her continue to share personal information with me at her own pace. I would be sensitive to her situation, realizing that a major relocation can be an extremely stressful experience, and do as much as I could to help her ease the transition. I'd put together a packet of information about the town and neighborhood she is considering that would focus on those things I know she's interested in: tennis and health clubs, churches, etc.

Appeal to her Perceiving: I would expect her to have lots of questions, and would prepare myself to provide as much additional information as she needed. I would not put pressure on her to make decisions she didn't yet feel ready to make, but I would gently try to get her to narrow her choices and ultimately make a decision in order not to miss out on a good opportunity.

CASE # 3: THE SOCCER COACH (PAGE 146)

HIS TYPE: ESTP
Your objective: to encourage him to be more sensitive with your son

Questions to answer:

1. **What drives him? Based on his temperament, what are the things he values most that relate to your problem that will help you meet your objective?**

As an Experiencer, he is driven by a desire to have the freedom to do what he loves doing, as he sees fit, without anyone else looking over his shoulder telling him how to act.

2. **Using what you know about his preferred communication style (based on his type preferences), what specific strategies would you use to connect with him?**

Appeal to his Extraversion: I would first try to engage him in some small talk, perhaps by commenting on the sports trophies and pictures that adorn his walls. Once we got down to business, I would keep the conversation light and moving, getting to the point quickly, and leaving out all extraneous information.

Appeal to his Sensing: In a step-by-step manner, I would relay to him the details of each specific incident that caused my son to feel uncomfortable, and, where possible, offer evidence (a friend of his told us same thing) to corroborate the story. I might also tell him about a similar problem our older child experienced, what the coach in that case did, and how he created a positive outcome.

Appeal to his Thinking: I would try to get him to see that treating kids differently —because of their different personalities and needs— is neither unfair nor inconsistent (two things that Thinkers rail against), but rather an effective strategy based on flexibility. I would also point out that if our son were to feel better about his experience, he would probably perform better, which would benefit the whole team.

Appeal to his Perceiving: Finally, I would make a few suggestions about how he might handle the situation based on how well we know our son, but I wouldn't require him to commit himself to one particular course of action now. Rather, I'd suggest that he think about the issues we'd raised as he observed our son in practice for the next week, and then talk again, after he's collected some more information.

CASE #4: THE HEADHUNTER'S CANDIDATE (PAGE 147)

HER TYPE: INTP
Your objective: to convince the candidate to switch companies

Questions to answer:

1. **What drives her? Based on her temperament, what are the things she values most that relate to a possible job switch and will help you meet your objective?**

As a Conceptualizer, she is driven by a strong desire to feel competent and intellectually challenged by her work. She values her independence and opportunities to exercise her creativity, continue to learn, and excel in a new situation.

2. **Using what you know about her preferred communication style (based on her type preferences), what specific strategies would you use to connect with her?**

Appeal to her Introversion: I would give her plenty of information to consider and review as much of it in writing as possible. I would listen carefully to her questions and give her plenty of time to think about issues or concerns before expecting her to discuss them.

Appeal to her Intuition: I would emphasize the many possibilities and opportunities that exist with this company, and talk about how this switch would positively affect her long-range career plans.

Appeal to her Thinking: I would be organized and logical when making my pitch, resisting any temptation to discuss her feelings about a move, or prying into her personal life by asking how it might affect her family or personal plans. I would "net out" the advantages to her in terms of pay and benefits, and try to compare them with her current employment situation.

Appeal to her Perceiving: I would try to anticipate her many questions, so I could best respond to her concerns, and extend the invitation to call with questions she has during the next few days as she considers the opportunity. I would also try to be prepared for her to want to negotiate various aspects of the arrangement, and I would try to remain flexible to her suggestions and/or demands.

CASE #5: THE DISSATISFIED CUSTOMER (PAGE 147)

HIS TYPE: INFJ
Your objective: to resolve his complaint and keep him as a customer

Questions to answer:

1. **What drives him? Based on his temperament, what are the things he values most that relate to his problem and your interaction and will help you meet your objective?**

As an Idealist, he is driven by a need to understand, be understood, and create harmonious relationships with others, while at the same time remaining faithful to his own convictions and beliefs.

2. **Using what you know about his preferred communication style (based on his type preferences), what specific strategies would you use to connect with him?**

Appeal to his Introversion: I would listen patiently and give him my undivided attention as he described his problem and how he would like it resolved.
Appeal to his Intuition: I would explain to him the big picture: how manufacturers' policies threaten the existence of small businesses like mine. I would spell out the dilemma of trying to stay in business and keep customers happy. I would demonstrate

how pervasive the problem is by citing local stores he knows that have been forced out of business by larger chains due to similar circumstances. Appealing to his creativity, I might ask him if he had any innovative suggestions about alleviating the problem if he were in my shoes.
Appeal to his Feeling: If he needed to, I would certainly give him adequate opportunity to vent his feelings, be careful not to talk him out of them, and remember to express my understanding of his position. I would apologize for any inconvenience the situation had caused him, tell him that I was disappointed at the way the boots performed and that I appreciated his taking the time to make me aware of the problem.
Appeal to his Judging: I would act decisively to resolve his problem. I might see how he felt about receiving a partial refund applied to a new pair of boots, but if he still was not satisfied, I would take the boots back at my expense.

Hopefully, this exercise has helped you learn key SpeedReaching techniques. Since these are sophisticated new skills, you will find that the more you use them, the more proficient you become. Eventually, they will become almost second nature to you. It is important to point out that in this chapter, we focused on how to use various components to SpeedReach people—specifically temperament (which reflects core values), and type preferences (which influence preferred communication style). This was a necessary approach, since it is much easier to learn the process by starting with the pieces. But in reality, no one is just a

Sensor or just an Intuitive. So after you've become proficient at SpeedReading and SpeedReaching people, you will relate to them as a whole type (INTPs, ESFJs, etc.) rather than just as Sensors or Intuitives.

In order to be able to do that, you need to know more about the subtleties and preferred communication styles of each of the individual sixteen types. That is what Part 3 is all about. In the following four chapters, which are devoted to providing in-depth insights into the sixteen types grouped together by temperament, you will learn the specific clues for SpeedReading, as well as detailed communication recommendations for SpeedReaching people of each type.

So, on to Part 3: "Getting to Know the Sixteen Types."

PART THREE

Getting to Know the Sixteen Types

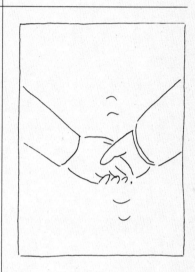

Congratulations! You have made great progress toward acquiring two new valuable and permanent life skills — the art of SpeedReading, and the art of SpeedReaching people. Having learned the underlying principles of Personality Type, the techniques for identifying these key characteristics in others, and for communicating with people in their favorite style, you have only one remaining task left before you will have truly mastered these skills: to understand and appreciate the subtleties and preferred communication styles of each of the sixteen types.

Chapters 8 through 11 are devoted to providing just such in-depth insights. We have grouped together by Temperament people of each type, and you will learn the specific clues for SpeedReading and receive detailed communication recommendations for SpeedReaching them.

This course will end with Chapter 12, where we will share some final thoughts and suggestions designed to help you maximize what you have learned in this book, and provide you with a list of resources you will find useful as you continue to sharpen your SpeedReading skills.

CHAPTER EIGHT

Getting to Know the Traditionalists: The Four SJ Types

In Chapter 4 we described the different temperaments as four different human natures and explained how temperament forms the core of one's type. Hence, in our in-depth look at the individual types, it is most helpful to start with their shared temperament characteristics, then talk about each type individually. As you learned in Chapter 4, all Traditionalists share certain core values, among them the belief in a strong work ethic, the need for people and institutions to be responsible, the importance of following the rules and of serving one's community.

COMMUNICATION RECOMMENDATIONS

As you know, some Traditionalists are Thinkers, while others are Feelers, and some are Extraverts, while others are Introverts. Since all four Traditionalists share so much in common, there are several *general* communication techniques that will be effective with all of them. But since there are also significant differences between the four Traditionalist types, there are several *specific* techniques that will be most effective with people of each type. To avoid repetition, below are presented the general recommendations once, followed by the specific ones for each type.

General Tips for Communicating with Traditionalists
• Be direct, straightforward, and to the point.

- Don't joke around while discussing serious or important matters.
- If you know them, refer to their values concerning the issue.
- Use simple, uncomplicated language.
- Be prepared and organized.
- Present information sequentially, step-by-step.
- Pay careful attention to the accuracy of your facts.
- Stress the practical implications or results.
- Point out why your suggestion is the most responsible course of action.
- Explain how your proposition is the "right thing" to do.
- Be prepared to back up your points with statistics, facts, and real-life experience.
- Offer examples of success based on past experience.

HOW TO SPOT AN ESTJ:

ESTJs may be the toughest of the Traditionalists. While they are generally friendly and may be somewhat physically animated, they prefer to keep things on a more cerebral level and generally avoid dealing with emotions and feelings, their own or others'. They are highly decisive people, quick to come to logical conclusions, which may result in being blunt and appearing insensitive to the needs of others. The language of ESTJs is direct, clear, and functional, and their appearance is typically neat, tailored, even classic in style. Above all, they dress and act conservatively and appropriately for all occasions.

ESTJs usually have a high energy level. They are eager to work hard and are also very productive. Because they instantly notice what needs doing

H O W   T O   S P E A K   "E S T J"

- Be assertive; you may have to push to get your point across. Don't worry about hurting their feelings; ESTJs take few things personally. They'll respect you more if you don't back down from your position.
- Try not to be put off by their frankness or even bluntness — they probably do not mean what they say personally, so try not to take it that way.
- Don't expect to score points with personal appeals. Be objective and base your argument or reasoning on the realistic, logical consequences of the action, rather than on its personal importance to you or others.
- Appeal to their sense of fairness and justice. Don't make frequent exceptions to the rule.
- Be prepared to discuss your ideas when you present them. They are action-oriented people and don't tend to take much time for reflection.
- Appeal to their need to get the job done.
- Come directly to your point or request. Be explicit, organized, and honest. Try numbering your points for clarity. Do not try to skirt around issues.

and are driven to get it done, they can usually be counted on to volunteer to take charge of any project. But they can also be domineering and bossy and, in the process, may unintentionally "roll over" people or hurt their feelings without any awareness that they did. Wherever they are, they are likely to be in charge, and so whether at work or at play, they usually assume a leadership role. ESTJs are often found in management or other positions of responsibility at work or at service in their communities, churches, or synagogues.

Attention grabbers: Words or phrases that are likely to get the attention of most ESTJs

- Let me net it out for you.
- Let's cut to the chase.
- Here's the bottom line.
- Here's the plan.

Special Challenges

Not surprisingly, the challenges for reaching ESTJs are greatest for people who are the most different from them. Specifically, Introverts need to prepare themselves for the quick action ESTJs will want to take. Intuitives need to present their global ideas in very specific ways, emphasizing their practical application and workability. Since Perceivers may find ESTJs rather inflexible, their special challenge is helping ESTJs to see the value in keeping options open until all the necessary information has been considered. They may also need to clearly state that a course of action has not yet been agreed to. Perhaps the greatest challenge, however, comes for Feelers, who may have to stretch the most by being assertive and not taking criticism or rejection of their ideas by ESTJs personally.

HOW TO SPOT AN ISTJ

ISTJs are generally quiet, yet extremely strong-willed people. Their lead Sensing makes them probably the most realistic, down-to-earth, practical type. They are also often the most conservative. Typically meticulous and thorough, they are especially precise and accurate with facts. Their appearance is usually neat, conservative, and understated. They do not tend to wear loud colors or trendy fashions, preferring a more classic, tailored look, especially when dressed for work. Their speech is usually slow, deliberate, and full of specific references. They tell stories in the correct time sequence and can rarely be diverted off a linear path.

Cautious by nature, ISTJs often hesitate when faced with a change or unfamiliar situation, and instead may want to review what has worked in the past. They have a great drive to accomplish their goals, are incredibly focused, and can concentrate all of their energy on one thing at a time. "Slow and steady wins the race" accurately describes the work style of most ISTJs, who do not like to be hurried or rushed. They are very private, especially about personal matters, and are comfortable spending long hours alone, either working or en-

HOW TO SPEAK "ISTJ"

- Provide them with plenty of facts and concrete documentation to support your position or idea.
- Stress the practical application of the idea and, if possible, specifically what it will accomplish, how it is to be implemented, where it has worked before, and with what results.
- Present your proposal in a sequential manner, one idea at a time. Lay out all the necessary steps and, if possible, provide a realistic schedule for accomplishing your goals.
- Give them plenty of time to think about ideas, especially new or unusual ones, before discussing them or expecting them to respond. When possible, submit all proposals in writing first, and be explicit about when you need to get their reaction or input.
- Don't ask them to brainstorm possibilities or to discuss things they haven't had adequate time to quietly and thoughtfully consider in advance.
- Simplify the message; boil it down to its basic components, and try to avoid long, complicated, or tangential explanations.
- Make logic-based arguments, rather than personally based ones.

joying hobbies such as reading, gardening, cooking, or other hands-on activities. While their ability to focus is among their greatest strengths, their single-mindedness can also result in their being stubborn and inflexible, and especially resistant to change. Always the straight arrow in work and in play, they take things seriously and get their responsibilities met before indulging in leisure activities. Their friends sometimes tease them about being so ultraresponsible because they seldom do anything remotely crazy.

Attention grabbers: Words or phrases that are likely to get the attention of most ISTJs

- Here's what's worked before.
- I have documentation.
- If it ain't broke, don't fix it.
- Step-by-step.
- Anything worth doing is worth doing right.

Special Challenges

Extraverts need to be sure to respect ISTJs' need to reflect before acting. Feelers need to make their presentations as logical as possible, and not take criticism and feedback personally. Perceivers need to realize that ISTJs may take a while deciding something, but once they do, it is very hard to change their minds. Therefore, the more bona fide and relevant facts they provide, the longer the ISTJ is likely to keep the door open to new possibilities. The greatest challenge may be for Intuitives, who need to go to great lengths to make sure their proposals are realistic and workable. They should prepare themselves for the ISTJ's characteristic resistance to new and untested ideas and ready critique of any realistic concerns or flaws in reasoning.

HOW TO SPOT AN ESFJ

ESFJs are perhaps the most friendly and outgoing of all the sixteen types. They are supremely helpful to others in a myriad of real and concrete ways. Usually polite and somewhat proper, ESFJs are also physically demonstrative; pumping your hand when shaking it, touching an arm or shoulder when making a point, or even giving bear hugs when appropriate. They wear their emotions on their sleeves, and their faces usually provide an accurate reflection of their feelings.

Their language reflects their strongly held beliefs and values; they may use the word "should" a lot and freely offer opinions and reactions to everything going on around them. ESFJs are often the first to volunteer when something needs to be done, and tend to take on projects with gusto and purpose. This can sometimes mean they may act somewhat controlling, determined to be sure every detail is done the way they think is best. They often see things in terms of black and white, and speak and act with great conviction.

Attention grabbers: Words or phrases that are likely to get the attention of most ESFJs

- Can you lend me a hand with something?
- Here's how I feel about it.
- What's the right thing to do?

H O W   T O   S P E A K   "E S F J"

■ Respect their feelings! Don't try to talk them out of feeling a certain way, even if you don't share their view. Never accuse them of being irrational.

■ Always mention points of agreement before offering criticism. ESFJs tend to take things personally and are less likely to be able to hear you clearly if they are offended.

■ Be aware they are run by their values; be careful not to propose an idea or course of action or behave in a way that may offend their personal value system.

■ Genuinely and explicitly express to them your appreciation when they do something that helps or benefits you; let them know they are valued for their contributions and cooperation.

■ Most ESFJs enjoy talking; be prepared to listen and to contribute.

■ Be clear and precise. Outline steps in an accurate sequence.

■ Try to adhere to agreed-upon plans. If they must be changed, appeal to the ESFJ's strong desire to help and please others.

- Please . . . thank you.
- I really appreciate your help.
- How do you usually do this?
- What has your experience been in the past?

Special Challenges

Introverts may find it hard to keep up with the quick-moving and long-talking ESFJs. Fortunately, most Introverts are good listeners, and ESFJs are sensitive to others' comfort levels, so they won't overwhelm Introverts. Intuitives may be frustrated by ESFJs' resistance to trying new things and their unwillingness to abandon old habits and beliefs. They need to make the ESFJ see exactly how the new suggestion will work (preferably based on past experience) or prove the change will be worth the stress and commotion it may initially cause. Per-

ceivers may find ESFJs' twin needs for control and closure stifling, and need to work hard to meet their deadlines and expectations. But the greatest challenge is probably for Thinkers, who need to realize that ESFJs take practically everything personally and are easily hurt and offended. This is particularly important to be mindful of because, once hurt, ESFJs may very well burn their bridges and write off the offending party permanently.

HOW TO SPOT AN ISFJ

ISFJs are quiet, modest, patient people who enjoy helping others without calling a lot of attention to themselves. They are most often comfortable working behind the scenes, both in their jobs and in their community or volunteer activities. They have considerable facility working with facts and

HOW TO SPEAK "ISFJ"

- Be specific; announce the topic you are addressing at the start of a conversation.
- Be explicit: let them know exactly what you expect and want, preferably providing detailed instructions as opposed to vague guidelines.
- Respect their privacy. Do not pry into their personal affairs or share information about them, even if it seems unimportant, without their permission.
- Be polite, considerate, and nice. If possible, keep your energy and voice level down, and don't in-

terrupt them when they are speaking. Apologize quickly and sincerely if you hurt their feelings.
- Don't rush them. Give them plenty of time to consider ideas, especially new ones. If you ask their opinion, wait patiently for them to give it; don't finish their sentences for them.
- Honor all your commitments to them. Be vigilant about meeting deadlines, fulfilling promises, being on time for dates and appointments, and generally doing what you say you will do.

details and are usually so tuned in to whatever they are doing in the present moment that they have excellent recall. They have excellent memories for details, especially pertaining to experiences they've had and those regarding people they care about.

Most ISFJs speak softly, slowly, and deliberately. Their language is uncomplicated and full of references to specifics based upon personal experience. They are neither highly animated nor physically demonstrative, especially when they are talking with someone they don't know well. ISFJs rarely make waves. Instead, they tend to faithfully follow the rules and work hard to do what is expected of them. Their unassertive nature can sometimes mean they get taken advantage of by others. Although they care deeply for people and are loyal, devoted friends, they are also intensely private and are uncomfortable sharing much about their personal lives with people they do not fully trust. Even after a full day's work, they often have a hobby, volunteer effort, or other commitment that keeps them busy.

Attention grabbers: Words or phrases that are likely to get the attention of most ISFJs

- I promise. You have my word on it.
- What would make you feel comfortable?

- Do you need some time to think about this?
- May I share something private with you?
- What's your recollection about that?

Special Challenges

Extraverts may be impatient with the slower, methodical, and contemplative style ISFJs prefer, and may find dealing with them somewhat tedious. Even if this is the case, you must try to be patient and respectful. Thinkers may not consider ISFJs tough enough to handle certain tasks or situations. And Thinkers may also fail to appreciate ISFJs' sensitivity to others' feelings rather than recognizing and valuing this as an innate ISFJ strength. Perceivers may be frustrated by ISFJs' discomfort or unwillingness to change gears or act spontaneously. Giving them information ahead of time will make it easier for ISFJs to try new things or make changes in their routines. However, the biggest challenge may be for Intuitives, who can become impatient dealing with the facts, details, and immediate applications rather than the big picture and possibilities. But slowing down and actually listening carefully to an ISFJs story can prove much more interesting and engaging than the Intuitive might have erroneously assumed.

CHAPTER NINE

Getting to Know the Experiencers: the Four SP Types

As you remember from Chapter 4, people who share the Experiencer temperament value spontaneity, excitement, fun, the freedom to respond to life's many adventures, and the opportunity to fully experience the physical sensations of their favorite activities.

COMMUNICATION RECOMMENDATIONS

Like Traditionalists, some Experiencers are Thinkers, while others are Feelers. And some are Extraverts, while others are Introverts. We begin with the communication recommendations for *all* Experiencers and then present an in-depth look at the four unique Experiencer types. Because they share so much in common, there are several general communication techniques that will be effective with all Experiencers. But since there are also significant differences between the four Experiencer types, there are also several specific techniques that will be most effective with people of each type.

General Tips for Communicating with Experiencers
- Be friendly, open, and responsive to their questions.
- Focus on the real, the practical, and the immediate; present tangible proof and supporting evidence.

- Give them plenty of options to consider.
- Be casual, and try not to take yourself too seriously around them. If possible, mix business with pleasure.
- If appropriate, make the experience as much fun and as entertaining as possible. To Experiencers, variety really is the spice of life, so try to keep the conversation or presentation lively, interactive, moving, and exciting. If possible, build in some payoff or source of immediate gratification.
- Appeal to as many of their senses as possible; when appropriate, include interesting and attractive audiovisual and tactile aids. Provide opportunities for hands-on demonstrations, site inspections, or field trips.
- Engage the person; encourage dialogue, and don't lecture.

HOW TO SPOT AN ESTP

ESTPs are sometimes described as chameleons because they can adapt their behavior so easily to new environments and situations. This can present a unique challenge in SpeedReading them, especially on the basis of a limited exposure, since they may look like another type, or even several different types. However, in general, they are gregarious, outgoing, energetic, and active people who enjoy being the center of attention. They love to be spontaneous and to have a good time, and especially like parties. In social interactions they are usually charming, animated, and flirtatious. They usually remember jokes and are good at telling them, although they may frequently be off-color or "earthy." Their language is straight-

HOW TO SPEAK "ESTP"

- Engage them in the process; expect and prepare for a vigorous, challenging, and even good-naturedly confrontational give-and-take.
- Lighten up! Make the conversation or presentation fun; don't misconstrue their casual, easygoing style and perhaps good-natured ribbing or comments as a lack of interest or support for your project.
- Base your reasoning and argument on the pragmatic outcome you desire, emphasizing practical benefits; avoid appeals based on emotion.

- Keep it simple. Present ideas in a straightforward way; avoid long, complicated, involved explanations or rationales. Use plenty of specific and sensory examples and action words to convey your meaning and intention.
- When possible, give them more than one option to consider and the opportunity to modify the plan.
- If appropriate, appeal to their willingness to take calculated risks.

forward and usually includes plenty of realistic and accurate sensory details.

ESTPs often move gracefully and with a true economy of motion. For the most part, they tend to be very much aware of their bodies and at ease within them. They are often comfortable touching others to demonstrate affection or to make a point. Their appearance is generally casual, and they may have a great sense of style. Aware of everything that goes on around them, including the impressions they make on others, they often are skillful at working a room, and are socially relaxed in a host of different environments. While ESTPs are found in many diverse occupations, they usually prefer their work, as well as spare-time activities, to involve physical activity, variety, and possibly even some risk. They often enjoy sports, both as participants and as observers.

Attention grabbers: Words or phrases that are likely to get the attention of most ESTPs

- I'm game if you are.
- The sky's the limit.
- What have you got to lose?
- You only go around once.
- Let's party!

Special Challenges

Introverts may be frustrated by ESTPs' lack of interest in exploring subjects in great depth and should try to condense any exhaustive background or documentation material into a sum-

mary and offer it in writing. Most ESTPs will find comfort in having a physical outline, even if they do not plan to study it thoroughly. Feelers may be put off by ESTPs' apparent failure to take important matters seriously. They may also misread ESTPs' Extraverted Feeling as an indication of agreement when none really exists. Feelers might try appealing to the ESTP's desire to be liked and have everyone as friend (and hope for the best!). Judgers may find ESTPs' preference for keeping options open and changing plans inconvenient or even maddening. They need to appeal to ESTPs as Thinkers, to point out the logical consequences of delaying action or changing plans.

Perhaps the greatest challenge faces Intuitives, who want to make the ESTPs see the big picture and the long-range implications of decisions, rather than to just pay attention to the present moment. They may have success by linking new ideas to past successful ones and offering as many relevant models and specifics as possible. If Intuitives run into resistance because the proposed idea is yet untried, they can appeal to the ESTP's love of adventure and risk-taking nature.

HOW TO SPOT AN ISTP

ISTPs are generally quiet, reserved, and very independent people. Because they are so private, they are often very difficult to get to know and, therefore, to SpeedRead. It may be much easier to identify them based on what they do, rather than what they say. They often are drawn to mechanical devices and have a natural affinity for using tools. They usually prefer to work with objects that can be logically understood—rather than with people, who are emotionally complex and much less predictable.

Most ISTPs would greatly prefer to engage in physical activities than social ones. And many are sometimes real adrenaline junkies, happiest when they are focusing all their attention like a laser beam on whatever (sometimes dangerous) activity they are engaged in at the moment. ISTPs are usually fun to be around and enjoy having a good time. More concerned that they are comfortable and that their clothes are functional, they do not tend to dress for others or especially care what others think of them. They do have very high needs with regard to their personal freedom and personal space and are seldom physically demonstrative

with others. They are attracted most to occupations that involve lots of physical activity, often with a component of danger or risk, such as fire fighting, police work, operating construction equipment, or being part of an emergency medical response team. Recreationally, they often seek activities that also involve adventure, physical challenges, and risk, such as motorcycle racing, flying airplanes, and "extreme" sports.

Attention grabbers: Words or phrases that are likely to get the attention of most ISTPs

- I'll leave you alone to work on that.
- Can you help me figure this out?
- Live and let live.
- Does that make sense to you?
- What's the logical choice here?

H O W   T O   S P E A K   " I S T P "

- Respect their privacy, give them plenty of space, and don't push yourself on them; avoid attempting intimacy unless they initiate or clearly desire it.

- Be pragmatic; make sure suggestions or requests are well thought out, realistic, practical, and workable.

- Appeal to their need for action; whenever possible, take advantage of their ability to stay calm, think clearly, and respond quickly in a crisis or emergency.

- Try not to overschedule their time or limit their ability to act spontaneously by imposing too many

rules or too much structure. Be explicit about the requirements you need or responsibilities you expect them to fulfill.

- Avoid making appeals based on emotion; rather, make sure there is a logical rationale for suggestions and proposals.

- Listen carefully when they do share personal information. Most ISTPs will say something only once, and if you miss it, they may still assume you heard them and not repeat it.

Special Challenges

Extraverts are most likely to be put off by ISTPs' strong need for privacy, the fact that they are so hard to get to know, and their insistence on participating only on their own terms. If Extraverts need ISTPs' participation, they should appeal to their natural desire for action, recognizing that may be their most potent motivation. Intuitives may find ISTPs' focus on the present and their tendency toward immediate action a bit short-sighted. They need to convince ISTPs — through their logical Thinking and ability to see cause and effect — that other factors, which may not yet be apparent, should be taken into consideration. Judgers may find ISTPs' general unwillingness to comply with anything that does not grab their attention and their resistance to working within narrowly defined boundaries like time, rules, and policies a real source of frustration. Understanding the independent nature of ISTPs is the first step. Next, they need to find a way for ISTPs to feel ownership in the project. Once they become invested in it, they will be more motivated to make sure it happens when it is supposed to. Feelers may be put off by how hard it is to establish a relationship with ISTPs and be easily wounded by their remoteness. It takes a long time to get close to ISTPs, and, even if you do, remember that it is essentially out of character and against their nature for these strong Introverted Thinkers to be outwardly warm and affectionate. Feelers also need to step back and accept criticism from ISTPs as the objective, honest feedback it is usually intended to be, not as the personal attack Feelers are likely to misinterpret it as.

HOW TO SPOT AN ESFP

ESFPs are warm, friendly, approachable, and usually have an easygoing nature. They truly enjoy people and doing nice things for them. They are also playful and energetic, love parties, and have a real zest for living. They enjoy being the center of attention by playing an instrument or telling stories and delight in getting others involved and making people laugh. ESFPs are extremely observant and aware of whatever is happening around them. Not particularly complicated, they are unassuming and down-to-earth people.

ESFPs' language is straightforward. They use words simply to communicate, and mean exactly what they say, without hidden agendas. Curious as well as friendly, they tend to ask a lot of questions and demonstrate genuine interest in other people. But since ESFPs prefer action and having fun above all else, they would much rather do something with a group of friends than sit around and have serious talks. Their dress and appearance also reflect their casual, free-flowing attitude toward life. They prefer sensual textures in fabric, and wear bold and bright colors more often than subdued ones. While they are happiest surrounded by people they like, they can be quite private about their deep, personal feelings, and are comfortable sharing these only with their closest friends. The kinds of jobs they gravitate toward often involve

H O W   T O   S P E A K   " E S F P "

■ Be direct and straightforward; do not present ideas in terms of complicated theories, concepts, or hypothetical situations. Stick with what is real and realistic.

■ Be friendly, relaxed, and casual, since ESFPs tend not to respond well to uptight people; be attentive to their physical needs and comforts.

■ Make your pitch based on the practical ways your idea or proposal will benefit others; appeal to their common sense.

■ Respect their privacy; don't misread their gregariousness as a desire to reveal intimate details or feelings.

■ Describe sequentially the way projects are to be completed, and be very clear about what is expected.

■ Be polite and complimentary. Show your appreciation for their efforts. If you have any criticism, make sure to point out something positive and tangible first.

■ Respond immediately to their requests. Don't ask them to wait too long or postpone activities into the future, if possible. These action-oriented people live for today.

■ Surprise them. Whenever appropriate, make a party or a game out of everyday chores or activities.

---

lots of interaction with the public that allows them to help people in concrete ways, such as through sales of products or providing a service. Recreationally, they often have a wide circle of friends and a large number of different hobbies, sports, and activities, all of which keep them very busy.

Attention grabbers: Words or phrases that are likely to get the attention of most ESFPs

• Surprise!
• Let's have a party.
• A bunch of us are going over to . . .

• I'm having a rotten day. Can you cheer me up?
• I need some help with this project. How about it?

Special Challenges

Introverts may find ESFPs too chatty and tiring to be around for extended periods of time. They may need to be prepared to discuss their thoughts or plans immediately. Introverts will also do well to keep their explanations brief, uncomplicated, and to the point. Thinkers are liable to consider ESFPs too sensitive and/or inconsistent in their decision making. They should realize that ESFPs place a high value on being nice and helping others whenever the need arises. While ESFPs can usually take a joke well, they are likely to be offended if they are criticized or dismissed as being too sensitive. Judgers may be frustrated by ESFPs' apparent lack of organization skills and/or their difficulty making and sticking to decisions. ESFPs' "live for the moment" mentality may result in their being unprepared for future events. Instead, appeal to the ESFP's desire for action, emphasizing that the sooner a decision is made, the quicker everyone can get the desired outcome and move on to something more fun. Intuitives may find these highly realistic people resistant to unusual or completely new ideas, and unwilling or unable to look beyond the moment to consider the future consequences or implications of their present actions. They need

to gently remind ESFPs that something that seems ideal today may not look as good tomorrow.

HOW TO SPOT AN ISFP

ISFPs are gentle, soft-spoken, and modest. While on the surface they may appear cool to strangers, they are extremely sensitive and nurturing people who are run by their own set of values. Once they get to know you, they can be very affectionate and warm. Easygoing and relaxed, ISFPs have very little need or desire to control or influence others, but will often go to great lengths to please the people they care about. Sensitive and concerned, they find it very important that people get along and that there is harmony around them. ISFPs

---

HOW TO SPEAK "ISFP"

- Respect their privacy; don't push them into doing things, especially in public, before they are comfortable.

- Don't be loud, overbearing, or argumentative; avoid confrontations at all costs. Speak quietly, privately, and gently.

- Be specific and explicit. If possible, refer to instances in their personal experience in which similar ideas or suggestions were successfully implemented.

- Appeal to their sensitivity and desire to help

people. Stress the practicality of your idea or proposal, and show how it will benefit others in a concrete way.

- Give them plenty of time to react to proposals or suggestions, especially new ones.

- Solicit their opinions and avoid trying to control them; don't misinterpret their compliant, cooperative nature as agreement with, or enthusiasm for, your plan or suggestion.

- Make it fun. Incorporate social and other downtime to break the project into manageable pieces.

tend to dress casually and comfortably, in clothes that are functional but are also soft, aesthetically pleasing, and colorful. However, they do not generally like to call a lot of attention to themselves. Not highly verbal, they prefer to express themselves through their actions and gestures, which often includes doing something thoughtful or considerate for someone in need. Just as they shy away from the limelight, unassuming ISFPs go to great lengths to avoid confrontation or arguments, and become anxious around loud, overbearing people.

When it comes to their careers, ISFPs may not be terribly ambitious, but they are fully engaged in whatever they are doing at the moment. They often seek work that involves helping people in tangible ways, such as child care and nursing. ISFPs generally treasure their free time and often enjoy exploring nature, beach combing, hiking in the mountains, and spending time with animals. They also enjoy a variety of sports, making crafts, and other sensory experiences such as going to the movies, concerts, or other cultural events.

Attention grabbers: Words or phrases that are likely to get the attention of most ISFPs

- Help!
- Can you keep a secret?
- How thoughtful of you.

- Take your time, I'll wait for you.
- Your good manners and considerate behavior are appreciated.

Special Challenges

Extraverts may be frustrated with the time it takes to get ISFPs moving on a project. They need to realize that ISFPs do love to act on things, but only after they've had time to think them through first. Intuitives may find ISFPs are unable or unwilling to see beyond the moment and consider the long-term implications of actions. They need to show ISFPs how factoring in these other considerations will benefit people in real ways, not only now, but in the future as well. Judgers may become annoyed with ISFPs who don't seem very ambitious or driven to make and stick with plans. They also may consider them too indecisive. Although Judgers can usually push ISFPs into doing what they want them to do, they will have better results if they can gently move ISFPs toward their position in small steps, rather than dominating them. But Thinkers are liable to find the greatest challenge lies in not offending these very sensitive people. The best advice for them is to remember they are speaking to people who first and foremost value their own and other people's feelings, regardless of whether others think they are being logical or rational.

CHAPTER TEN

Getting to Know the Conceptualizers: the Four NT Types

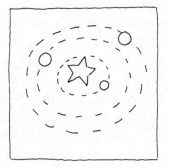

You'll remember that people who share the Conceptualizer temperament value competence above all else, so they are naturally driven to excel at whatever they do. Global thinkers, they pride themselves on their creative problem-solving abilities — especially those involving complex issues.

COMMUNICATION RECOMMENDATIONS

While all Conceptualizers share preferences for Intuition and Thinking, some are Extraverts and others Introverts. And some are Judgers, while others are Perceivers. We begin with the communication recommendations for all Conceptualizers and then present an in-depth look at the four Conceptualizer types. Since they share so much in common, there are several general communication techniques that will be effective with all Conceptualizers. But since there are also significant differences between the four Conceptualizer types, there are also several specific techniques that will be most effective with people of each type.

General Tips for Communicating with Conceptualizers

- Challenge their intellectual curiosity.
- Focus on the big picture and the patterns, rather than on the specifics; address the future implications of actions.
- Use analogies and metaphors.
- Reinforce your points with other ideas and compatible theories.
- Engage their imaginations.

- Demonstrate confidence in your position.
- Don't overwhelm them with details, or bore them with minutiae.
- Stress the logical consequences of your position; avoid emotional appeals.
- Appeal to their sense of fairness and gift for objectivity.
- Expect them to be creative and resourceful, and not to be bound by tradition or precedent.
- Be consistent and, above all else, demonstrate your competence.

HOW TO SPOT AN ENTJ

No shrinking violets, ENTJs make their presence known and are the ultimate take-charge types. Usually friendly and outgoing, ENTJs have lots of energy and think, speak, and move briskly, often leaning forward with intent and purpose. Great strategic thinkers, ENTJs grasp things quickly, even issues that are complicated and complex. Because they generally exude such great confidence, they may appear condescending or even, at times, arrogant. Usually very organized and decisive, ENTJs frequently juggle several projects at once, completing them all with great efficiency. Creative and innovative, they understand and like to use power, but may have a tendency to overpower people into doing their bidding. Their language is generally sophisticated, and they often have extensive vocabularies. Most ENTJs are extremely career driven, and although they can be found in many occupations, they almost always

HOW TO SPEAK "ENTJ"

- Get to the point; don't beat around the bush and waste their time; be conscientious about meeting deadlines and delivering on your promises.
- Do your homework! Be prepared to defend your position; expect them to challenge you and to play the devil's advocate.
- Prepare yourself to be assertive; don't worry about hurting their feelings, and don't let them intimidate you, which they may unintentionally do.
- Keep in mind how your proposal or idea fits into the big picture and their own and/or their organization's long-range plans and objectives.

- Don't be afraid to offer bold and innovative approaches, as long as they are well thought out and logical.
- Sell yourself as someone who is competent on your own but also capable of being a team player. Communicate self-sufficiency and the ability to need little direct assistance.
- Tell them immediately if they hurt your feelings or offend you. But be sure to tell them precisely what they did that bothered you, and do it honestly and calmly.

gravitate to positions of leadership; an inordinately high percentage of top-level managers and administrators are ENTJs. Their spare-time activities often involve self-improvement, or if they are involved in organizations, once again they are usually in charge.

Attention grabbers: Words or phrases that are likely to get the attention of most ENTJs

- Damn the torpedoes, full steam ahead!
- We need someone to take charge of this project.
- What do you think our strategy should be?
- What's wrong with this picture?

Special Challenges

Introverts may have difficulty with ENTJs' desire to initiate bold actions so quickly. The more competent and expert the Introvert is seen as, the better his or her chance to get the ENTJ to spend more time in the reflecting and planning stages. Sensors may question whether the ENTJ's new ideas are practical enough to actually work the way they want. They need to convince ENTJs that their realistic input and focus on the specifics are crucial to the success of the larger idea. Perceivers may be frustrated by ENTJs' quick decision-making style and strong opinions that they tend to present as cast in concrete. They need to use logic to convince ENTJs of the importance of keeping decisions fluid until all the necessary options have been

considered and information gathered. But Feelers face perhaps the greatest challenge dealing with ENTJs, who can easily, and inadvertently, hurt their feelings with their insensitivity and blunt criticism. Feelers need to realize such comments are almost always intended to be helpful and constructive, rather than hurtful and undermining. They do well to summon their courage and be as objective and assertive as possible. ENTJs have strong personalities and they most admire others who possess that same quality.

HOW TO SPOT AN INTJ

INTJs are typically the most independent of all types. They are generally quiet and reserved, and cool and formal in their interactions with others. However, they become more excited when talking about projects that are important to them or about which they possess extensive knowledge or expertise. Unless they are completely prepared, they usually avoid being the center of attention and are embarrassed by too much flattery or praise. They are most comfortable inside the intellectual world and spend good amounts of time in a reverie of deep thoughts. Because INTJs are such complex people, their sentences are frequently so long and complicated, and usually involve so many related thoughts, that others may have difficulty understanding them. They can also be vague and imprecise, since they are least interested in the details of a project. But they will often toil through a surprising number of details in order to make their

HOW TO SPEAK "INTJ"

- Submit new ideas and/or proposals in writing, and give them plenty of time to think about them before discussing. Preview new experiences ahead of time.
- Pay careful attention to the *strategy* necessary for implementing your ideas. Remember that INTJs place a very high value on competence.
- Don't expect effusive appreciation or lavish praise for a job well done. INTJs often consider both unnecessary, meaningless, and, therefore, insulting.

- Resist the temptation to finish their sentences. Even if they seem to be rambling and you think you know where they are heading, it is far better to let them get there on their own.
- Remember to make your case based on logic — not personal preferences or extenuating circumstances.
- Remember they are most concerned with the big picture and how the idea fits in with their larger mission.

ideas or projects perfect. They can be very impatient with, and even dismissive of, others who don't quickly grasp their meaning or whom they consider incompetent.

INTJs' movements are usually thoughtful and deliberate. While most dress fairly conservatively, they may have quite an individual look, since they are not particularly concerned about what others think of them. Since they set very high standards for themselves and others, they are often demanding bosses and parents. Both their work and recreational activities usually involve some form of self-improvement or intellectual challenge, such as learning a new language, playing bridge, chess, doing difficult crossword puzzles, reading, or exploring the Internet and using complex computer programs.

Attention grabbers: Words or phrases that are likely to get the attention of most INTJs

- We've got a very complicated problem.
- We need a completely original approach.
- What's your opinion?
- What are the long-range implications?
- With all due respect . . .

Special Challenges

Extraverts may be frustrated by the depth to which INTJs wish to explore issues, and the pace at which they make decisions. They need to recognize that if the INTJ is forced to act without benefit of reflection, the answer may well be no. Feelers may be put off by INTJs' lack of warmth, sometimes brusque manner, and apparent lack of concern for people issues and concerns. They need to not take comments personally, nor expect a lot of compliments or enthusiastic approval. With INTJs, silence often indicates consent. They need to convince INTJs of the importance and logical consequences of not factoring in the human element, enlightening them as to the simple truths of how others' reactions will affect their support for their initiatives. Perceivers may find INTJs too rigid and stubborn. They need to logically make the case for not closing down options, and force themselves to meet the INTJ's deadlines. But they might just do better to accept the need to give these highly individualistic people wide latitude and stop trying to make them more accommodating. Sensors may have the hardest time dealing with INTJs because of their capacity for creativity. Sensors should wait before discounting the INTJ's radical ideas and strive to see their practical use.

HOW TO SPOT AN ENTP

ENTPs are often very charming, charismatic, and even flirtatious people. Enthusiastic and energetic, they love people and come alive in the spotlight. Clever and quick studies, they often seem to be working on some new creative idea or scheme. Of-

HOW TO SPEAK "ENTP"

- Be prepared to talk about your idea and especially to answer a myriad of questions that may occur to the ENTP spontaneously.

- Emphasize the way your idea/proposal/suggestion is new and different. The more innovative, the more appealing it will be to the ENTP.

- Don't overwhelm them with details. It's the big picture that is important to them. They have innate confidence that if the idea is good, the bugs can be worked out later.

- Be flexible and solicit their suggestions. They will likely see ways of improving the idea and may want to put their own thumbprint on it as well. Be prepared for the possibility they will want to share any credit derived from the project's success.

- If feasible, always present them with several different options to consider, rather than just one.

- Don't force them to make decisions before they are ready. However, you may well have to nudge them into ultimately making a decision, and lobby convincingly for letting some decisions stand once made, since their natural inclination might be to revisit it repeatedly as new information becomes available.

ten masterful communicators and great story or joke tellers, ENTPs have a great affinity and facility for language. They especially like using unusual words, and concocting puns and plays on words. Given their flair for the dramatic and their capacity to express a great range of emotion—smiling or even crying easily—it is sometimes hard to tell if they are being genuine. They also use their bodies to connect with others, and are often comfortable placing their hand on a shoulder, giving someone a hug, or standing close and speaking intimately. Curious and observant, they are surprisingly perceptive about people and quick to point out their insights. ENTPs like to impress others and are very conscious of their image. They typically dress well and surround themselves with as much luxury as they can afford. Spontaneous and impulsive, they are ready to go at a moment's notice and rarely resist an opportunity to have fun, leaving their commitments to finish later.

ENTPs are happiest in jobs or other activities that involve a lot of interaction with people, variety, and the opportunity to use their considerable creativity. They may have a wide variety of outside interests, but most involve being around people, such as playing team sports, coaching, acting, or entertaining.

Attention grabbers: Words or phrases that are likely to get the attention of most ENTPs

- How about this good idea?
- Let's brainstorm some possibilities.
- I've got a proposition for you.
- This may be a little off the wall, but . . .
- There're some people I'd like you to meet.

Special Challenges

Introverts are likely to find ENTPs' pace dizzying and their energy level draining. It may help them to try and anticipate the kind and volume of questions they are likely to encounter from the ENTP and rehearse some of their answers in advance. Feelers are likely to connect with ENTPs on a superficial level, but may get their feelings hurt or feel betrayed if the ENTP turns out not to be as sensitive or genuine as he or she first appeared. They need to recognize that ENTPs like to please people and be liked, and sometimes they simply overextend themselves and make promises they cannot keep. But in the final analysis, ENTPs will usually make the tough decisions based on what is logical, regardless of how they or others personally feel. Judgers may become exasperated by ENTPs' inability and/or unwillingness to make decisions and stick with them! They need to gently push them toward closure by reassuring the ENTP that few decisions are irrevocable, and most can always be changed later. Finally, Sensors may find these creative and imaginative people too impractical and unrealistic to take seriously. They need to recognize the ENTP's gift for naturally seeing what they cannot, while at the same time try to temper the ENTP's vision with reality.

HOW TO SPOT AN INTP

INTPs are often hard to get to know because they are intensely private and are highly selective about whom they will share their inner selves with. Often brilliant, these strategic thinkers are most in their element when they are quietly and independently analyzing some complex and interesting problem. INTPs are so internally focused, they may remind you of the classic absentminded professor, not noticing the little details around them that make up ordinary life. Their thought processes are so complex, they are sometimes unable to communicate their ideas and vision in a way that's easily understood by others, especially Feelers. They tend to pause frequently during conversations, and even look away as they mentally turn ideas and words over in their minds until they find the right one that accurately conveys their meaning. In a group, many INTPs remain somewhat detached and aloof, taking their time and participating in discussions only to the extent they are comfortable with or feel is worthwhile. They are not particularly appearance conscious, usually preferring to dress casually rather than stylishly. INTPs are often in jobs that allow and require them to work for long stretches by themselves, engaging in creative problem solving by applying their considerable talent for analysis based on logic and objectivity. Not surprisingly, many INTPs have a natural affinity for and enjoy working with computers. Although they may have diverse recreational interests, many are voracious readers who often have eclectic tastes in books, movies, and music. And many love to spend time working or playing at their computers.

HOW TO SPEAK "INTP"

- Be prepared to consider as many options as possible, and anticipate that decisions which have been made may change as new information becomes available.

- Challenge their creative problem-solving skills. INTPs seldom encounter a problem that they cannot solve. The trickier the issue, the more they will enjoy it, and the more energized they will become.

- Give INTPs adequate time to "noodle" ideas around before expecting them to act on them.

- If possible, spare them the boredom of working out the details. Instead, let them focus on the creative, more challenging aspects of a problem or situation.

- Let them know that you respect their competence and expertise.

- Respect their privacy and don't probe for information about their personal lives unless they are willing to share. Even close friends are wise to let the INTP initiate personal discussions.

Attention grabbers: Words or phrases that are likely to get the attention of most INTPs

- Would you give this some thought?
- Take all the time you need.
- Here's an interesting challenge.
- I don't know how we're going to figure this one out.
- I respect your privacy.

Special Challenges

Extraverts are liable to be frustrated by the depth INTPs apply to their analysis. Therefore, Extraverts need to carefully think their ideas through in advance, but may benefit from checking them out with other Introverts to see if they consider them substantial or too superficial. Sensors may not appreciate INTPs' long-range vision and may find their explanations unnecessarily complicated and confusing. They need to ask for clarification at times and recognize the INTP's future orientation as an asset. Judgers may find pinning INTPs down an exercise in futility. While they can gently push for closure, and appeal to the INTP's natural need for logical order, it is essentially impossible to hurry or control these independent people. But Feelers may have the most difficulty dealing with superlogical INTPs. Feelers need to learn not to take comments, critiques, and lack of praise personally, but rather to view them as an opportunity to receive some honest, constructive feedback.

CHAPTER ELEVEN

Getting To Know the Idealists: the Four NF Types

People who share the Idealist temperament value uniqueness and originality and are driven to understand the inner meaning of their life experiences. Like Conceptualizers, Idealists prefer Intuition to Sensing, but since they are Feelers, they make decisions based on their personal values. Some NFs are Extraverts and some are Introverts. And some are Judgers, while others are Perceivers. Following are the communication recommendations for dealing with all Idealists.

General Tips for Communicating with Idealists

- Appeal to their empathetic nature. Stress how the action proposed will benefit people, preferably how it will improve their long-term psychological and/or spiritual well-being.
- Communicate the intensity of your belief in, and your commitment to, your position, proposal, or idea.
- Seek harmony and a cooperative relationship; try not to be combative or competitive.
- Whenever possible, make points with personal stories and examples: use metaphors and analogies liberally.
- Try to win their friendship. How they feel about you personally may have a significant impact on how eager they are to hear your point, or how willing they are to collaborate or compromise.
- Appeal to their desire to be unique and original; appreciate their leanings toward the unconventional and the unusual.
- Challenge their creativity and imagination. They are often excellent solvers of personal or interpersonal problems.

- Share your personal feelings with them; generally, the more genuine personal disclosure offered, the more connected to them you will become.
- Be sincere. Idealists value integrity and react strongly to people they consider not genuine or phony.

HOW TO SPOT AN ENFJ

Energetic, friendly, talkative, and articulate, ENFJs often have the best communication skills of all types. ENFJs enthusiastically maintain good eye contact, touch people frequently but always appropriately, lean into conversations, and register approval and disapproval on their faces. They use verbal and nonverbal language to express their many value-based opinions. They prefer talking about personal topics, and can spend long periods of time discussing relationships.

Comfortable and poised in social settings of all sizes and varieties, ENFJs instantly respond to the emotional climate of a person or a group. Often charismatic, they easily persuade others to go along with their good ideas, which inevitably involve helping people in some way. However, they can be so nice and try so hard to please others that some people may doubt their sincerity. ENFJs actively avoid confrontation and may be quick to apologize and forgive. They are very sensitive to criticism and may withdraw from a contentious discussion rather than express their hurt feelings. ENFJs — especially women ENFJs — are very

HOW TO SPEAK "ENFJ"

- Let them know *verbally* how much you appreciate them and their contributions. With ENFJs, words often speak louder than actions.
- If you need to offer criticism, make sure to point out any areas of agreement first. Alert them to incoming criticism and ask them to receive it in the spirit in which it is given.
- Never discount, dismiss, or make light of their personal feelings about an issue, even if you don't feel there is a rational or logical basis for them to feel that way. Never try to talk them out of how they feel. Listen, rather than try to fix their problem.
- Avoid confrontation whenever possible. Try to cooperate and find middle ground.
- Make sure to follow through on commitments you make to them. Don't change plans unless it is absolutely necessary. And if it is, give them plenty of time to adjust to the changes and to shift gears.
- When pitching an idea or proposal, make sure you have fully considered how the action will affect others, and emphasize all positive aspects.
- Use their first name and maintain eye contact. Be patient with their sometimes long and tangential story-telling style.

conscious about their appearance and concerned about how others will judge them. Therefore, they dress appropriately for the occasion; their outfits and accessories are well coordinated. While they are often attracted to helping professions, such as counseling or teaching, they also enjoy a great variety of jobs as long they believe in the product or service and the job involves lots of positive interaction with others. Whether at work or at a social gathering, ENFJs are frequently in leadership roles and are typically found organizing other people or juggling many ideas and projects at the same time.

Attention grabbers: Words or phrases that are likely to get the attention of most ENFJs

- Can I tell you how I feel?
- How do you feel about this?
- I have a problem.
- What's the plan?
- What's your opinion?
- Give compliments freely.

Special Challenges

Some Introverts may feel overwhelmed by ENFJs' energy and enthusiasm. In the case of a strong Introvert dealing with a strong Extravert, they may even need to limit the time they spend with that person to avoid getting burned out. Sensors may feel ENFJs are unrealistic, too idealistic, and at times impractical. They need to not overwhelm ENFJs with lots of details, but instead should focus on those specifics that relate to the ENFJ's larger vision and concerns. Perceivers are likely to be frustrated by ENFJs' drive for closure and what Perceivers may consider a premature decision-making style. They need to gently try to keep ENFJs from foreclosing options too early, and get them to agree to a particular point in time when the decision really will be made (and then they need to stick to it!). The greatest challenge may be for Thinkers, who might see ENFJs as hypersensitive, illogical, and overly emotional. They need to be especially careful not to offend ENFJs. For if they do, even unintentionally, they run the risk of jeopardizing their relationship permanently.

HOW TO SPOT AN INFJ

INFJs are complex, creative people with deep feelings and strong convictions, but are often somewhat difficult to get to know. Usually reserved, and sometimes a bit uncomfortable in social situations, INFJs generally prefer dealing with people one-to-one, where they can really zero in and concentrate all their attention on the other person. They are usually very good listeners, skilled at generating enlightened and creative solutions to people's problems. INFJs are generally not very demonstrative, either verbally or physically. Their posture is usually erect and they walk and move with real purpose. INFJs often have strong opinions based on their values and convictions, and once they have staked out a position, it may be very difficult to convince them to change it. Their language is thoughtful, figurative, and filled with deep mean-

HOW TO SPEAK "INFJ"

- Give them plenty of time to consider your idea or proposal in-depth before expecting feedback or discussion.
- Present the idea in terms of your vision—the big picture, and how it may fit into their larger personal or organizational goals, rather than focusing on the specifics and details.
- Discuss the benefits it will have on people—especially how it will positively affect them in the future as well as in the present.
- Especially with regard to problem solving, solicit

their ideas, appeal to their creativity, and talk about possibilities.
- Be patient with what might be long, complicated explanations; don't hesitate to take your time carefully considering their proposals—they like to do the same.
- If relevant, provide information regarding the timing of the implementation of the plan; be sure to meet all agreed-upon deadlines, and honor your commitments.

ing. But it is often complex and sometimes difficult to follow. Since INFJs are rather formal, their appearance tends toward the conservative. They are seldom flashy dressers, and since they may also be both frugal and resourceful, they may consider expensive clothes more of a luxury than a necessity. The jobs that appeal most to them are ones that allow them to be "thinker-uppers," leaving the details and execution to others. While there are INFJs in all fields, they tend to be drawn to occupations that let them work one-on-one with people, like counseling or teaching. They also enjoy writing. Whatever they do, they must feel a sense of personal integrity for it to have any meaning or real satisfaction. INFJs have varied interests, but often enjoy hobbies that can be done alone or with their family or a few close friends.

Attention grabbers: Words or phrases that are likely to get the attention of most INFJs

- I need a creative solution. Can you help me?
- What am I not seeing?
- What do you feel is the right thing to do?
- Take your time, and we'll talk when you're ready.
- Let's plan it out.

Special Challenges

Some Extraverts may be impatient with INFJs' slower, thoughtful, more reflective pace, as well as the depth they naturally apply to their analysis. Extraverts need to slow down and try to focus their attention on only the issue being discussed.

Thinkers may find INFJs both too sensitive and too subjective. Instead, they might view the INFJ's acute perceptiveness about people as a valuable asset that can be very useful in many practical ways. Perceivers may find INFJs stubborn, resistant, inflexible, and unable to be spontaneous. They need to tap into INFJs' love of possibilities, which represents the more open-ended side of their personalities. But Sensors may have the most difficulty dealing with these imaginative, theoretical, and sometimes mysterious people. Likely to see them as impractical dreamers, Sensors need to appeal to INFJs' desire to turn their ideas into a tangible result — something that also appeals to the more practical, results-driven Sensors.

HOW TO SPOT AN ENFP

ENFPs are first and foremost energized by new ideas and possibilities. Outgoing, friendly, and talkative, they love being around people, and often have a large and varied assortment of friends and acquaintances. ENFPs are usually quick and clever, and commonly use language to capture people's attention and entertain them, as well as to express their creative, offbeat personalities. They like to tell stories, jokes, and use puns and plays on words. Naturally irreverent, they usually speak rapidly, their language is peppered with humor and metaphors, and they may even swear more often than some other types. Insatiably curious, ENFPs are

HOW TO SPEAK "ENFP"

- Be prepared to discuss many topics and answer a lot of questions.

- Don't overwhelm them with details, especially those concerning projects or ideas they are not already heavily invested in.

- Challenge their creativity. ENFPs love nothing better than seeing possibilities and generating unique, helpful solutions.

- Present them with lots of options. If at all possible, don't limit their choices or restrict their ability to come up with alternatives. Never immediately point out why their ideas won't work.

- Appeal to their enormous sense of the possible, especially with regard to getting what they want or helping others achieve something that is important to them.

- Respect their personal privacy. Don't ask them to share their feelings publicly. While they like to be appreciated for their contributions, they are often embarrassed when praised publicly.

- Keep presentations interesting and the pace moving. The more you involve them, the more invested they will become. Make chores and required tasks fun.

- Don't be too formal or structured, or overwhelm them with too many rules or procedures. If at all possible, encourage (or at least tolerate) their desire to act spontaneously.

quick to strike up conversations with strangers, ask lots of questions, and tend to finish other peoples' sentences. Their conversation can be very scattered as they move from one thought to the next without finishing the first as new inspirations strike them. With regard to appearance, ENFPs often have an original, artsy look, and dress more for themselves than for others, or to make a statement.

Privately, ENFPs are very sensitive and sentimental, but tend to be more reluctant to share their deep personal feelings unless they are with those they know well and trust. ENFPs have enormously varied occupational interests and often change jobs or careers frequently. The most satisfying jobs for ENFPs are ones that allow them to be creative and spontaneous while in the service of others. ENFPs also have a wide range of recreational interests, but enjoy most being with friends and having a good time with friends.

Attention grabbers: Words or phrases that are likely to get the attention of most ENFPs

- It's impossible. . . . It just can't be done.
- We're having a reunion.
- We've got plenty of time; let's finish it tomorrow.
- I've got a great idea!
- Do you know anyone who can . . . ?
- There's some people I'd like you to meet.

Special Challenges

Some Introverts may be worn out by the high energy level and frenetic pace many ENFPs prefer.

Instead, talk with them one-on-one, when they will be more responsive and quieter. Keep in mind that with ENFPs, the larger the group, the greater the ENFP's energy. Thinkers may be irritated by ENFPs' inconsistent behavior and eagerness to find extenuating, albeit compelling circumstances. Couching any objections or resistance in terms of fairness to people is usually the most effective strategy. Judgers may find it challenging and frustrating to get ENFPs to make choices, stick to decisions, and respect deadlines. Judgers can help nudge ENFPs into committing themselves to a course of action by reminding them that decisions aren't irrevocable; they can always be changed. This is often all it takes to relieve ENFPs' stress around decision making. As for deadlines, Judgers may try setting up two deadlines for ENFPs: the first one is when they tell the ENFP the work is due, the second, when they actually need to have it done. Since they are remarkably resourceful, even when it looks as though they'll never make their deadline, they usually pull it off. Sensors may have the hardest time with ENFPs' wildly imaginative style. They may need to work particularly hard at not putting a damper on ENFPs' creativity and enthusiasm. They may also need to trust the fact that just because they cannot see a viable option at the moment, doesn't mean one doesn't exist.

HOW TO SPOT AN INFP

INFPs are the most idealist of the Idealists, and of all types in general. Absolutely driven by their innermost personal values, they are extremely sensi-

H O W   T O   S P E A K   "I N F P"

- INFPs are very sensitive to criticism and view everything personally. However, they may never come out and tell you that you've hurt their feelings. If in doubt, stay away from or tread lightly with topics you think they may be sensitive about.

- Be very careful not to dismiss, discount, or make light of things they consider important. If you do, you run the risk of damaging your relationship permanently, since INFPs may hold grudges longer than other types.

- If possible, find out how your idea, suggestion, or proposal fits in with one of their passions, and try to link the two, or point out commonalties.

- Give them plenty of time to consider your ideas. Be prepared to discuss the impact they will have on others, including the future implications.

- If relevant, convey your sincere belief in the value of what you are proposing. If you are not genuine, it will be obvious to them, and they will immediately, and perhaps permanently, reject your idea or proposal.

- Respect their style of decision making, which usually requires time and privacy to mull ideas over, consider alternatives all along the way, change plans as new information is discovered, perhaps even start all over if the central mission or concept is corrupted by too much external influence.

- Remember that INFPs are process people. Build time for revision, modification, and reflection into any schedule.

tive and feel things very deeply. Many INFPs have an otherworldly quality about them, and seem to be unconcerned about many of the more mundane, day-to-day requirements of modern life. They seem nearly oblivious to the details of daily living, like being on time, knowing where their glasses are, or keeping up with the Joneses. The least practical of all types, they march to the beat of a different drummer, which is defined completely by them. INFPs are usually thoughtful and soft-spoken, and use language carefully and as a means of self-expression. Many have a natural talent for poetry and other creative writing. They are seldom aggressive and are not especially ambitious, except when it comes to their own projects, about which they can be surprisingly protective and at which they will work tirelessly. While they like to help people and are natural counselors, most INFPs are very selective and share their true selves with only a few very special people. With strangers, they may appear cold and aloof. Their appearance is often original and they dress to please themselves. They may wear funky clothes from another era that appeals to them, or mix and match styles. But their clothing and accessories, while making a statement about their uniqueness, are also selected to make them comfortable. Many INFPs are drawn to the arts — music, literature, painting — and to psychology, both in their occupations and in their spare time.

Attention grabbers: Words or phrases that are likely to get the attention of most INFPs

- What feels right to you?
- Can I speak with you privately about something?
- I'd love to hear about your latest project.
- There's no rush. Take all the time you need.

Special Challenges

Some Extraverts may find INFPs very difficult to get to know and even harder to get moving. They need to slow their pace and recognize that INFPs need plenty of time to do their best work. They also need to be careful not to rush INFPs into relationships before they are ready. Sensors may be likely to consider INFPs impractical and their suggestions unrealistic and unworkable. They need to be patient to hear the INFP all the way out before they see the value of their ideas. Judgers may become frustrated with INFPs' apparent lack of organization and how long it takes them to make decisions. They can shorten the decision-making process by presenting a select few options for the INFP to consider, being absolutely clear about any deadline, and by not leaving things completely open-ended. But the greatest challenge will be for Thinkers, who are likely to feel they need to walk on eggshells in order to avoid hurting the feelings of INFPs. In fact, they *do* have to be careful dealing with INFPs and may benefit from first testing out ideas on other Feelers (friends or coworkers) to get their reactions and suggestions for presenting the information in the most positive way.

Now that you have mastered the SpeedReading and SpeedReaching system, and have gotten to know all sixteen types, you're *almost* ready to go out and start using these techniques to understand and be more effective with everyone you meet. But before we leave you, we have some final words and important suggestions, warnings, and resources for you in Chapter 12.

CHAPTER TWELVE

"How Will I Ever Look at People the Same Way Again?"

Final Thoughts on a New Beginning

At the beginning of this book, we told you that mastering the art of SpeedReading people would forever change the way you look at and relate to people. Hopefully, you've achieved an understanding of the tremendous power of Personality Type, and gained the skills necessary to facilitate effective communication.

SpeedReading people is a sophisticated life skill. And like most new skills, the more you use it, the better you become. However, SpeedReading people is different from learning to ride a bike, build a house, or learn a foreign language, because it involves understanding and predicting human behavior. This has been a subject of intense study for thousands of years and one that is so complex, scientists readily admit they've only just scratched the surface of what they someday hope to learn.

We are certain that long before you've reached this page, you may have tried practicing your new SpeedReading skills. And you may have made a simple, yet oftentimes painful observation: some people do not *like* to be figured out and may feel quite threatened by your ability to do so. Potentially, this can be a real problem, since the whole point of learning to SpeedRead people is to enable you to *connect* with others, not alienate them. Fortunately, there a few steps you can take to minimize the likelihood of this happening:

1. Resist the urge to show people how smart you are. Amazing your friends and coworkers by making SpeedReading into a parlor game may temporarily please your ego but is likely to come back to haunt you.

2. Don't portray yourself as some kind of mind reader. Being able to SpeedRead people doesn't make you clairvoyant.

3. Never insist that you know something about a person that he or she considers private. And never share that information with anyone else.

4. Practice your newly developing skills cautiously, in a safe environment where the stakes aren't too high. It would be as foolish for you to make major decisions based upon SpeedReading people while still a novice as it would be to try and fly a plane without *really* knowing what you are doing.

5. Always allow for the possibility that your guess about a person's type could be wrong. Rather, consider it a working hypothesis, subject to greater refinement as you gather more information until you reach the point where you have to ask yourself the ultimate confirming question: "What else could he or she be?"

If you follow these suggestions, we are confident that you will be able to use your SpeedReading people skills effectively, ethically, and to everyone's best advantage. Best of luck!

The next page describes the SpeedReading People video, an exciting resource which can help you in your quest to implement SpeedReading people more quickly and effectively. We also list several organizations and books that we recommend for further reading or study.

The SpeedReading People Advanced Video Training Kit
The Quickest Way to Master the Art of SpeedReading People

This book has been designed to be self-contained—that is, you can learn the art of SpeedReading people from this book alone. However, there is another resource available to you that can enhance your learning and drastically reduce the time it takes to fully master these techniques.

Developed exclusively and *only* for those who have first learned the art of SpeedReading people by studying this book, the Advanced Video Training Kit gives you something we simply could not provide in a book format: a visual demonstration of what each SpeedReading clue—type preferences, temperaments, and a person's E/I-Feeling pattern—looks like in real people. If "one picture is worth a thousand words," then one *moving* picture—i.e., videotape—is worth many times that. An additional advantage of the SpeedReading People kit is that you can stop the videotape and rewatch the clues as many times as necessary until you are comfortable you can identify them in others.

The SpeedReading People kit comes with a comprehensive workbook, which includes additional skill-building exercises so you can test yourself to determine how well you've learned the clues. Also included is a set of audiotapes that allows you to use otherwise unproductive "car time" to hone your SpeedReading and SpeedReaching skills. One tape is devoted entirely to helping you SpeedRead people over the phone.

The kit also comes with the Portable Speed-Reader—a sort of crib sheet that summarizes key clues for Speed**Reading** and Speed**Reaching** each of the sixteen types and is small enough to fit into a jacket pocket or purse for discreet use.

PLEASE NOTE: The SpeedReading People kit is *not* a stand-alone course. While you *can* learn how to SpeedRead people without the kit, you *cannot* learn it using *only* the kit. It is not sold separately and it can be purchased only by people who have already bought the book, or as part of a **complete package that includes: a copy of *The Art of SpeedReading People,* the video, the audiotapes, the User's Guide, and the Portable SpeedReader.** The cost of the complete package is $149.95. The cost of the kit *without* the book is: $129.95.

ORDERING INFORMATION

To order, see the inside back cover. Please have your copy of this book handy.

Your total satisfaction with the kit or complete package is absolutely guaranteed. If for *any* reason you are not 100 percent satisfied, you will promptly receive a complete refund.

Organizations and Resources

Now that you have learned of the power of Personality Type and how relevant it is to so many aspects of your life, we encourage you to increase your depth of understanding, and learn how Type can be applied in specific areas of interest to you, such as careers, personal relationships, business, education, spirituality, and so forth. We have assembled a comprehensive list of books, journals, training opportunities, and organizations to assist you in this endeavor. Some of the books referenced here are available at bookstores. But many can only, or can more easily, be found through organizations that specialize in publishing and distributing books about Personality Type. All the organizations listed also provide training courses relating to Personality Type. Call or write them for information.

Organizations

Communication Consultants, LLC
20 Beverly Road
West Hartford, CT 06119
800-YOUR-TYPE
Fax: 860-232-1321
Communication Consultants, LLC, provides specialized training for career professionals from introductory to advanced-level programs. Programs based on our books, *Do What You Are*, *Nurture by Nature*, and *The Art of SpeedReading People*, are open to the public or can be arranged for organizations and companies.

Association for Psychological Type (APT)
9140 Ward Parkway
Kansas City, MO 64114
816-444-3500
APT is an international membership organization open to all people interested in Type. APT conducts training workshops, and publishes material including the *Bulletin of Psychological Type* and the *Journal of Psychological Type*, and conducts the APT Myers-Briggs Type Indicator training program. APT sponsors international and regional conferences as well as local groups throughout the country and around the world that meet to share information about Type.

Center for Applications of Psychological Type (CAPT)
2815 N.W. 13th St., Suite 401
Gainesville, FL 32609
800-777-CAPT
CAPT provides training programs in Type for professionals and the public, offers consulting services for training and research, publishes Type-related books and materials, compiles research to advance the understanding of Type, does computer scoring of the Myers-Briggs Type Indicator, and maintains the Isabel Briggs Myers Memorial Library.

Consulting Psychologists Press (CPP)
3803 E. Bayshore Road
Palo Alto, CA 94303
800-624-1765
The publisher of the Myers-Briggs Type Indicator instrument and other psychological instruments and materials.

KBA, The Human Resource Technology Company
P.O. Box 116
Rockwall, TX 75087
214-771-3991 phone and fax
An international consulting/training firm that assists a wide range of professionals, including teachers, educational consultants, and career counselors in the new physiological insight known as the Benziger Breakthrough. The Benziger Type Assessment is an exciting and useful next-step tool that tracks Falsification of Type, while identifying the person's true natural type when it differs from the manner in which the individual is currently using his or her brain. Dr. Benziger's book, *The Art of Using Your Whole Brain,* is available through KBA.

The La Jolla Group
2410 First Avenue
San Diego, CA 92101
800-658-5387
Fax: 619-232-3052
The La Jolla Group is a management consulting and interactive multimedia firm specializing in improving personal, team, and corporate effectiveness.

Otto Kroeger Associates
3605 Chain Bridge Road
Fairfax, VA 22030
703-591-6284
Fax: 703-591-8338

A training and consulting organization specializing in the use of the Myers-Briggs Type Indicator instrument. Programs include the qualifying workshop as well as other workshops for individuals and groups. Otto Kroeger Associates offers a variety of books, tapes, and videos.

The Temperament Research Institute
16152 Beach Boulevard
Suite 119
Huntington Beach, CA 92647
714-841-0041
800-700-4TRI
An organization specializing in applications of Keirseyan Temperament Theory and Type dynamics, the Temperament Research Institute provides a variety of services, workshops, and products to promote the growth and development of individuals and organizations.

Type and Temperament, Inc.
Box 200
Gladwyne, PA 19035-0200
800-447-8973
The publisher and distributor of a variety of papers, books, and materials regarding Personality Type.

Type Resources
101 Chestnut Street, H-135
Gaithersburg, MD 20877-2139
310-840-8575 or 800-456-6284
An organization that specializes in consulting and training professionals to use Type theory and the Myers-Briggs Type Indicator instrument in the areas of team building, counseling, conflict resolution, and quality management. They also distribute a wide range of Type and Jungian-related books.

WORKSHOP WAY®
P.O. Box 850170
New Orleans, LA 70185-0170
504-486-4871
Located on the campus of Xavier University, WORK-SHOP WAY® is an entire system of education in which human growth is central to the process. Its Five Freedoms nurture the needs of all learning styles. WORKSHOP WAY® offers consulting and training services for educational professionals and entire school systems.

Psychometrics Canada Ltd.
7125-77 Avenue, Edmonton, Alberta,
Canada T6B 0B5
403-469-2268
The Canadian distributor of the MBTI® and related materials.

Books about Personality Type

General Introduction to Personality Type

Brownsword, Alan. *It Takes All Types*. Herndon, Va.: Baytree Publication Company, 1987.

Duniho, Terence. *Patterns of Preference*. Providence, R.I.: Career Designs, 1993.

Giovannoni, Louise C., Berens, Linda V., and Cooper, Sue A. *Introduction to Temperament*. Huntington Beach, Calif.: Cooper, Berens, 1986.

Hirsh, Sandra, and Kummerow, Jean. *Lifetypes*. New York: Warner Books, 1989.

Keirsey, David, and Bates, Marilyn. *Please Understand Me*. Del Mar, Calif.: Prometheus Nemesis, 1978.

Kroeger, Otto, and Thuesen, Janet A. *Type Talk*. New York: Delacorte Press, 1988.

Kroeger, Otto, and Thuesen, Janet A. *Type Talk at Work: How the 16 Types Determine Your Success on the Job*. New York: Delacorte Press, 1992.

Myers, Isabel Briggs, with Myers, Peter. *Gifts Differing*. Palo Alto, Calif.: Consulting Psychologists Press, 1980.

Myers, Isabel Briggs. *Introduction to Type: A Description of the Theory and Application of the Myers-Briggs Type Indicator*. Palo Alto, Calif.: Consulting Psychologists Press, 1987.

Myers, Isabel Briggs, and McCaulley, Mary H. *Manual: A Guide to the Development and Use of the Myers-Briggs Type Indicator*. Palo Alto, Calif.: Consulting Psychologists Press, 1985.

Myers, Isabel B., with revisions by Myers, K. and Kirby, L. *Introduction to Type*. Palo Alto, Calif.: Consulting Psychologists Press, 1993.

Myers, Katharine D., and Kirby, Linda K. *Introduction to Type Dynamics and Development*. Palo Alto, Calif.: Consulting Psychologists Press, 1994.

Quenk, Naomi L. *Beside Ourselves: Our Hidden Personality in Everyday Life*. Palo Alto, Calif.: Consulting Psychologists Press, 1993.

Saunders, Frances. *Katharine and Isabel: Mother's Light, Daughter's Journey*. Palo Alto, Calif.: Consulting Psychologists Press, 1983.

Saunders, Frances. *Katharine and Isabel*. Palo Alto, Calif.: Consulting Psychologists Press, 1991.

Tieger, Paul D., and Barron-Tieger, Barbara. *Do What You Are: Discover the Perfect Career for You Through The Secrets of Personality Type*, rev. ed. Boston: Little, Brown, 1995.

The Type Reporter. Published five times a year. Contains articles and information on various topics of interest concerning psychological type. Susan Scanlon, Editor, 11314 Chapel Road, Fairfax Station, VA 22039 (703-764-5370).

Yabroff, William. *The Inner Image: A Resource for Type Development*. Palo Alto, Calif.: Consulting Psychologists Press, 1990.

Personality Type and Children/Education

Bargar, June R., Bargar, Robert R., and Cano, Jamie M. *Discovering Learning Preferences and Learning Differences in the Classroom*. Columbus, OH.: Ohio Agricultural Education Curriculum Materials Service, Ohio State University, 1994.

Bowman-Kruhm, Mary, and Wirths, Claudine G. *Are You My Type or Why Aren't You More Like Me?* Palo Alto, Calif.: Consulting Psychologists Press, 1992.

Fairhurst, Alice M., and Fairhurst, Lisa. *Effective Teaching, Effective Learning: Making the Personality Connection in Your Classroom*. Palo Alto, Calif.: Davis-Black Publishing, 1995.

Ginn, Charles W. *Families: Using Type to Enhance Mutual Understanding*. Gainesville, Fla.: Center for Applications of Psychological Type, 1995.

Golay, Keith. *Learning Patterns and Temperament Styles*. Newport Beach, Calif.: Manas-Systems, 1982.

Lawrence, Carolyn M., Galloway, Ann W., Lawrence, Gordon D. *The Practice Centers Approach to Seatwork: A Handbook*. New York: McKenzie Press, 1988.

Lawrence, Gordon. *People Types and Tiger Stripes: A Practical Guide to Learning Styles*. Gainesville, Fla.: Center for Applications of Psychological Type, 1979, 1993.

Meisegeier, Charles, Murphy, Elizabeth, and Meisegeier, Constance. *A Teacher's Guide to Type*. Palo Alto, Calif.: Consulting Psychologists Press, 1988.

Murphy, Elizabeth. *The Developing Child: Using Jungian Type to Understand Children*. Palo Alto, Calif.: Consulting Psychologists Press, 1992.

Neff, LaVonne. *One of a Kind*. Portland, Ore.: Multnomah Press, 1988.

Penley, Janet P., and Stephens, Diane W. *The M.O.M.S. Handbook: Understanding Your Personality Type in Mothering*. Wilmette, Ill.: Penley and Associates, 1995. (Self-published: available through 847-251-4936)

Provost, Judith A., and Anchors, Scott. *Applications for the Myers-Briggs Type Indicator in Higher Education*. Palo Alto, Calif.: Consulting Psychologists Press, 1987.

Tieger, Paul D., and Barron-Tieger, Barbara. *Nurture by Nature: Understand Your Child's Personality Type—And Become a Better Parent*. Boston: Little, Brown, 1997.

Van Sant, Sondra, and Payne, Diane. *Psychological Type in Schools: Applications for Educators*. Gainesville, Fla.: Center for Applications of Psychological Type, 1995.

Wickes, Frances. *The Inner World of Childhood*. Old Tappan, N.J.: Prentice Hall, 1978.

Personality Type and Counseling/Relationships

Duniho, Terence. *Personalities at Risk: Addiction, Codependency and Psychological Type*. Gladwyne, Pa.: Type & Temperament, 1992.

Duniho, Terence. *Understanding Relationships*. Providence, R.I.: Life Patterns Institute, 1988.

Faucett, Robert, and Faucett, Carol Ann. *Intimacy and Mid-life: Understanding Your Journey . . .* New York: Crossroads Publishing, 1990.

Grant, Richard D. *Symbols of Recovery: The 12 Steps at Work in the Unconscious*. Gladwyne, Pa.: Type & Temperament, 1990.

Hartzler, Margaret. *Using Type with Couples*. Gaithersburg, Md.: Type Resources, 1988.

Isachsen, Olaf, and Berens, Linda V. *Working Together: A Personality-Centered Approach*, 3rd ed. San Juan Capistrano, Calif.: Institute for Management Development, 1995.

Kroeger, Otto, and Thuesen, Janet A. *16 Ways to Love Your Lover: Understanding the 16 Personality Types So You Can Create a Love That Lasts Forever*. New York: Delacorte Press, 1994.

Milner, Nan Y. B., and Corlett, Eleanor S. *Navigating Mid-life: Using Typology as a Guide*. Palo Alto, Calif.: Consulting Psychologists Press, 1993.

Provost, Judith A. *A Casebook: Applications of the Myers-Briggs Type Indicator in Counseling*. Gainesville, Fla.: Center for Applications of Psychological Type, 1984.

Stein, Murray, and Hollwitz, John, eds. *Psyche at Work: Workplace Applications of Jungian Analytical Psychology*. Wilmette, Ill.: Chiron Publications, 1992.

Ward, Ruth McRoberts. *Blending Temperaments: Improving Relationships—Yours and Others*. Grand Rapids, Mich.: Baker Book House, 1988.

Personality Type and Religion/Spirituality

Duniho, Terence. *Wholeness Lies Within: Sixteen Natural Paths to Spirituality*. Gladwyne, Pa.: Type and Temperament, 1991.

Faucett, Robert, and Faucett, Carol Ann. *Personality and Spiritual Freedom*. New York: Doubleday, 1987.

Golden, Bonnie J. *Self Esteem and Psychological*

Type: Definitions, Interactions, and Expressions. Gainesville, Fla.: Center for Applications of Psychological Type, 1994.

Grant, Harold, Thompson, Magdala, and Clarke, Thomas E. *From Image to Likeness: A Jungian Path to the Gospel Journey.* Mahwah, N.J.: Paulist Press, 1983.

Grant, Richard D. *The Way of the Cross: Christian Individuation and Psychological Temperament.* Gladwyne, Pa.: Type & Temperament, 1990.

Harbough, Gary L. *God's Gifted People.* Minneapolis, Minn.: Augsburg Fortress Publishers, 1988.

Keating, Charles. *Who We Are Is How We Pray: Matching Personality and Spirituality.* Mystic, Conn.: Twenty-third Publications, 1987.

Michael, Chester P., and Morrissey, Marie C. *Prayer and Temperament.* Charlottesville, Va.: Open Door Press, 1984.

Pearson, Mark A. *Why Can't I Be Me?* Grand Rapids, Mich.: Chosen Books, 1984.

Oswold, Roy, and Kroeger, Otto. *Personality Type and Religious Leadership.* Washington, D.C.: Alban Institute, 1988.

Personality Type and Research

CAPT Bibliography. A semiannual listing of more than 1,700 research papers, articles, dissertations, and books. Gainesville, Fla.: Center for Applications of Psychological Type.

Journal of Psychological Type. Edited and published by Thomas G. Carskadon, Ph.D., Box 6161,

Mississippi State University, MS 39762 (601-325-7655).

Macdaid, Gerald P., McCaulley, Mary H., and Kainz, Richard. *Atlas of Type Tables.* Gainesville, Fla.: Center for Applications of Psychological Type, 1986. A compendium of hundreds of tables reflecting the type distribution of people in a variety of occupations.

Personality Type and Business/Management

Barger, Nancy, and Kirby, Linda. *Challenge of Change in Organizations: Helping Employees Thrive in the New Frontier.* Palo Alto, Calif.: Consulting Psychologists Press, 1995.

Barr, Lee, and Barr, Norma. *Leadership Development: Maturity and Power.* Austin, Tex.: Eakin Press, 1994.

Barr, Lee, and Barr, Norma. *Leadership Equation: Leadership, Management and the MBTI.* Austin, Tex.: Eakin Press, 1989.

Berens, Linda, and Isachsen, Olaf. *Working Together—A Personality Centered Approach to Management.* Coronodo, Calif.: New World Management Press, 1988.

Benfari, Robert. *Understanding Your Management Style.* Lexington, Mass.: Lexington Books, 1991.

Bridges, William. *The Character of Organizations: Using Jungian Types in Organization Development.* Palo Alto, Calif.: Consulting Psychologists Press, 1992.

Brock, Susan. *Using Type in Selling.* Palo Alto, Calif.: Consulting Psychologists Press, 1994.

Hartzler, Margaret, and Hartzler, Gary. *Management Uses of the MBTI*. Gaithersburg, Md.: Type Resources, 1987.

Hirsh, Sandra. *MBTI Team Building: Leader's Resource Guide*. Palo Alto, Calif.: Consulting Psychologists Press, 1992

Hirsh, Sandra, and Kummerow, Jean. *Introduction to Type in Organizational Settings*. Palo Alto, Calif.: Consulting Psychologists Press, 1987.

Kroeger, Otto, and Thuesen, Janet. *Type Talk at Work: How the 16 Personality Types Determine Your Success on the Job*. New York: Dell Publishing, 1993.

Index

Also by Paul D. Tieger & Barbara Barron-Tieger

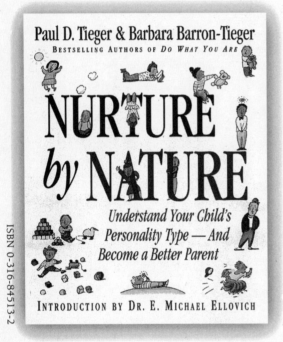

ISBN 0-316-84513-2

Every parent knows that children, even babies, have distinct personalities. So it's only natural that parenting strategies that work with one child may be less effective with another child. How can you be sure that your nurturing is well suited to your child? With this one-of-a-kind parenting guide, you can use Personality Type analysis — a powerful and well-respected psychological tool — to understand your child as never before and become a more loving and effective parent.

In *Nurture by Nature* you'll learn:

- Which of the 16 different types best matches your child's personality

- How this personality type affects your child in each of three stages
  of development — preschool, school age, and adolescence

- How other parents deal with a wide array of parenting joys and
  challenges you may encounter with your child

- Strategies for adapting your parenting style to your child's type

Whether your child is a tantrum-prone toddler, a shy third-grader, a rebellious teen, or somewhere in between, *Nurture by Nature* will give you the power to understand your child and become the best parent you can be.

Available in paperback at bookstores everywhere

Little, Brown and Company

Also by Paul D. Tieger & Barbara Barron-Tieger

ISBN 0-316-84522-1

This perennial bestseller shows you step-by-step how to achieve career satisfaction by unlocking the secrets of Personality Type. You'll discover your own personality type through an easy self-evaluation — and then get specific advice for your particular type, including real-life examples and information on today's hottest job tracks.

If you're a student or a recent graduate, or if you're thinking about switching jobs or careers, *Do What You Are* gives you the key to on-the-job satisfaction and professional success.

"Every job hunter or career changer needs this book."
— Kevin Harrington, Career Services,
Harvard Graduate School of Education

"An indispensable resource."
— John Madigan, Director of Staffing, ITT
Hartford Life Company

"Loaded with real-world examples and practical applications. . . . When you are armed with this new self-awareness, the directions toward your own job-and-career satisfaction become clear."
— William Corwin, Office of Career Services,
Princeton University

"Provides pertinent information that is very validating. . . . People are motivated by what they read about Personality Type. This information gives them the confidence to take off on their own."
— Carol Dunne,
Apple Computer Human Resources

"Discover your personality strengths, then get the right job."
— *Business Week*

Available in paperback at bookstores everywhere

Little, Brown and Company

Let's Talk

An Invitation to Join the Personality Type Community

Since we often hear the best stories about the benefits of using Personality Type from you, our readers, we invite you to join us in an ongoing dialogue on our web site at

www.personalitytype.com

Just click "Join the Community" to leave your name, address, and e-mail address so we can stay in touch with you. And if you're not Internet-connected, you can write to us at

Communication Consultants, LLC
20 Beverly Road
West Hartford, CT 06119

Your stories may very well end up in one of our books — with your permission, of course. And we'll be happy to share with you new and practical ways of improving your personal and professional lives using Personality Type.

We look forward to hearing from and communicating with you soon and often.

Paul D. Tieger and Barbara Barron-Tieger